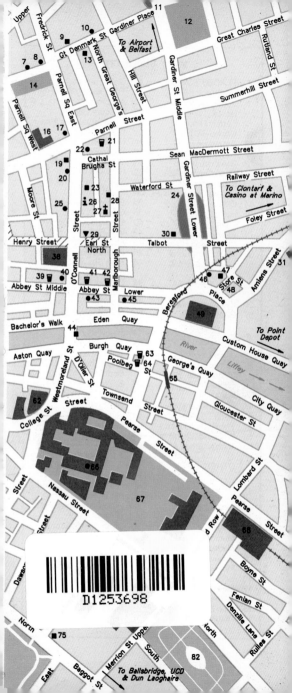

MAP 1 DUBLIN CITY

■ PLACES TO STAY

5 Young Traveller Hostel
9 Barry's Hotel
11 Cheap B&Bs
13 Belvedere Hotel
19 Royal Dublin Hotel
23 Gresham Hotel
24 More Cheap B&Bs
28 Marlborough Hostel
30 Cardijin House Hostel
44 Clifton Court Hotel
47 Isaac's (Dublin Tourist Hostel)
72 Avalon House
75 Shelbourne Hotel
80 Mont Clare Hotel
81 Davenport Hotel

▼ PLACES TO EAT

29 Kylemore Café
37 Bewley's Café

⬦ PUBS

4 Joxer Daly's
21 Fibber Magee's (Gate Hotel)
35 Slattery's
39 The Oval
41 Abbey Mooney's
42 Sean O'Casey's
51 The Brazen Head
63 White House Inn
64 John Mulligan's

OTHER

1 Hospital
2 Hospital
3 King's Inns
6 National Wax Museum
7 Municipal Gallery of Modern Art
8 Dublin Writers' Museum
10 Belvedere College
12 Mountjoy Square
14 Parnell Square
15 Sinn Féin Bookshop
16 Rotunda Hospital
17 Gate Theatre
18 The Laundry Shop
20 Aer Lingus
22 Telecom Centre
25 Dublin Bus (Bus Átha Cliath) Office
26 Dublin Tourism Office
27 St Mary's Pro-Cathedral
31 Connolly Station
32 St Paul's Church
33 St Michan's Church
34 Four Courts
36 St Mary's Abbey
38 GPO
40 Eason Bookshop
43 Irish Rail
45 Abbey Theatre
46 Rent-a-Bike
48 Main Bus Station (Busáras)
49 Custom House
50 Guinness Hop Store
52 Adam & Eve's Church
53 St Audoen's Churches
54 Dublin Corporation Civic Offices
55 The Liberties
56 Tailor's Hall
57 Christ Church Cathedral
58 St Werburgh's Church
59 Dublin Castle
60 City Hall
61 Temple Bar
62 Bank of Ireland
65 Tara Station
66 Trinity College Library & Book of Kells
67 Trinity College
68 Pearse Station
69 St Patrick's Cathedral
70 Marsh's Library
71 Whitefriars Carmelite Church
73 St Stephen's Green Shopping Centre
74 St Stephen's Green
76 National Museum
77 National Library
78 Leinster House (Irish Parliament)
79 National Gallery
82 Merrion Square

Dublin
city guide

Tony Wheeler

Dublin – city guide
  1st edition

Published by
  Lonely Planet Publications
  Head Office: PO Box 617, Hawthorn, Vic 3122, Australia
  Branches: PO Box 2001A, Berkeley, CA 94702, USA
              12 Barley Mow Passage,
              Chiswick W4 4PH, UK

Printed by
  Colorcraft Ltd, Hong Kong

Photographs by
  Tony Wheeler (TW) & John Murray (JM)
  Page 28 & 29 (TW)
  Page 216 top & middle (JM), bottom (TW)
  Page 217 (TW)
  Front cover: Sunlight Chambers (TW)
  Front cover gatefold: Top: Davy Byrne's (TW)
                            Middle: Trinity College (JM)
                            Bottom: Dublin Doors (TW)
  Back cover: Patrick Kavanagh Statue, Grand Canal (TW)
  Back cover gatefold: Top: Ha'penny Bridge (JM)
                           Bottom: Christ Church Cathedral (TW)

First Published
  June 1993

Although the authors and publisher have tried to make the information as accurate as possible, they accept no responsibility for any loss, injury or inconvenience sustained by any person using this book.

National Library of Australia Cataloguing–in–Publication Data

Wheeler, Tony
  Dublin city guide

  1st ed.
  Includes index
  ISBN 0 86442 184 2.
  1. Dublin (Ireland) - Guidebooks. 1. Title.
  (Series: Lonely Planet city guide)

  914.183504824

Tony Wheeler

Tony was born in England but grew up in Pakistan, the Bahamas and the USA. He returned to England to do a degree in engineering at Warwick University, worked as an automotive design engineer, returned to university to complete an MBA in London, then dropped out on the Asian overland trail with his wife Maureen. Eventually settling down in Australia they've been travelling, writing and publishing guidebooks ever since, having set up Lonely Planet Publications in the mid-1970s. Travel for the Wheelers is considerably enlivened by their daughter Tashi and their son Kieran.

From the Author

Thanks to the Irish Tourist Board (particularly Gordon Stepto at their Australian office and Tim Magennis in Dublin), to John Murray (who, along with Sean Sheehan, is helping to write our forthcoming Ireland guidebook) and to the many Dubliners who offered help, advice, suggestions and amusement.

From the Publisher

This first edition of *Dublin – city guide* was edited at the Lonely Planet office in Australia by Adrienne Costanzo. Sandra Smythe and Valerie Tellini drew the maps and Margaret Jung and Valerie Tellini designed the cover. Vicki Beale was responsible for the layout and photograph selection.

Thanks also to Sue Mitra for editorial guidance and support, and to Sharon Wertheim for help with the indexing.

Warning & Request

Things change – prices go up, schedules change, good places go bad and bad places go bankrupt – nothing stays the same. So if you find things better or worse, recently opened or long since closed, please write and tell us and help make the next edition better.

Your letters will be used to help update future editions and, where possible, important changes will also be included in a Stop Press section in reprints.

We greatly appreciate all information that is sent to us by travellers. Back at Lonely Planet we employ a hard-working readers' letters team to sort through the many letters we receive. The best ones will be rewarded with a free copy of the next edition or another Lonely Planet guide if you prefer. We give away lots of books, but, unfortunately, not every letter or postcard receives one.

Contents

PLACES TO STAY...187

Maps

Introduction

Dublin's Top 10:

Ireland's capital and its largest and most cosmopolitan city, Dublin is a city of great contrasts. It's a place that can swing so rapidly from rich to poor, black to white that it's virtually impossible to pin it down. The elegant and prosperous-looking Georgian squares can quickly give way to areas where any sign of elegance has long since faded into decay, and there's little modern architecture of any note. Despite its faults, Dublin is a curious and colourful place, an easy city to like and a fine introduction to Ireland.

Dublin celebrated its millennium in 1988 but in fact its history dates back to even earlier years. Traces of those earliest years are hard to find, but there are many reminders of Dublin's medieval period and its Georgian heyday during the 18th century when majestic streetscapes and regal squares reflected its wealth and importance. That century of elegance was followed by a century of disaster which saw the loss of the limited self-government Ireland had previously enjoyed and the escalation of the struggle for independence from Britain. The horrors of the potato famines combined with these problems to produce a century of stagnation and even decline.

Since Ireland finally achieved independence in 1921, Dublin has had a new role as the capital of the country. It's still one of the smallest European Community (EC) capitals, and compared to London and other larger cities in Continental Europe it's a quiet and slow-moving place. However, it's also a place with soul. The city's literary history seems to bump against you at every corner and Dublin's pub doors are open to all comers. An evening with a succession of pints of Guinness, that

Dublin Coat of Arms (TW)

noble Irish black brew, is as much a part of the Dublin
experience as the Georgian streets and the fine old buildings.

It's not only the pubs which are easily accessible.
Dublin is a city on a human scale so it's easy to get
around on foot. Accommodation is plentiful and varied,
ranging from cheap and cheerful backpacker hostels to
elegant five-star hotels. The food is surprisingly varied,
with restaurants from every corner of the world as well
as down-to-earth local specialities such as Irish stew or
Dublin coddle. It's a city which fits comfortably, like a
warm old coat; it may not always be fashionable, but it's
always a pleasure to slip on.

Facts about Dublin

HISTORY

Dublin officially celebrated its millennium in 1988 but it's fairly certain that there were settlements here long before 988 AD. The first early Celtic habitation was on the banks of the River Liffey and the city's Gaelic name, Baile Átha Cliath, 'the Town of the Hurdle Ford', comes from an ancient river crossing that can still be pinpointed today. St Patrick's Cathedral is said to be built on the site of a well used by Ireland's patron saint for early conversions in the 5th century.

Viking & Norman Invasions

It was not until the Vikings turned up that Dublin became a permanent fixture. By the 9th century raids from the north had become a fact of Irish life, but some of the fierce Danes chose to stay rather than simply rape, pillage and depart. They intermarried with the Irish and established a vigorous trading port at the point where the River Poddle joined the Liffey in a black pool, in

River Liffey (JM)

Gaelic a *dubh linn*. Today there's little trace of the Poddle, which has been channelled underground and flows under St Patrick's Cathedral to dribble into the Liffey by the Capel St (or Grattan) Bridge.

After their defeat by the Irish at the Battle of Clontarf in 1014, the Danes became a permanent fixture, adopting Christianity and building churches, traces of which can still be seen. The Norman Conquest of England in 1066 moved west to Ireland in the 12th century but, like their Viking predecessors, the Normans soon merged with the Irish rather than ruling over them. Until Elizabeth I (ruled 1558-1603) real English control over Ireland was restricted to the narrow east coast strip known as 'the Pale'. Beyond the Pale, Ireland remained unbowed, and raids from the fierce Irish warriors encamped in the Wicklow Mountains were a constant threat to the Norman stronghold in Dublin.

Medieval Dublin

Norman and then early English Dublin was still centred around the black pool which gave the city its name. The Olympia Theatre in the Temple Bar district would probably have been in that black pool, as the excavations under Dublin Castle, which you can visit today, show that the river banks extended to that point less than 1000 years ago. A little farther downstream Trinity College stands on reclaimed land, once part of the river's estuary. The black pool to the north and the estuary to the east bounded ancient Dublin, so when the city started to grow it expanded not eastward towards the heart of the modern city but westward. High St, the extension of Dame St and Christ Church Place beyond Christ Church Cathedral into the Liberties, was the spine of the medieval city. Patrick St, Francis St and other streets running off that ancient thoroughfare date back to the city's earliest development. Fishamble St, which winds down to the Liffey from right beside the Kinlay House Refectory, still has a medieval twist to it, quite unlike the straighter, more modern streets. The name comes from 'fish shambles' or fish market.

Dublin's history in the following centuries was a series of peaks and troughs. The 14th century brought an attempted invasion in 1316 and the devastation of the Black Death in 1348. In the 16th century there was Silken Thomas Fitzgerald's failed revolt in 1534 and Henry VIII's dissolution of the monasteries in 1537. In 1592, however, Elizabeth I founded Trinity College and gave Dublin an educational tradition which has been maintained to the present day.

The Protestant Ascendancy

The 17th century brought more disasters, as Cromwell took the city in 1649 and seized swathes of Ireland's best land to distribute among his soldiers. Worse was to come when Ireland found itself tangled up in greater European struggles and backed the wrong side at the Battle of the Boyne in 1690, in which England's William of Orange (1650-1702) defeated the deposed James II (1633-1701; king of England, Ireland and, as James VII, of Scotland). When the Catholic King James II scuttled away to safety, his supporters found themselves excluded from parliament and from many basic rights by the punitive anti-Catholic Penal Laws.

The period of the Protestant Ascendancy led Dublin into its 18th century boom years when fortunes were made, and for a time London was the only larger city in the British Isles. As the city expanded the nouveau riche abandoned medieval Dublin, which was squashed up against the Liffey around Dublin Castle and the two great cathedrals of St Patrick's and Christ Church. They moved north across the river to a new Dublin of stately squares surrounded by fine Georgian mansions. The planning of this magnificent Georgian Dublin was assisted by the establishment in 1757 of the Commission for Making Wide & Convenient Streets! At that time Mountjoy Square and Henrietta St to the north of the Liffey were Dublin's finest addresses.

Dublin's teeming masses were not so easily abandoned, however, and the city's slums soon spread north in pursuit of the rich, who turned back south to new homes on Merrion Square, Fitzwilliam Square and St Stephen's Green. When James Fitzgerald, the Earl of Kildare, commenced construction in 1745 of Leinster House, his magnificent mansion south of the Liffey, he was mocked for this foolish move away from the centre and into the wilds. 'Where I go society will follow,' he confidently predicted and he was soon proved right. Today Leinster House is used as the Irish Parliament building and it is right in the centre of modern Dublin.

Disasters of the 19th Century

The Georgian boom years of the 1700s were followed by more than a century of trouble and unrest. Even before the 18th century had ended the problems had started, with the abortive French-backed invasion by Wolfe Tone in 1796 and the equally unsuccessful rebellion of Lord Edward Fitzgerald, member of the United Irishmen, in 1798. Only five years later in 1803 there was another revolt, but, in what was becoming the Irish fashion, it was ill-conceived and badly planned though very romantic. Robert Emmet, the ringleader of this uprising, was executed outside St Catherine's Church in the Liberties and joined what would become an increasingly long list of eloquent Irish martyrs in the struggle against England.

In 1800 the Act of Union ended the separate Irish Parliament, subsuming it into the British Parliament at Westminster. This was achieved with more than a little bribery and corruption along the way, but the dramatic growth that had characterised Dublin in the previous century came to an almost immediate halt.

In 1823 Daniel O'Connell launched his campaign to recover basic rights for Ireland's Catholic population. For a time he made real progress and became known as 'The Liberator' but in the 1840s his efforts began to fade and Ireland was struck by its greatest disaster. The food needs of the burgeoning rural population had become overwhelmingly dependent on the easily grown potato, and when a disease devastated the potato crop the human cost was staggering, compounded as it was by the British government's shameful lack of assistance. Although Dublin escaped the worst effects of the great potato famines between 1845 and 1851, the streets and squares were still packed with refugees from the impoverished countryside, and the city's remorseless decline continued at an accelerated pace.

The clamour for Home Rule, effectively calling for a return to the pre-1800 situation when Ireland had its own parliament, grew louder in the 1870s. Charles Stewart Parnell (1846-91), leader of the Home Rule movement, was elected to the British Parliament in Westminster in 1875 and campaigned tirelessly for a Dublin parliament but, despite support from the British Prime Minister Gladstone, the Home Rule Bill was repeatedly defeated. Parnell himself, who at his peak had been dubbed the 'King of Ireland', suffered a dramatic fall from power when his liaison with Kitty O'Shea, a married woman, was revealed. The scandal reflected badly on Irish society and the Catholic Church, which found Parnell to be morally unfit as a leader. This was also a cause of the often bitter mistrust with which the church, in its conservative mode, is still held by many Irish.

The Struggle for Independence

Resentment against British rule began to show a violent side, and in 1882 the British Chief Secretary, Lord Frederick Cavendish, was assassinated in Phoenix Park by a group known as The Invincibles. The formation of the republican political movement Sinn Féin ('ourselves alone') in 1905 was further evidence of increasing anti-British resentment and in 1913 the general strike organised by Jim Larkin, a trade union leader, threw Dublin into chaos. At the same time agitation against Home Rule was growing in the Protestant-dominated northern Irish counties of Ulster, and the authorities turned a blind eye to arms shipments coming into Ireland for irregular Protestant forces. This was not to be the case when the *Asgard* slipped into Howth Harbour with a shipment of rifles for the Irish nationalist cause.

Despite well over a century of discontent, punctuated by occasional acts of violence or ill-planned revolts, there was still no across-the-board support for Irish independence and the departure of the British. Thousands of Irish volunteers marched off to the trenches in WW I but at home opposition to British rule continued to simmer. It came to the boil in 1916 in yet another ill-planned and poorly executed revolt – the Easter Rising.

The Easter Rising should have taken place on Easter Sunday, but was delayed at the last moment and rescheduled for Easter Monday. The end result of this bungling was a much smaller turnout than planned, but despite this the stirring words read out by Patrick Pearse (leader of the Rising) and his supporters from the steps of the GPO on O'Connell St were to lead inexorably to Ireland's division and independence.

Secrecy had been a key element in the planning of the Easter Rising since so many previous rebellions had been ruined by betrayals. Unfortunately, the secrecy was so pervasive that many supporters had little idea of what was happening. Nevertheless, the General Post Office (GPO), the headquarters for the Rising, was quickly taken, other key points in the city were secured and Dublin Castle itself would probably have fallen to the rebels had they known that it was virtually undefended. Initially the British troops in Dublin were taken completely by surprise but they quickly moved into action and the Irish forces were soon outnumbered and outgunned.

The rebels still managed to hold out for a week, by which time large tracts of Dublin were in ruins and the GPO, along with much of O'Connell St, was a smoking shell. Finally the revolt was crushed, the garrisons surrendered and the leaders were marched off to jail. That might have been the end of the matter, as they enjoyed little popular support and were openly jeered as they were taken away. But the British administration over-reacted disastrously and, in the words of W B Yeats, 'A terrible beauty is born'.

On 3 May, just three days after the Rising ended, Patrick Pearse and two other leaders faced the firing squad. Four more were executed on 4 May. Another was executed on 5 May, followed by four more on 8 May. In all, 77 death sentences were passed and, though most of them were not carried out by the time the 16th and final execution, that of James Connolly on 12 May, had taken place, the leaders of the Rising had been transformed from public nuisances into national heroes.

When prisoners from the Rising were released in 1917, after the British government suddenly decided to let the lot out, they returned to Dublin to a heroes' welcome. The whole country was now seething and when WW I dragged to an end Ireland was in turmoil. Parliamentary elections saw Sinn Féin candidates score turnround victories, winning nearly three-quarters of the Irish parliamentary seats. At the same time terrorist strikes against symbols of British control started to occur, led by the military wing of Sinn Féin, the Irish Republican Army (IRA). A prime force in this reversal of Irish opinion was Michael Collins, a visionary political leader of Sinn Féin and a master of ruthless but effective guerrilla tactics.

The British countered violence with violence by increasing the strength of the Royal Irish Constabulary and adding a tough-minded auxiliary force. They became known as the Black and Tans (because of the colour of their uniforms), but their use of violence simply increased resentment against the British and support for the Irish nationalist cause. The death from a hunger strike of Terence MacSwiney, the Mayor of Cork, further crystallised Irish opinion and in November 1920 Ireland's first 'Bloody Sunday' signalled a further escalation in the struggle. Michael Collins organised the prebreakfast killing of 14 undercover British intelligence officers in Dublin and that afternoon, in reprisal, spectators were fired on with machine guns at a football match. Twelve people, including one of the players, died. Later that night two IRA men and a Sinn Féin supporter were murdered in Dublin Castle.

A month later, in another act of reprisal by British forces, the centre of Cork city was burnt and looted. Fire brigades were deliberately prevented from fighting the blaze and a British enquiry into the event was never released. The violence continued despite British Prime Minister Lloyd George announcing in early 1921 that: 'We have murder by the throat!' In May IRA forces burnt down Dublin's Custom House, the centre of British administration in Ireland, but by this time exhaustion was setting in on both sides and a truce was signed on 11 July 1921.

Independence & the Civil War

The Anglo-Irish Treaty was finally signed, after months of argument, on 6 December 1921. Unfortunately for both sides, it was far from being a neat agreement and Michael Collins clearly saw its huge problems when he announced, 'I have signed my death warrant'. The treaty did not create the Irish Republic for which the IRA had fought, it merely created the Irish Free State, still subservient to Britain on many important issues. Worse, from the Irish perspective, it allowed the six Ulster counties that make up Northern Ireland to opt out of the new country. Thus were the seeds planted for a problem that will continue to fester into the next century.

The immediate result was the division of Ireland into pro and antitreaty supporters. Although the Dáil, the new parliament of independent Ireland, narrowly ratified the treaty and the general public did the same by a larger margin, a Civil War broke out in June 1922. Antitreaty IRA forces had occupied the Four Courts building on the banks of the Liffey in Dublin and when they refused to surrender, Collins shelled them from across the river. The Four Courts building, one of the classic buildings of Georgian Dublin, soon went up in flames, just as the equally beautiful Custom House had done a year earlier. In a repeat of the 1916 Rising, O'Connell St followed into the fire and antitreaty IRA forces were soon mounting ambushes of Free State forces, just like those against the Black and Tans a year or two before. On 22 August Michael Collins died in an ambush near Cork, thus fulfilling his dire prophecy.

The Dáil then passed a bill mandating the death sentence for any IRA member possessing a gun when captured. On 24 November Robert Erskine Childers, whose yacht the *Asgard* had brought arms for the republican cause to Howth in 1914, was executed for possessing a revolver which had actually been given to him by Michael Collins. By May 1923, 77 executions had taken place and Eamon de Valera, president of Sinn Féin, who had himself been imprisoned by the Free State authorities for a year, ordered the IRA to drop their arms. The Civil War ground to a halt and a wedge was driven between Sinn Féin, as a political force, and the IRA, as a terrorist organisation.

Top & Bottom: Derelict Buildings (JM)

The Irish Republic

Ireland was finally at peace but many questions were left unanswered. The substantial minority of members of parliament who had been elected on the republican and antitreaty platform refused to take up their seats, particularly as it would involve an oath of allegiance to the British king. The IRA, without an armed struggle to pursue, was becoming a marginalised force in independent Ireland and as a result Sinn Féin was falling apart. In 1926 Eamon de Valera, took his supporters to a new party, Fianna Fáil, and in 1927 almost won power, despite the fact that they still refused to sit in parliament. In 1927 he managed to lead his party into the Dáil by the simple expedient of not taking the oath but signing in as if he had.

In 1932 de Valera and Fianna Fáil won the election and repeated the performance, with an increased majority, in 1933. In fact what had happened was that the forces who lost the Civil War in 1922 had taken power by the ballot box 10 years later. They soon set about jettisoning the treaty clauses with which they disagreed. The oath to the British crown went, the British governor general soon followed, and, by the outbreak of WW II, Ireland was a republic in all but name, and even that had been changed from the Irish Free State to Eire. The actual creation of the Irish Republic followed in 1948, when Fianna Fáil finally fell from power.

The only unresolved problem that remains from 1921 is Northern Ireland but, though bitterness and violence have racked the north since 1969, the problem may yet be solved by more peaceful methods. The development of the EC may simply erase the border (one Europe may also mean one Ireland) or demographics may do the job (sometime early in the next century northern Catholics will outnumber northern Protestants).

Dublin's expansion has continued south to Ballsbridge, Dun Laoghaire and beyond, but the Liffey has remained a rough dividing line between southern haves and northern have-nots. The country's long-term population decline finally reached its trough in the 1960s and there has subsequently been modest growth. For a time EC investment promised a brighter future, but Ireland still suffers massive unemployment and ongoing emigration.

GOVERNMENT

The Republic of Ireland has a parliamentary system of government. The lower house, or house of representatives, is known as the Dáil Éireann, usually shortened to the Dáil and pronounced 'doil'. The upper house or senate is the Seanad Éireann. The prime minister is the Taoiseach (pronounced 'tee-shuck') and the 166 members of parliament are known as Teachtái Dála and referred to as TDs.

The main political parties are Fianna Fáil (Soldiers of Destiny), Fine Gael (Tribe of the Gaels) and the Labour Party. The current prime minister is Albert Reynolds, the leader of Fianna Fáil, which governs in coalition with the Labour Party. There is also an appointed president, who is currently the very popular Mary Robinson. Parliament meets in Leinster House (see that section in the Things to See & Do chapter for more information).

ORIENTATION

Dublin lies about 53° north of the equator, a similar latitude to Warsaw and some pretty chilly places in Canada. Luckily, Dublin enjoys a much milder climate than its northerly position might indicate.

Greater Dublin sprawls around the arc of Dublin Bay, bounded to the north by the hills at Howth and to the south by the Dalkey headland. The central city area of Dublin is neatly divided by the River Liffey into southern and northern halves. The Viking and medieval city of Dublin developed first to the south of the river. The city spread north in the early years of its Georgian heyday then moved south again as the northern part peaked and then declined.

North of the river the important streets for visitors are O'Connell St, the major shopping thoroughfare, and Gardiner St, with many bed and breakfasts (B&Bs). Most of the hostels are located in this area and the main bus station and one of the two main railway stations are near the southern end of Gardiner St, which becomes very run down as it continues north. Immediately south of the river is the intriguing old Temple Bar area and the expanse of Trinity College. Nassau St along the southern edge of the campus and pedestrianised Grafton St are the main shopping streets south of the river.

The post codes for central Dublin are Dublin 1 immediately north of the river and Dublin 2 immediately south. The posh Ballsbridge area south-east of the centre is Dublin 4.

Finding Addresses

There are several problems inherent with finding addresses in Dublin and these same problems also exist in other Irish towns. One is the tendency for street names to change every few blocks. Another is that streets are subdivided into upper and lower or north and south parts. It doesn't seem to matter if you put the definer in front of or behind the name – thus you can have Lower Baggot St or Baggot St Lower, South Anne St or Anne St South. Street numbering often runs up one side of a street and down the other, rather than a more logical system of having odd numbers on one side and even on the other.

CLIMATE

Ireland has a relatively mild climate. May and June are the sunniest months and December is the most overcast. The sea around Ireland is surprisingly warm for the latitude because of the influence of the North Atlantic Drift, or Gulf Stream. That merely means it's decidedly chilly rather than downright freezing. It's not much warmer at the height of summer (about 15°C) than in the depths of winter (10°C).

Rainfall

It does tend to rain in Ireland; even the drier parts of Ireland, and Dublin is one of the driest, get rain on 150 days in a typical year and it often rains every day for weeks on end. Dublin receives about 75 cm of rainfall annually, so there's much local terminology and humour about the rain – a 'soft day', for instance, is a damp one. Bring an umbrella. December and January are the coldest, dullest and wettest months but major snowfalls are rare.

Sunshine

May and June are the sunniest months and you can expect five to 6½ hours of sunshine a day. December is the opposite extreme with a daily average of only one to two hours of sunshine.

Temperatures

In January and February, average temperatures range from 4°C to 7°C. Average maximums in July and August range from 17°C to 20°C, so even at the height of summer it's wise to have a sweater or light coat at the ready. Winters tend to be damp and cold.

POPULATION & PEOPLE

The total population of Ireland is about five million – 3.5 million in the south, 1.5 million in the north. This figure is remarkable in that it is less than it was 150 years ago. Prior to the potato famines between 1845 and 1849, the population was probably around eight million. Deaths and huge numbers of emigrants reduced the population to around six million, and Irish emigration continued at a high level for the next 100 years. It was not until the 1960s that Ireland's population finally began to increase again. Dublin's population is about one million, approximately 20% of that of the whole island. Since the days of 'The Pale', when English power in Ireland was centred in Dublin and barely seeped out into the rest of the country, Dublin has been the centre of British influence. Even a century ago the term 'West British' was derisively applied to Irish whose hearts were really British. The term is still used today.

ARTS & CULTURE

Literature

Of all the arts it is in literature that Ireland has had the most impact. No other city, Dubliners are proud to boast, can claim three Nobel Prize winners for literature. There's even a Dublin Writers' Museum, purely to trace the country's literary history. Books also take centre stage at Marsh's Library, the Chester Beatty Library and, of course, at the Book of Kells exhibit in the Library of Trinity College.

Although writing goes back so far in Ireland – Irish monks were copying Bibles and spreading their learning abroad while England was still plunged in the Dark Ages – it's the Irish mastery of English that is most renowned. Jonathan Swift (1667-1745), the master satirist, was the greatest Dublin writer of the early Georgian period but he was followed by many others, such as Oliver Goldsmith (1728-74), author of *The Vicar of Wakefield*, and Thomas Moore (1779-1852), whose poems formed the repertoires of generations of Irish tenor singers.

William Butler Yeats (1865-1939), better known as W B Yeats, is perhaps best remembered as a poet though he also wrote plays, was a founder of the Abbey Theatre, served as a senator in the early years of the Irish Free State and carried off one of Dublin's trio of literary Nobel Prizes in 1938. George Bernard Shaw (1925) and Samuel Beckett (1969) were the other two prizewinners. James

Joyce (1882-1941) is this century's best known Irish author and was probably destined to add a fourth Nobel Prize to the Dublin tally had not WW II and his death intervened. *Dubliners* and *A Portrait of the Artist as a Young Man* were his first two books, but it is the monumental *Ulysses* for which he is chiefly remembered.

Dublin is also notable for its literary boozers and hell raisers. Brendan Behan (1923-64), author of *Borstal Boy* and *The Quare Fellow*, managed to fall into both categories and drink himself to death to boot. The poet Patrick Kavanagh (1905-67) was another writer with a fond attachment to pub life. He was a great chronicler of central Dublin and can still be found sitting, in statue form, by the Grand Canal.

Although Dublin and Ireland have played such a central part in the work of writers like James Joyce, others have become such international names that their Dublin antecedents are virtually forgotten. In fact Oscar Wilde (1854-1900) and George Bernard Shaw (1856-1950) were both products of Dublin. It was Dubliner Bram Stoker (1847-1912) who invented Dracula and in an earlier era it was a Dubliner named Richard Steele who founded those resolutely English magazines the *Tatler* (in 1709) and the *Spectator* (in 1711).

See the Books section in the Facts for the Visitor chapter for more information on Dublin writers and books about Dublin.

Theatre

Dublin has a theatrical history as long as its literary one. The first theatre was founded in Werburgh St in 1637 and, though it was closed by the Puritans only four years later, another theatre named Smock Alley Playhouse or Theatre Royal opened in 1661 and continued for over a century.

The turn-of-the-century Celtic Revival and the establishment of the Abbey Theatre by W B Yeats and Lady Gregory may be the first images that spring to mind when Irish theatre is mentioned today but many plays from an earlier era are still staged. Oliver Goldsmith found fame as a novelist as well as for writing plays like *She Stoops to Conquer* in 1773. Richard Brinsley Sheridan (1751-1816) introduced the word 'malapropism' to the English language via the tongue-twisted Mrs Malaprop in *The Rivals* in 1775.

The opening of the Abbey Theatre in 1904 also brought controversy to centre stage. J M Synge (1871-1909) was already a subject of discussion for his earlier plays before *The Playboy of the Western World* caused near riots in 1907. It was subjected to equally vociferous audience reaction when it was taken to the USA. *Juno & the Paycock* by Sean O'Casey (1880-1964) was well received in 1924 but *The Plough & the Stars* in 1926 sparked a violent reception from its audience. Synge's Playboy had upset a romantically idealised view of rural Ireland, and O'Casey's play raised patriotic ire as it was seen to be mocking the events of the 1916 Rising. More recently, *Waiting for Godot* by Samuel Beckett (1906-89) may not have pleased everybody (Sean O'Casey certainly had no time for Beckett's bleak outlook on life) but it did contribute to his winning the Nobel Prize in 1969.

See the Theatre sections in the Things to See & Do and Entertainment chapters for more details about Dublin's theatres and theatre performances.

Painting

Although Ireland does not have a tradition of painting anything like its literary history, the National Gallery does have an extensive Irish School collection, much of it chronicling the personages and pursuits of the Anglo-Irish aristocracy. Just as W B Yeats played a seminal role in the Celtic literary revival, his younger brother Jack Butler Yeats (1871-1957), inspired an artistic surge of creativity. Their father, John Butler Yeats, was also a noted portrait painter.

Music

Literature may be the field in which Irish artists have had the greatest worldwide influence but music is the art that you are most likely to come across while visiting Dublin. Just as pubs are an intrinsic part of the Dublin lifestyle, music is an intrinsic part of the pub lifestyle. It's not even necessary to enter a pub to find music, as buskers are busy in Dublin's streets at all hours of the day and far into the night.

The most time-honoured form of Irish music is folk or traditional music, which has managed to survive with much greater vigour in Ireland than has comparable music in other European countries. Irish music enthusiasm has not, however, been confined solely to traditional music. There is also great enthusiasm for imported musical forms – particularly country and western – and a great deal of Irish influence can be heard in the music played by modern Irish musicians like Clannad, Van

Morrison, Paul Brady, Luka Bloom or even U2. See the Entertainment chapter for information about music in Dublin and where to find it.

A wide variety of instruments are used in traditional Irish music but the most uniquely Irish include the harp, which is also the country's national emblem; the bodhrán, a goatskin drum; and the uillean pipes, which are played with a bellows squeezed under the elbow (*uillean* in Irish). The fiddle is less purely Irish but is a mainstay of traditional music, along with the accordion, the banjo, and simple tin whistles or spoons.

Architecture

Dublin's architectural prime was in the Georgian period, which lasted from the accession of King George I in 1714 to the death of King George IV in 1830. During this period a number of Georgian styles were followed but the unifying theme was a simpler and more severe style that contrasted with the Baroque designs of the preceding period. Architecture of the Georgian era was influenced at first by the Italian Renaissance and later by the designs of classical Greece and Rome.

Dublin's Georgian-era economic boom financed the city's rapid development in this period. Although there are many fine Georgian set pieces – such as James Gandon's Custom House and Four Courts buildings – it is the Georgian squares and streetscapes which are the city's most potent reminder of the times. Unfortunately, the economic boom ended with the close of the 18th century. The 1800s were tough years for Ireland and the country has certainly not produced any great architectural inspiration this century.

Sports

Ireland has a number of unique sports which are followed with great enthusiasm, though none has its strongest following in Dublin. Hurling is probably the most authentically Irish with a history that stretches back to Celtic myths. Gaelic football is the most popular sport in Ireland and has similarities with both soccer and rugby but particularly with Australian Rules football. The All Ireland Hurling and Football finals both take place in Dublin in September. See the Sports & Activities section in the Things to See & Do chapter for more information on Irish sports.

Dublin's Architects & Architecture

Dublin's wonderfully unified feel can be credited to a rough-and-tumble history, a century of elegant wealth, a further century of neglect and a final tough century leading up to the present day. Dublin's tangled history from its pre-Viking Celtic beginnings to its Viking, Norman and English periods saw fine buildings thrown up, and equally rapidly torn down. As a result the survivors from Dublin's earliest days are either inconsequential (the Protestant St Audoen's Church), fragmentary (bits and pieces of Dublin Castle) or heavily restored (St Patrick's and Christ Church cathedrals).

Dublin's peak was reached during the 1700s, when it was one of the great Georgian cities whose wealth led to the creation of magnificent streetscapes and fine squares. The reason the architecture of this era survived is because of the century of neglect that followed, for the 1800 Act of Union not only destroyed the Irish Parliament but also the basis of Ireland's wealth. The mid-century potato famines and the ensuing depopulation of Ireland simply compounded the disaster, so nothing much was built in the 1800s. Ireland's decline continued into the 1900s, and independence in the 1920s, the Depression in the 1930s and WW II in the 1940s all contributed to the slow pace of change.

The end result is that despite a spate of destructive modern development since the 1960s and the influx of money from the EC, large chunks of modern Dublin are still of a piece – of an 18th century piece. The Georgian house style that is so powerfully and consistently displayed in Dublin follows a very standard pattern. Starting with the basement, Dublin town houses typically have four storeys with symmetrically arranged windows and an imposing, centrally located front door. Granite steps lead up to the door, which is further embellished with, in the best examples, a delicate leaded fanlight. A wide variety of door knockers, door handles and letterboxes decorate the often brightly painted doors, while foot scrapers, once used to scrape mud from gentlemen's boots, can still be seen beside many doors. The formal exteriors of these houses was often counterpointed internally by exuberant plasterwork and complex staircase railings.

In spite of its many fine Georgian streetscapes and town houses, Dublin would be just another Georgian city if it had only private houses to show for the period. The city's real glory is its wonderful public buildings and for these it has one particular architect to thank – James Gandon.

Of all of Dublin's architects, during its prime, James Gandon (1743-1823) was the greatest. Among his works are his two riverside masterpieces, the Custom House and the later Four Courts, as well as the King's Inns, the O'Connell Bridge (originally the Carlisle Bridge) and the final part of the Houses of Parliament, now the Bank of Ireland. Gandon was English but of Huguenot descent and he looked across the Channel for his inspiration, so his greatest works owe more to Paris' River Seine than to London's Thames.

Francis Johnston (1760-1829) was responsible for numerous buildings, such as the Chapel Royal in Dublin Castle, St George's Church in north Dublin, the Royal Hibernian Military School in Phoenix Park (now St Mary's Hospital) and the GPO. He was also called in for a number of important additions and alterations, including work on King's Inns and the building which is now the Irish president's residence, Áras an Uachtaráin. It was Johnston who redesigned the Irish Parliament building when it was taken over by the Bank of Ireland.

The work of Sir William Chambers (1723-96) in Dublin included buildings at Trinity College and Charlemont House on Parnell Square (now the Hugh Lane Municipal Gallery of Modern Art), but his Dublin masterpiece is the wonderfully eccentric Casino at Marino. Remarkably, Chambers never visited Dublin. In England his work featured the remodelling of Buckingham House (now Buckingham Palace) and the designing of Somerset House.

From a slightly earlier era Richard Castle (1690-1751) can cause some confusion in Dublin as he is frequently referred to as Richard Cassel. He was born in Hesse-Cassel in Germany and came to Ireland in 1727. Among the buildings he created are those at Nos 80 and 85 St Stephen's Green (now Iveagh House and Newman House respectively), Tyrone House on Marlborough St (near the Pro-Cathedral), a number of Trinity College buildings (most of which were later replaced, except for the Printing House) and some of Ireland's finest country homes, such as Powerscourt (County Wicklow) and Westport (County Mayo). His crowning achievements were Leinster House (now the Dáil or Irish Parliament) and the Rotunda Hospital, construction of which started just before he died.

Another of Dublin's prominent architects was Thomas Burgh (1670-1730), who built the original Custom House, Dr Steeven's Hospital near Heuston Station and Trinity College Library. Sir William Robinson was responsible for Marsh's Library and the Royal Hospital Kilmainham, built between 1680-87 and said to be Dublin's finest building in that century.

A number of Dublin's buildings are crowned by fine statuary, and Edward Smyth created the statues which top the Four Courts and the Custom House. Dublin's finest Georgian houses, whose exteriors were so simple and severe, were often decorated inside with superbly crafted plasterwork. Some of the finest is the work of Michael Stapleton which can be seen in Trinity College, Powerscourt House, Ely House near St Stephen's Green and Belvedere House in north Dublin. Also notable is the work of the Francini brothers in Newman House on St Stephen's Green and that of Robert West on the building next door (the home of Richard Chapel Whaley) and in Newbridge House at Donabate. West's own house is still standing at 20 Dominick St, near King's Inns in north Dublin.

Of course, architects are nothing without developers to employ them, and the greatest of all the Georgian Dublin property speculators was Luke Gardiner (1745-98), later Viscount Mountjoy. Dublin in its Georgian prime started north of the river, then spread back to the south. Gardiner's Mall was one of the viscount's greatest achievements, and when a bridge linked it (as Sackville St) with south Dublin it became the new central axis of the city. It remains so to this day, though it is now known as O'Connell St. Mountjoy Square, which began as Gardiner's Square, was another Luke Gardiner creation. The very first of Dublin's great Georgian streets was Henrietta St, leading to King's Inns in north Dublin, and Luke Gardiner lived there at No 10.

William Dargan (1799-1867) also played a major part in the development of Dublin. He opened the Dublin-Dun Laoghaire railway line in 1834 and mounted the Dublin Industrial Exhibition on the lawn in front of Leinster House in 1853. The proceeds from that exhibition were then used to found the National Gallery in 1864. ∎

CULTURAL CENTRES

With its new EC role Dublin has an international selection of cultural centres. The city is also a very popular centre for English-language instruction, particularly for students from Spain who flock to Dublin every summer and have become a colourful part of the city scene. The city's cultural centres include:

Alliance Française
    1 Kildare St, Dublin 2 (☎ 676 1732)
British Council
    Newmount House, 22/24 Mount St Lower, Dublin 2 (☎ 676 4088, 676 6943)
Goethe Institute
    37 Merrion Square, Dublin 2 (☎ 661 1155)
Italian Cultural Institute
    11 Fitzwilliam Square, Dublin 2 (☎ 676 6662)
Spanish Cultural Institute
    58 Northumberland Rd, Dublin 4 (☎ 668 2024)

RELIGION

Ireland is a strongly Catholic country but it also has a substantial Protestant minority, as well as smaller numbers of other faiths. The undeniably powerful position of the Roman Catholic Church in Ireland is a subject of considerable controversy and is frequently cited by the Northern Irish as a major barrier to unification. The new constitution introduced by Eamon de Valera in 1937 noted the church's 'special position' in Ireland as the religion of 'the great majority of its citizens'. However, it did not make Catholicism the official religion of the country even though the church had pressed for that position.

In 1970 even the constitutional 'special position' was rescinded but the reality is that the church still wields great power in Ireland. Some of the church's influence has been cut back in recent years – the enormous list of banned books has been drastically curtailed and in 1992 the controversial film *Basic Instinct* was shown uncut in Ireland, when even in the USA it suffered some cuts. On the other hand the contraceptive pill is still banned in Ireland, though condoms are freely available even if they cannot be openly displayed. Divorce is still banned in Ireland, as is abortion. Despite this, Ireland is believed to have a greater abortion rate than liberal countries like the Netherlands – Irish abortions are simply exported to England.

BEHAVIOUR

Ireland is a relaxed and easy-going country with few rigid rules and regulations. There is nobody you have to be particularly wary of offending, and there are few rigid rules of behaviour and dress code regulations, apart from those dreamed up by bad-tempered Leeson St nightclub bouncers. You can jaywalk with impunity and lots of Irish cyclists even seem to get away with chaining their bicycles up to the 'do not park bicycles here' signs. Be aware, however, that discussions about religion or politics can get very heated.

LANGUAGE

English is spoken throughout Ireland, but there are still parts of western Ireland known as the Gaeltacht, where Irish (a Gaelic language) is the native language. Officially, the Republic of Ireland is bilingual but in practice few people outside the Gaeltacht speak it fluently.

Some useful words in Gaelic include *fáilte* (welcome), *céad míle fáilte* (a hundred thousand welcomes), *gardaí* (police), *mná* (woman), *fir* (man), *an lár* (town centre). In Irish, Dublin is *Baile Átha Cliath*.

Although English is, in reality, the main language of Ireland, it's spoken with a peculiar Irish flavour and lilt. Indeed the Irish accent is one of the most pleasant varieties of English to be heard. Some of the peculiarly Irish sentence constructions are closely related to Gaelic; for instance, the usual word order in Irish sentences is verb, subject, object. The present participle is also used more frequently in constructions like 'Would you be wanting a room for the night, then?'. The Irish also have a notable bias towards scatological speech, in particular, as anyone who has seen the film *The Commitments* will confirm, towards use of the word 'fucking' or, more correctly in Irish use, *fooking*.

Facts for the Visitor

VISAS & EMBASSIES

Citizens of most Western countries do not need a visa to visit Ireland. UK nationals born in Great Britain or Northern Ireland do not require a passport. Irish diplomatic offices overseas include:

Australia
    20 Arkana St, Yarralumla, Canberra, ACT 2600 (☎ 06-273 3022)
Canada
    170 Metcalfe St, Ottawa, Ontario K2P 1P3 (☎ 416-745 8624)
Denmark
    Ostbanegade 21, ITH, DK-2100 Copenhagen (☎ 423 233)
France
    12 Ave Foch, 75116 Paris (☎ 45 00 20 87)
Germany
    Godesberger Allee 119, 5300 Bonn 2 (☎ 37 69 37/38/39)
Italy
    Largo del Nazzareno 3, 00187 Rome (☎ 678 25 41/42/43/44/45)
Japan
    Kowa Building No 25, 8-7 Sanbancho, Chiyoda-ku, Tokyo (☎ 263 06 95)
Netherlands
    9 Dr Kuperstraat, 2514 BA The Hague (☎ 070-63 0993/4)
Portugal
    Rua da Imprensa (a Estrela) 1-4, 1200 Lisbon (☎ 396 1569)
Spain
    Claudio Coello 73, 1st floor, Madrid 1 (☎ 576 3500)
Sweden
    Ostermalmsgatan 97 (IV), 114 59 Stockholm (☎ 661 80 05, 661 74 09 & 661 32 41)
Switzerland
    Eigerstrasse 71, Berne 3007 (☎ 46 23 53/54)
UK
    17 Grosvenor Place, London SW1X 7HR (☎ 071-235 2171)
USA
    2234 Massachusetts Ave NW, Washington, DC 20008 (☎ 202-462 3939)

In addition there are Irish consulates in the USA in Boston, Chicago, New York and San Francisco.

Foreign Embassies in Dublin

You will find embassies of the following countries in Dublin. For citizens of New Zealand and Singapore, the closest embassies are in London.

Australia
    6th floor, Fitzwilton House, Wilton Terrace, Dublin 2 (☎ 676 1517)
Canada
    65/68 St Stephen's Green, Dublin 2 (☎ 478 1988)
Denmark
    121 St Stephen's Green, Dublin 2 (☎ 475 6404)
France
    36 Ailesbury Rd, Dublin 4 (☎ 269 4777)
Germany
    31 Trimleston Ave, Booterstown (☎ 269 3011)
Italy
    63 Northumberland Rd, Dublin 4 (☎ 660 1744)
Japan
    22 Ailesbury Rd, Dublin 4 (☎ 269 4244)
Netherlands
    160 Merrion Rd, Dublin 4 (☎ 269 3444)
New Zealand
    (in London) New Zealand House, Haymarket, London SW1 4QT (☎ 071-930 8422)
Norway
    Hainault House, 69 St Stephen's Green, Dublin 2 (☎ 478 3133)
Portugal
    Knocksinna House, Foxrock (☎ 289 4416)
Singapore
    (in London) 2 Wilton Crescent, London SW1X 8HG (☎ 071-235 8315)
Spain
    17A Merlyn Park, Dublin 4 (☎ 269 1640)
Sweden
    Sun Alliance House, Dawson St, Dublin 2 (☎ 671 5822)
Switzerland
    Ailesbury Rd, Dublin 4 (☎ 671 5822)
UK
    33 Merrion Rd, Dublin 4 (☎ 269 5211)
USA
    42 Elgin Rd, Dublin 4 (☎ 668 8777)

Work

With unemployment in Ireland running at nearly 20%, this is not a good country in which to look for casual employment, though there is a great deal of seasonal work in the tourist industry. Ireland is a member of the EC so citizens of any other EC country can work in Ireland.

CUSTOMS

The usual tobacco, alcohol and perfume regulations apply to duty-free imports. Dublin and Shannon airports place great emphasis on their competitive duty-free shopping.

MONEY

Currency

The Irish pound or punt (IR£) is, like the British pound, divided into 100 pence (p). There are coins of 1, 2, 5, 10, 20 and 50p and IR£1. Notes come in IR£5, IR£10, IR£20, IR£50 and IR£100.

Don't confuse Northern Irish pounds (issued by the Bank of Ireland or Allied Irish Banks) with Republic of Ireland pounds (issued by the Central Bank of Ireland). 'Sterling' or 'Belfast' are giveaway words on the Northern Irish notes, which are worth the same as the pound sterling. After many years of being worth slightly less than the British pound sterling, in early 1993 the punt was worth slightly more.

Most major currencies and brands of travellers' cheques are easily exchanged in Ireland. If you carry them in pounds sterling, you can change them without exchange loss or commission if you visit Northern Ireland or Britain. Eurocheques can also be cashed in Ireland.

When your finances have you by the balls... (JM)

Exchange Rates

A$1	=	IR£0.47
C$1	=	IR£0.52
NZ$1	=	IR£0.33
US$1	=	IR£0.66
UK£1	=	IR£0.95
IR£1	=	A$2.15
IR£1	=	C$1.90
IR£1	=	NZ$3.00
IR£1	=	US$1.50
IR£1	=	UK£1.05

Banks & Exchange Bureaus

The best exchange rates are obtained at banks, which are usually open from 10 am to 12.30 pm and 1.30 to 3 pm Monday to Friday. In Dublin they stay open until 5 pm on Thursday. The custom of closing for lunch may soon be dropped. *Bureaux de change* and other exchange facilities usually stay open longer but the rate or commission will be worse.

The foreign exchange counter at Dublin Airport is in the baggage collection area and opens from around 7 am to 9.30 pm in summer, 7.30 am to 8.30 pm in winter. There are numerous banks around the centre, all of which have exchange facilities. American Express and Thomas Cook are across the road from the Bank of Ireland and the Trinity College entrance.

The main offices of major Irish banks in Dublin are:

Allied Irish Banks
    Bankcentre, Ballsbridge, Dublin 4 (☎ 660 0311)
Bank of Ireland
    Baggot St Lower, Dublin 2 (☎ 661 5933)
National Irish Bank
    7/8 Wilton Terrace, Dublin 2 (☎ 678 5066)
Ulster Bank
    33 College Green, Dublin 2 (☎ 677 7623)

Currency Regulations

You can bring in as much currency as you wish but on departure you are not allowed to take out more than IR£150 in Irish notes, and notes must be no larger than IR£20. Foreign currency in excess of IR£1200 may be taken out of the country only if you brought it in with you. There are no limits on the import and subsequent export of travellers' cheques or letters of credit.

Cheques

Eurocheques can be cashed in Dublin but special arrangements must be made in advance if you wish to use personal cheques.

Credit Cards

Major credit cards, particularly Visa and MasterCard (often called Access), are widely accepted. You can obtain cash advances on these cards from a bank or from Allied Irish Bank (AIB) automated teller machines (ATMs). The AIB has a number of conveniently central ATMs.

Costs

Costs in Dublin are lower than in London or other major European cities but they are certainly not cheap. Many places to stay, particularly hostels, have different high and low-season prices. Some places may have not just a high season but a *peak* high-season price. In all cases the highest price levels are quoted. Entry prices are usually lower for children or students than for adults. The student and child price may sometimes differ.

At the bottom of the scale a hostel bed will cost IR£6 to IR£10 a night. A cheap B&B will cost about IR£15 to IR£20 per person, and a more luxurious B&B or guest-house with attached bathroom would cost about IR£20 to IR£40. Dinner with a glass of wine or a beer in a reasonable restaurant will cost from IR£8 to IR£15.

Sightseeing Discounts

Many parks, monuments and gardens in the Republic of Ireland are operated by the Office of Public Works (OPW). From any of these sites, you can get a Heritage Card for IR£10 (children IR£4), giving you unlimited access to all of these sites for one year.

If you're planning a serious onslaught on Ireland's plentiful supply of castles, monasteries and other sites, this card can be worthwhile. OPW sites in Dublin which charge an entry fee are the Casino Marino (IR£1), St Mary's Abbey (IR£1) and Kilmainham Jail (IR£1.50). OPW sites within day-trip distance of Dublin are Mellifont Abbey (80p), Knowth (IR£1) and Newgrange (IR£1.50) in the Boyne Valley to the north; Glendalough to the south charges an entry fee to the visitors' centre (IR£1) but not to the site itself.

A 'Passport to Dublin's Heritage' costs IR£15 (students IR£11) and gets you into the Dublin Writers'

Museum, the zoo, Malahide Castle, Newman House and Trinity College and gives you various freebies at other sites. It's available from the tourist offices or at the sites.

Tipping

Tipping is less prevalent in Ireland than elsewhere in Europe. Fancy hotels and restaurants usually add a 15% service charge and no additional tip is required. Simpler places usually do not add service, and if you decide to tip, it's acceptable to round up the bill or add 10% at most. You do not have to tip taxi drivers, but if you do 10% is fine. For porters 50p per bag is OK.

Consumer Taxes

Value-added tax (VAT) applies to most goods and services in Ireland. Visitors can claim back the VAT on large purchases that are subsequently exported outside the EC. If you are a resident of a country outside the EC and buy something from a Cashback Store, you will be given a Cashback Voucher that can be refunded at Dublin Airport or stamped at the ferry port and mailed back for a refund.

WHEN TO GO

Dublin is definitely a summer destination, but in July and August it will be at its most crowded and expensive. In the quieter winter months, however, you may get miserable weather and many tourist facilities will be shut.

WHAT TO BRING

The Irish climate is changeable and even at the height of summer you should be prepared for cold weather and sudden rainfall. A raincoat or an umbrella is a necessity. Otherwise, Dublin presents few surprises, dress is usually casual and you are unlikely to come across many coat and tie-type regulations except in the most deluxe restaurants.

TOURIST OFFICES

There are tourist offices operated by Dublin Tourism and the Irish Tourist Board or Bord Fáilte. The services of both offices are more or less identical. If you arrive by air or sea, you will find tourist offices at the airport

(☎ 844 5387) and on the waterfront at Dun Laoghaire
(☎ 280 6984).

In the city the Dublin Tourism office (☎ 874 7733) is at
14 O'Connell St Upper. This office is open from 8.30 am
to 8 pm Monday to Saturday and 10.30 am to 2 pm on
Sunday in the summer months, but it can get very
crowded, with long queues for accommodation bookings and information. The head office of the Irish Tourist
Board (☎ 676 5871) at Baggot St Bridge has an information desk and though it is less conveniently located it is
also much less crowded.

An Óige (☎ 30 4555, fax 30 5888), the Irish Youth
Hostel Association, has its office at the hostel at 61
Mountjoy St, Dublin 7. The Automobile Association or
AA (☎ 677 9481) is at 23 Suffolk St, Dublin 2.

Tourist Offices Abroad

Offices of the Irish Tourist Board or Bord Fáilte can be
found in the following countries:

Australia
    5th floor, 36 Carrington St, Sydney, NSW 2000 (☎ 02-299
    6177)
Belgium
    Avenue de Beaulieu 25, 1160 Brussels (☎ 02-673 9940)
Canada
    160 Bloor St East, Suite 934, Toronto, Ontario M4W 1B9
    (☎ 416-929 2777)
Denmark
    Box 104, 1004 Copenhagen K (☎ 033-15 8045)
France
    33 Rue de Miromesnil, 75008 Paris (☎ 1-47 42 03 36)
Germany
    Untermainanlage 7, W 6000 Frankfurt Main 1 (☎ 069-23
    64 92)
Italy
    Via Santa Maria Segreta 6, 20123 Milano (☎ 02-869 05 41)
Netherlands
    Leidsestraat 32 1017 PB Amsterdam (☎ 020-622 31 01)
New Zealand
    Dingwall Building, 87 Queen St, Auckland 1 (PO Box 279,
    ☎ 09-379 3708)
Northern Ireland
    53 Castle St, Belfast BT1 1GH (☎ 071-493 3201)
Sweden
    Box 5292, 102 46 Stockholm (☎ 08-662 8510)
UK
    150 New Bond St, London W1Y 0AQ (☎ 071-493 3201)
USA
    757 Third Ave, New York, NY 10017 (☎ 212-418 0800)

HOLIDAYS & FESTIVALS

Ireland has the following public holidays:

New Year's Day – 1 January
St Patrick's Day – 17 March
Good Friday
Easter Monday
June Holiday – first Monday in June
August Holiday – first Monday in August
October Holiday – last Monday in October
Christmas Day – 25 December
St Stephen's Day/Boxing Day – 26 December

St Patrick's Day and St Stephen's Day holidays are taken on the following Monday should they fall on a weekend.

CULTURAL & SPORTING EVENTS

Highlights of the Dublin year include the following events:

March – The St Patrick's Day Parade features an international marching band competition and up to a quarter of a million spectators.

May – At the Royal Dublin Society Showground, the Spring Show features agricultural and farming pursuits.

August – The August Bank Holiday weekend (the first Monday in August and the preceding weekend) is the time for Féile, Ireland's major annual rock festival, which is held in Thurles, County Tipperary. A large proportion of the city's rock music fans leave Dublin for the weekend, and pray for good weather.
At the Royal Dublin Society Showground the Dublin Horse Show features showjumping and other horse-related activities.

September – The All Ireland Hurling Finals and All Ireland Football Finals both take place in September.

October – The Dublin Theatre Festival takes place over two weeks in October.

POST & TELECOMMUNICATIONS

Postal Services

Post offices are open from 8 am to 5.30 or 6 pm Monday to Saturday, but smaller offices close for lunch. Mail can be addressed to poste restante at post offices but is officially held for two weeks only. If you write 'hold for collection' on the envelope they may keep it for a longer period.

Dublin's famed GPO is on O'Connell St, north of the river, and has longer opening hours: 8 am to 8 pm Monday to Saturday, 10.30 am to 6 pm Sunday and holidays. For stamp collectors there's a Philatelic Office in Henry St Arcade near the GPO. There's a handy post office on Anne St South, just off Grafton St, which is well patronised by foreign visitors and used to dealing with their curious requests.

Postal Rates

Postal rates by air for letters up to 20 grams and other items are:

aerograms	all destinations	45p
postcards	Ireland & EC countries	28p
	Other countries	38p
letters	Ireland & EC countries	32p
	Non-EC Europe	44p
	Other countries	52p

Telephone

The area code for calls to Dublin from outside the city is 01. If you are calling Ireland from overseas, drop the leading zero. Old-fashioned payphones where you rolled coins down ramps and pressed buttons mysteriously labelled A and B have disappeared from Dublin and most phones now are modern electronic wonders. Phonecards can be bought in IR£2 (10 units), IR£3.50 (20 units), IR£8 (50 units) and IR£16 (100 units) denominations. You can dial international calls directly from payphones.

Overseas Calls To dial direct overseas from Ireland dial the international access code 00, the country code (1 for the USA or Canada, 44 for Britain, 61 for Australia, 64 for New Zealand, 65 for Singapore, 852 for Hong Kong, etc), the area code (dropping the leading 0) and then the number. The one variation is that to call Northern Ireland from Ireland you do not dial 00-44 as for Britain. Instead you dial 08 and then the Northern Irish area code *without* dropping the leading 0. For reverse-

Facts for the Visitor

Top: Guinness Float, St Patrick's Parade (JM)
Bottom: GPO, O'Connell St (TW)

charge calls or enquiries call the international operator
on ☎ 114.

The full rate for a three-minute directly dialled call
from Ireland is:

	private phone	phone box
UK	IR£0.50	IR£0.97
Other EC countries	IR£0.64	IR£1.00
North America	IR£1.18	IR£1.80
Australia	IR£1.83	IR£2.80

Reduced rates are available at certain times to the UK,
the rest of Europe or North America but not to Australia
and Asia.

Home Direct Calls Rather than placing reverse-
charge calls through the operator in Ireland, you can dial
direct to your home country operator and then reverse
the charges or charge the call to a local phone credit card.
To use the home direct service dial the following codes
then the area code and, in most cases, the number you
want. Your home country operator will come on the line
before the call goes through:

Australia	1 800 5500 61
New Zealand	1 800 5500 64 + number
USA – AT&T	1 800 5500 00 + number
MCI	1 800 551001 + number
Sprint	1 800 552001 + number

Dublin Phone Numbers By the end of 1994 all
Dublin telephone numbers will have been converted to
seven digits. Where possible, we have given the new
phone numbers in this book. If you have difficulties
with a six-digit number, it may have already been
converted.

Payphones & Phonecards Phonecards are available in 10, 20, 50 and 100-unit versions. Each unit gives
you one local phone call. Phonecards are very useful for
making international calls since you do not have to carry
a sack of coins to the phonebox. Note that you cannot
make international calls via the operator from a card-
operated phone.

Fax & Telegrams You can send faxes from post offices
or other specialist offices. Phone the operator on ☎ 196
to send international telegrams.

Area Codes Some area codes in Ireland and Northern Ireland include:

Athlone	0902	Glendalough	0404
Bantry	027	Kilkenny	056
Belfast	08 023 2	Killarney	064
Cork	021	Kilronan	099
Derry	08 050 4	Limerick	061
Dingle	066	Shannon	061
Donegal	073	Tipperary	062
Drogheda	041	Waterford	051
Dublin	01	Wexford	053
Galway	091		

TIME

Dublin is on GMT (Greenwich Mean Time) or UTC (universal time coordinated), as is London. Without making allowances for daylight-saving time changes, when it is noon in Dublin or London it is 8 pm in Singapore, 10 pm in Sydney or Melbourne, 7 am in New York and 3 am in Los Angeles or San Francisco.

Also as in Britain, clocks are advanced by one hour from mid-March to the end of October. During the summer months it stays light until very late at night; you could still just about read by natural light at 11 pm.

Business Hours

Offices are open from 9 am to 5 pm Monday to Friday, but shops open a little later. On Thursday and/or Friday shops stay open later. Many are also open on Saturday or Sunday. Tourist attractions often have shorter opening hours, may be open fewer days per week or may be shut completely during the winter months.

ELECTRICITY

Electricity is 220 volts, 50 Hz AC, and plugs are usually of the flat three-pin type, as in Britain.

LAUNDRY

Most of the hostel-style accommodation offers laundry facilities at lower than commercial rates. Irish self-service laundries almost all offer a service wash facility where for IR£3 to IR£4 they'll wash, dry and neatly fold your washing. Many guesthouses and hotels will offer a similar service in conjunction with a local laundry, simply tacking on an extra IR£1 or so delivery charge.

Otherwise, there are a number of convenient laundries, including the Laundry Shop at 191 Parnell St, Dublin 1, off Parnell Square in north Dublin. Also in north Dublin is the Launderette at 110 Dorset St Lower near the An Óige Hostel. South of the centre and just north of the Grand Canal is Powders Launderette at 42A Richmond St South, Dublin 2. If you're staying northeast of the centre at Clontarf there's the Clothes Line at 53 Clontarf Rd. If you're staying at Dun Laoghaire there's the Star Laundrette (☎ 280 5074) at 47 George's St Upper.

WEIGHTS & MEASURES

As in Britain, progress towards metrication is slow and piecemeal. Meanwhile, Ireland mainly uses the imperial system.

BOOKS & MAPS

Books

English may be an adopted language but the Irish truly have a way with it. A glance in most Dublin bookshops will reveal huge Irish interest sections, whether it's fiction, history and current events, or the numerous local and regional guidebooks. It's definitely worth dipping into Irish writing as it features renowned writers like W B Yeats, James Joyce, Oscar Wilde, Sean O'Casey, Samuel Beckett, Flann O'Brien or Brendan Behan, as well as many modern writers who are resolutely carrying on the Irish literary tradition.

Dublin is the only city in the world which can boast three winners of the Nobel Prize for Literature – George Bernard Shaw in 1925, W B Yeats in 1938 and Samuel Beckett in 1969. Ireland's first president, Douglas Hyde (1860-1944), was also a poet and wrote in Irish. He is commemorated today by an art gallery bearing his name in Trinity College. The Irish pride in this literary track record is exemplified in the Dublin Writers' Museum on Parnell Square in north Dublin.

For many years Ireland also suffered under an absurdly restrictive censorship code. The *Censorship of Publications Act* of 1929 became sillier and more farcical as time went on. At one time Ireland was in the peculiar position of providing taxation advantages to encourage authors to live and work in the country and at the same time banning whatever they wrote. Even between 1960 and 1965, when censorship was definitely on the wane, nearly 2000 books were banned.

Books about Dublin

Fiction Of course no book describes Dublin like Joyce's immortal *Ulysses* (first published in 1922), and, though much has changed since Bloomsday 1904, there is still enough left to sustain a steady flow of Joyce admirers bent on retracing the events of 16 June 1904 (the day in which the novels events unfold). Joyce's *Dubliners* (published in 1914 after 10 years of censorship tangles) and *A Portrait of the Artist as a Young Man* (published in serial form from 1914) also recreate turn-of-the-century Dublin and are readily available in paperback.

Oliver St John Gogarty (1878-1957) bore a lifelong grudge against Joyce because of his appearance as Buck Mulligan in *Ulysses*, but it didn't prevent him from presenting his views of Dublin in *As I Was Going Down Sackville Street* (published in 1937) and other volumes of his memoirs. He was also a renowned wit, a brand of humour which Oscar Wilde had already pioneered.

The Informer (published in 1925) by Liam O'Flaherty (1896-1984), was the classic book about the divided sympathies that plagued Ireland throughout its struggle for independence and the ensuing Civil War. More recently Irish authors writing with a flavour of Ireland include Edna O'Brien (1936-), with books like *The Country Girls* (1960), which enjoyed the accolade of being banned.

Dublin schoolteacher Roddy Doyle has recently made a big name for himself with his comic descriptions of north Dublin life, most notably with *The Commitments*, which was made into a successful film. His other books tracing the trials and tribulations of the Rabbitt family are *The Snapper* and *The Van*, all available in Penguin paperbacks. Christy Brown's marvellous *Down all the Days* summed up Dublin's backstreet energy with equal abandon from a slightly earlier era. *The Ginger Man* by J P Donleavy (1926-) was another high-energy foray around Dublin, this time from the Trinity College perspective. It received the church's seal of approval by lingering on the Irish banned list for many years.

Dermot Bolger's *The Journey Home* (1990) would certainly have been banned in the old days, for it depicts the underside of modern Dublin at its darkest. Political corruption, drugs, violence, unemployment and a pervading sense of hopelessness make this a decidedly gloomy book, though it still hurtles along at a flat-out pace. John McGahern is another familiar name among modern Irish writers, with titles like *The Barracks* (1963) and *Amongst Women* (1990) to his credit. Aidan Carl Mathews' work includes the novel *Muesli at Midnight*.

Finally, *A New Book of Dubliners* edited by Ben Forkner (Methuen Paperbacks, London, 1988) is a fine collection of Dublin-related short stories written by authors old and new, including James Joyce, Oliver St John Gogarty, Liam O'Flaherty, Samuel Beckett, Flann O'Brien, Sean O'Faolain, Benedict Kiely and others.

Non-Fiction *A Concise History of Ireland* by Máire & Conor Cruise O'Brien (Thames & Hudson, London, revised 1985) is a readable and comprehensively illustrated short history of Ireland. *Ireland – A History* by Robert Kee (Abacus paperback, London, 1980) covers similar ground in a similar format in a book developed from a BBC/RTE TV series.

Dublin – One Thousand Years by Stephen Conlin (The O'Brien Press, Dublin, 1988) is a fascinating book about the development of Dublin today with a series of illustrations showing how the city would have looked at various times in its history. The paintings of the area around the black pool *(dubh linn)* in 988 and the same scene again in 1275, with the addition of Dublin Castle, are particularly interesting.

Dublin by V S Pritchett (The Hogarth Press paperback, London, 1967) is a little old but gives an evocative and engaging account of an often eccentric city. For all sorts of minutiae about Dublin buildings and streets check the *Encyclopaedia of Dublin* by Douglas Bennett (Gill & Macmillan, Dublin, 1991).

The Irish bookshop chain Eason publishes a series of slim booklets on specific fields of Irish interest, including several on personages and buildings of Dublin. Interesting, specifically Dublin-related titles in this series are *The American Ambassador's Residence, Christ Church Cathedral, The City Hall, Georgian Dublin, Guinness, Joyce's Dublin, Malahide Castle, Masterpieces of the National Gallery of Ireland, The National Library, The Royal College of Surgeons, The Shelbourne Hotel, St Mary's Pro-Cathedral, St Patrick's Cathedral, Swift's Ireland, Trinity College* and *The World of George Berkeley*.

Irish Literature & James Joyce *Literary Dublin – a History* by Herbert A Kenny (Gill & Macmillan, Dublin, 2nd edition, 1991) traces the history of Dublin's diversely rich literary culture.

Serious Joyce groupies can make their own Bloomsday tour of the city with a number of books which follow the wanderings of *Ulysses'* characters in minute detail.

Joyce's Dublin – A Walking Guide to Ulysses by Jack McCarthy (Wolfhound Press, Dublin, 1988) traces the events chapter by chapter with very clear maps. *The Ulysses Guide – Tours through Joyce's Dublin* by Robert Nicholson (Mandarin Paperbacks, London, 1988) concentrates on certain areas and follows the events of the various related chapters. Again there are clear and easy-to-follow maps.

James Joyce & Sites from Ulysses

Ireland's most famous author, the man who claimed Dublin could be rebuilt from scratch using his descriptions as a plan, spent most of his adult life overseas. James Joyce was born in Dublin in 1882 and was the eldest of the 10 Joyce children to survive beyond infancy. His father's roller-coaster financial situation led to a rather varied education, which included a two-year spell of self-education at home. He finally completed his school years at Belvedere College (the building still stands on Great Denmark St in north Dublin) and went on to University College, Dublin. He was already determined to become a writer when he graduated in 1902 but then wavered towards studying medicine and wandered between Dublin and Paris for the next couple of years.

In 1904 three short stories appeared in an Irish farmers' magazine, written under the pseudonym Stephen Dedalus; these were later to form part of *Dubliners*. In late 1904 Joyce abandoned Ireland and moved to Pula in what was then Austria-Hungary with Nora Barnacle, whom he was not to marry until 27 years later. In 1905 they moved on to Trieste where their two children were born and where he reworked *Stephen Hero*, a novel he had started in Dublin, into *A Portrait of the Artist as a Young Man*. He returned to Ireland twice in 1909 but his efforts to find a publisher for *Dubliners* were unsuccessful. It was finally published in 1914 but not until after the first edition had been destroyed when the publisher objected to its use of real locations, its language and the stories.

The outbreak of WW I forced the Joyce family to shift to Zürich in 1915, where Joyce commenced work on *Ulysses*. He was always convinced of his own genius but English lessons and grants from literary societies and admirers were his only means of support at the time. His life was further complicated by recurrent eye problems that led to 25 operations for glaucoma, cataracts and other difficulties. *A Portrait of the Artist as a Young Man* was finally published in 1916 and in 1918 the American magazine *Little Review* started to publish extracts from *Ulysses*. Notoriety was already pursuing his epic work and the censors prevented further episodes from being published after 1920.

In 1920 Ezra Pound persuaded Joyce to move to Paris where, in 1922, Sylvia Beach of the Paris bookshop Shakespeare & Co finally managed to put *Ulysses* into print. Its earlier censorship difficulties made it an instant success. *Ulysses* follows its characters around Dublin during a single day stretching from 8 am one morning to 2 am the next. During this remarkable journey Stephen Dedalus retraces the voyage of Homer's *Odyssey*, but this literary invention was only a small part of the novel's total achievement. The book ends with Molly Bloom's famous stream of consciousness discourse, a chapter of eight huge and totally unpunctuated paragraphs. Hardly surprisingly for the time, Joyce was immediately labelled a pornographer, and the book, 20th century masterpiece or not, was banned. It was finally published in the USA in 1933, but not until much later in the UK, and much much later in Ireland.

Ulysses has been described as one of the 'great unread works of the English language' and may have bent English into totally new and hitherto unthought-of shapes, but Joyce's final work, *Finnegan's Wake* (published in 1939), was even more complex and went part way to inventing a new language, adding further complications through multilingual wordplays. In 1940 WW II drove the Joyce family back to Zürich where the author died in 1941.

Many of the places visited on that well-documented 1904 journey around Dublin can still be found. The tourist office's *Ulysses Map of Dublin* locates some of them, but serious Joyce groupies should get a copy of Jack McCarthy's book *Joyce's Dublin: A Walking Guide to Ulysses* (Wolfhound Press, Dublin, 1988), which traces the events of each chapter, or *The Ulysses Guide: Tours through Joyce's Dublin* by Robert Nicholson (Mandarin Paperbacks, London, 1988), which concentrates on certain areas and follows the events of the various related chapters. Both books have clear and easy-to-follow maps. An annual retracing of the journey takes place on Bloomsday, 16 June. Some of the interesting relics of Joyce's Dublin and the chapters of *Ulysses* in which they appear are described here. The names in parentheses refer to episodes in Homer's *Odyssey*.

The Martello Tower, Sandycove near Dun Laoghaire
   Chapter 1 (Telemachus) After the open-air shave with which the book commences, Buck Mulligan goes for a swim in the nearby 40 Foot Pool. The tower houses the James Joyce Museum and it's still traditional to swim unclothed in the pool before 9 am.

St Andrew's Church & Sweny's Chemist Shop, south Dublin Chapter 5 (Lotus Eaters) On his way into the centre, Leopold Bloom stops to observe part of the mass at All Hallows Church. This is now St Andrew's on Westland Row, just east of Trinity College and right beside Pearse Station. From there he goes to Sweny's Chemist Shop on Lincoln Place, which is still a chemist shop, still has the name Sweny prominently displayed and still sells lemon soap, though a bar will now cost you IR£1.95 or IR£2.95, rather than the fourpence Bloom paid in 1904.

The Oval & Mooney's, north Dublin Chapter 7 (Aeolus) Leopold Bloom and Stephen Dedalus both visit the office of the *Freeman's Journal* and the *Evening Telegraph* on Prince's St North. A branch of British Home Stores now occupies the site. Visits are then made to two pubs. The Oval on Abbey St Middle is still the Oval, but Mooney's on the other side of O'Connell St on Abbey St Lower has changed markedly since Joyce's day and is now the Abbey Mooney. In 1988 a series of 14 pavement plaques were placed in the city to trace Bloom's peregrinations from Abbey St Middle in this chapter to the National Library in Chapter 9.

Thomas Moore Statue, north Dublin Chapter 8 (Lestrygonians) Leopold Bloom crosses the Liffey by the O'Connell Bridge and walks down Westmoreland St by the Bank of Ireland, ruminating on the amusing position of the statue of poet Thomas Moore on the traffic island where College St meets Westmoreland St. To this day it's a local joke that the author of the poem 'The Meeting of the Waters' should have his statue plonked in front of a public urinal.

Davy Byrne's, Duke St, south Dublin Chapter 8 (Lestrygonians) Having 'crossed under Tommy Moore's roguish finger' Bloom continues by Trinity College, noting the provost's house where the college provost still resides, and various shops along Grafton St, particularly Brown Thomas, still one of Dublin's best known shops. Finally he turns into Duke St and having glanced into Burton's (no longer there) decides he doesn't like the look of the patrons and turns back to Davy Byrne's. Bloom would hardly recognise Joyce's 'moral pub' today as it was extensively remodelled in the 1940s and then yuppified in the 1980s. If Joyce turned up today he would probably be turned away by the bouncers.

National Library, Kildare St, south Dublin Chapter 9 (Scylla & Charybdis) From Davy Byrne's, Bloom continues down Molesworth St to the National Library, after a brief diversion to the National Museum, both on Kildare St. Stephen Dedalus is also in the library, discussing Shakespeare with a group of famous Dubliners, including Æ (George Russell).

Ormond Hotel, Ormond Quay, north Dublin Chapter 11 (Sirens) Although it has been changed considerably during this century, the Ormond Hotel still overlooks the Liffey from Ormond Quay Upper and a plaque outside commemorates its role in *Ulysses*. On the way there from the National Library, Bloom walks along Wellington Quay on the Temple Bar side of the Liffey and contemplates a stop at the Clarence Hotel (also still operating) before crossing the Liffey to the Ormond.

James Joyce Statue, O'Connell St (TW)

Bella Cohen's & Olhausen's, north Dublin Chapter 15 (Circe) The red-light district of north Dublin, called Nighttown in *Ulysses* though it was known as Monto to Dubliners of the time, is no more. The prostitutes departed with the British army after Ireland's independence, but Bella Cohen was indeed a brothel madam in 1904 though her premises were at 82, not 81, Railway St (then known as Tyrone St Lower). This area has been totally redeveloped and is of zero interest today. In this chapter Bloom also drops into Olhausen's, the pork butcher, at 72 Talbot St to pick up a pig's trotter and a sheep's hoof as a snack. Olhausen's is still in business.

Amiens St, north Dublin Chapter 16 (Eumaeus) Leopold Bloom and Stephen Dedalus, whose paths have crossed several times during the day, finally meet in Nighttown and wander down Amiens St, the main road into the city from Clontarf which passes Connolly Station and ends by the Busáras. On the way they pass Dan Bergin's Pub (now Lloyd's), Mullett's (still there), the Signal House (now J & M Cleary), the North Star Hotel (still there) and the 1842 Dock Tavern (which, after a spell as the Master Mariner Bar, is now Kenny's Lounge) before turning into Store St (beside the Busáras today) past the Dublin City Morgue (still there) and the City Bakery (now the Kylemore Bakery).

Gardiner St to Eccles St, north Dublin Chapters 17 & 18 (Ithaca & Penelope) Bloom and Dedalus make the long walk up Gardiner St, now a favourite strip for centrally located B&Bs. At Mountjoy Square they turn left then right to pass by St George's Church and end up at Bloom's home at 7 Eccles St. A private hospital now occupies the site where Molly Bloom's soliloquy ends *Ulysses*, but similar Georgian houses still stand on the opposite side of the street. The door from No 7 can now be seen in The Bailey, a pub right across the road from Davy Byrne's, which was visited in Chapter 8. ∎

Maps

For most purposes giveaway maps of Dublin are quite adequate. If you need an indexed street directory, the *Dublin Street Guide* published by the Ordnance Survey is the best on offer though it's not very detailed or easy to use.

Bookshops

Directly opposite Trinity College at 27/29 Nassau St is Fred Hanna's (☎ 677 1255) excellent bookshop. Round the corner at 57 Dawson St is the large and well-stocked Hodges Figgis (☎ 677 4754). Directly across the road is Waterstones (☎ 679 1415) at 7 Dawson St, which also carries a wide range of books.

At 24 Grafton St the Dublin Bookshop (☎ 677 5568) has a particularly good selection of books of Irish interest. North of the Liffey, Eason (☎ 873 3811) at 40 O'Connell St near the post office has a wide range of books and one of the biggest selections of magazines in Ireland. All these bookshops have an extensive choice of books on Ireland.

A number of bookshops cater to special interests. Forbidden Planet (☎ 671 0688) at 36 Dawson St, Dublin 2, is a wonderful science fiction and comic book specialist. The Sinn Féin Bookshop is at 44 Parnell Square West, Dublin 1. An Siopha Leabhar on Harcourt St, just off St Stephen's Green, has books in Irish.

The IMMA at the Royal Hospital Kilmainham and the National Gallery on Merrion Square both have bookshops offering a good range of art books. There's a bookshop in the Dublin Writers' Museum on Parnell Square North, Dublin 1. The Library Book Shop at Trinity College has a wide selection of Irish interest books, including, of course, various titles on the Book of Kells.

George Webb (☎ 677 7489) at 5 Crampton Quay, Dublin 1, has old books of Irish interest. So do Green's Bookshop (☎ 676 2554) at 16 Clare St, Dublin 2, and Cathach Books (☎ 671 8676) at 10 Duke St, Dublin 2.

FILMS

Dublin has made numerous movie appearances, most recently in *The Commitments*, a wonderful, bright and energetic 1991 hit about a north Dublin soul band. The film accurately records north Dublin's scruffy atmosphere, though Dublin audiences (well, north Dublin ones at least) were somewhat amused by the geographical jumps around the city that the characters managed to make.

The Tom Cruise and Nicole Kidman vehicle *Far & Away* was less of a hit in 1992 but did provide some intriguing views of the Temple Bar district standing in for Boston. You might still notice the alternative name painted on the popular Temple Bar pub The Norseman.

Older films featuring Dublin include *Educating Rita*, which used Trinity College as its quintessentially English university! The movie *My Left Foot* was as wonderful as the book it came from, *Down all the Days*. It also managed to make some interesting peregrinations around Dublin, including visits to John Mulligan's, the pub reputed to pull the best Guinness in Ireland. Renowned director John Huston's final film, *The Dead*, released in 1987, was based on a James Joyce story from *Dubliners*.

MEDIA

Newspapers & Magazines

English papers and magazines are readily available but the main Irish papers are the *Irish Times* and the *Irish Independent*. The *Irish Times* is famous for its highly opinionated letters page. Eason on O'Connell St has a wide selection of foreign newspapers.

Radio & TV

Ireland has two state-controlled TV channels, RTE 1 and Network 2, and an independent station, TV3. British BBC and ITN programmes can also be picked up. There are three state-controlled radio stations. Two of them – RTE 1 and 2 FM – are broadcast in English, and Radio na Gaeltachta is in Irish. There are also various independent stations – 98 FM and 104 FM, for instance, both play classic rock. Irish radio, however, whether AM or FM, can be pretty dreadful as it has a tendency to waffle on interminably or play the same records endlessly!

FILM & PHOTOGRAPHY

Ireland is a photogenic country but often a surprisingly gloomy one, so keen photographers should bring high-speed film. Remember the rain as well and bring a plastic bag to keep your camera dry.

Fast developing services are readily available. Developing and printing a 24-exposure print film typically costs around IR£7 for one-hour service or IR£4 to IR£5 for slower turnround. Although print film is widely available, slide film is not always so easy to find.

HEALTH

Ireland poses no serious health problems apart from the dangers posed by the Irish high-cholesterol diet. The

Irish distaste for contraception does not prevent condoms from being sold through pharmacies (that is, if the pharmacist isn't morally opposed).

Medical Services

Citizens of EC countries are eligible for medical care, but other visitors should have medical insurance or be prepared to pay. The Eastern Health Board Dublin Area (☎ 671 9222) at 138 Thomas St, Dublin 8, has a Choice of Doctor Scheme which can advise you on a suitable doctor from 9 am to 5 pm Monday to Friday. Your hotel or your embassy can also suggest a doctor.

WOMEN TRAVELLERS

Although women are in some ways treated as second-class citizens in Ireland (the church influence), they're also generally treated respectfully (the Irish mother influence). Nevertheless, women should exercise the usual care. See the next section for more information.

DANGERS & ANNOYANCES

Ireland is probably safer than most countries in Europe, but the usual precautions should be observed. Dublin has its fair share of pickpockets and sneak thieves waiting to relieve the unwary of unwatched bags. If you have a car, do not leave valuables inside the car when it is parked. Dublin is notorious for car break-ins, and foreign registered cars and rental cars are a particular target. See the Car section of the Getting Around chapter for more details.

Cyclists should always lock their bicycles securely and be cautious about leaving bags on their bikes. Certain areas of Dublin are not safe at night and visitors should avoid run-down, deserted-looking and poorly lit areas. Phoenix Park is not safe at night and campers should avoid the temptation to set up tent there.

EMERGENCIES

For emergency assistance phone 999 and then specify the type of assistance required:

Fire
Police (Gardaí)
Ambulance
Boat or Coastal Rescue

Other emergency services include:

Poisons Information Centre
 Beaumont Hospital, Beaumont Rd, Dublin 9 (☎ 37 9964,
 37 9966)
Rape Crisis Centre
 70 Leeson St Lower, Dublin 2 (☎ 661 4911, 661 4564)
Drugs Advisory & Treatment Centre
 30/31 Pearse St, Dublin 2 (☎ 677 1122)

Getting There & Away

For student travel information in Ireland, contact USIT (Union of Students in Ireland Travel), the Irish youth and student travel association. The USIT Travel Office (☎ 679 8833) in Dublin is at 19 Aston Quay, right by the river and O'Connell Bridge. Its London office is at London Student Travel (☎ 071-730 3402), 52 Grosvenor Gardens, London SW1W OAG. In the USA it can be found at the New York International AYH Hostel (☎ 212-663 5435), 895 Amsterdam Ave (at 103rd St), New York, NY 10025. USIT issues International Student Identity Card (ISIC) cards.

AIR

Dublin is Ireland's major international airport gateway with flights from all over Europe. Flights from North America have to come via Shannon. There is no airport departure tax from Dublin.

To/From Other Cities in Ireland

Aer Lingus has flights to Cork, Galway, Kerry, Knock, Shannon and Sligo.

To/From the UK

Dublin is linked by a variety of airlines to a number of cities in the UK, including all the major London airports. Aer Lingus and British Midland fly to/from Heathrow, Aer Lingus flies to/from Gatwick, Ryanair flies to/from Luton/Stansted. British Airways does not fly to Dublin. Connections are generally very frequent; in the summer Aer Lingus may have 15 Heathrow-Dublin services daily and British Midland another seven or eight.

The standard one-way London-Dublin economy fare is £70, but advance-purchase fares are available offering return tickets for as low as £60 to £70. These must be booked well in advance as seats are often limited.

The airlines' UK addresses and phone numbers are as follows:

Aer Lingus
    228 Regent St, London W1 (☎ 081-899 4747)
British Midland
    PO Box 60, Donington Hall, Castle Donington, Derby DE7 2SB (☎ 071-589 5599)
Ryanair
    235-37 Finchley Rd, London NW3 6LS (☎ 071-435 7101)

From Dublin the Aer Lingus or British Midland fare to Heathrow or Gatwick is IR£125 for a standard one-way fare, or IR£83 for a budget or off-peak one-way fare. There is a host of return fares requiring a variety of advance-purchase arrangements, minimum stays and so on. They range from as low as IR£92 to as high as IR£187 or IR£250 if you simply want to turn up and take the next flight in each direction. Fares to Manchester are roughly the same as those to London, but to other cities in Britain the Aer Lingus fares are even higher.

Special budget fares are often available and if you're 12 to 25 years old you can fly Dublin-London for IR£50 one way.

Ryanair fares between Dublin and Stansted, north of London, are slightly cheaper than those of Aer Lingus or British Midland. There are regular trains between Stansted and Liverpool St Station in central London.

Other cities in the British Isles connected with Dublin and the relevant airlines are:

Birmingham	Aer Lingus, British Midland
Blackpool	Manx Airlines
Bristol	Aer Lingus
Cardiff	Manx Airlines
East Midlands	Aer Lingus
Edinburgh	Aer Lingus
Glasgow	Aer Lingus
Isle of Man	Manx Airlines
Jersey	Manx Airlines & Aer Lingus
Leeds/Bradford	Aer Lingus
Liverpool	Manx Airlines & Ryanair
Luton	Ryanair
Manchester	Aer Lingus
Newcastle	Aer Lingus, Gill Air

To/From North America

There are no direct flights to Ireland from Canada, and all flights from the USA must put down in Shannon on their way to Dublin. Because competition on flights to London is so much fiercer, it will generally be cheaper to fly to London first and then pick up a London-Dublin-London flight. Delta connects Dublin (via Shannon) with Atlanta. Aer Lingus flies (again via Shannon) to Boston, New York and Los Angeles. During the summer high season, Aer Lingus' return fare is US$750 mid-week, or US$780 on weekends. Usually there are advance-purchase fares offered early in the year which allow you to fly New York-Dublin-New York for around US$600 return. In the low season, discount return fares from New York to London will be in the US$350-450 range, and in the high season, US$550-650. Check the Sunday travel sections of papers like the *New York Times*, *Los Angeles Times*, *San Francisco Chronicle-Examiner* or *Chicago Tribune* for the latest fares. The *Toronto Globe & Mail*, the *Toronto Star* or the *Vancouver Province* will have similar details from Canada. Offices of Council Travel or STA in the USA or Travel CUTS in Canada are good sources of reliable discounted tickets.

To/From Australia & New Zealand

Excursion or Apex fares from Australia or New Zealand to Britain can have a return flight to Dublin tagged on at no extra cost. Return fares from Australia vary from around A$1600 (low season) to A$2500 (high season) but there are often short-term special deals available. STA and Flight Centres International are good sources of reliable discounted tickets in Australia or New Zealand. The cheapest fares from New Zealand will probably take the east-bound route via the USA but a round-the-world ticket may well be cheaper than a return.

To/From Europe & Russia

Dublin is connected with major centres in Europe. From Paris, for instance, fares to Dublin range from 755 to 915 FF one way, 1205 to 1730FF return.

Other cities and the relevant airlines with connections to Dublin are:

Amsterdam, Netherlands	Aer Lingus
Barcelona, Spain	Iberia
Brussels, Belgium	Aer Lingus & Sabena
Cologne, Germany	Lufthansa
Copenhagen, Denmark	Aer Lingus & SAS
Düsseldorf, Germany	Aer Lingus
Frankfurt, Germany	Aer Lingus & Lufthansa
Lisbon, Portugal	TAP
Madrid, Spain	Aer Lingus & Iberia
Málaga, Spain	Viva Air
Milan, Italy	Aer Lingus & Alitalia
Moscow, Russia	Aeroflot
Munich, Germany	Lufthansa & Ryanair

Paris, France	Aer Lingus & Air France
Rome, Italy	Aer Lingus & Alitalia
Zürich, Switzerland	Aer Lingus

Airline Offices

You will find the following airline offices in Dublin:

Aer Lingus (☎ 37 7777 for UK enquiries, 37 7747 for elsewhere)
    42 Grafton St, Dublin 2
    41 O'Connell St Upper, Dublin 1
    12 George's St Upper, Dun Laoghaire
Aeroflot
    Dublin Airport (☎ 842 5400)
Air France
    29/30 Dawson St, Dublin 2 (☎ 677 8899)
Alitalia
    60/63 Dawson St, Dublin 2 (☎ 677 5171)
Birmingham
    European Airways (☎ 021-27 2211)
British Midland
    Nutley, Merrion Rd, Dublin 4 (☎ 283 8833)
Delta Airlines
    24 Merrion Square, Dublin 2 (☎ 676 8080)
Iberia Airlines
    54 Dawson St, Dublin 2 (☎ 677 9486)
Lufthansa
    Grattan House, Mount St Lower, Dublin 2 (☎ 676 1595)
Manx Airlines
    Dublin Airport (☎ 84 23555)
Ryanair
    3 Dawson St, Dublin 2 (☎ 677 4422)
Sabena World Airlines
    7 Dawson St, Dublin 2 (☎ 671 6677)
SAS
    Dublin Airport (☎ 842 1922)
TAP Air Portugal
    54 Dawson St, Dublin 2 (☎ 679 8844)
Viva Air
    54 Dawson St, Dublin 2 (☎ 677 9846)

Note that British Airways does not fly to Dublin. For British Airways enquiries call ☎ 1-800 62 6747.

FERRIES

Ferry services from Britain and France operate to a variety of ports in Ireland. There are two direct services to Dublin – one from Holyhead on the north-west tip of Wales to Dublin, and the other from Holyhead to Dun Laoghaire, the port on the southern side of Dublin Bay. On either route the crossing takes 3½ hours. Passenger fares are from £17 in the off season and up to £23 in the peak season. For a car including up to four passengers, the fare varies from £94 to £180.

Sealink Stena (☎ 0233-64 7047), Charter House, Ashford, Kent TN24 8EZ, operates Holyhead-Dun Laoghaire. B&I Line (☎ 071-734 4681), 150 New Bond St, London W1Y 0AQ, operates Holyhead-Dublin. In Dublin, Sealink Stena (☎ 280 7777) is at 15 Westmoreland St, Dublin 2, and at Adelaide House, Haddington Terrace, Dun Laoghaire. B&I Line (☎ 679 7977) is at 16 Westmoreland St, Dublin 2.

Other ferry services to Ireland from Britain include Swansea to Cork (Swansea Cork Ferries), Fishguard to Rosslare (Sealink Stena), Pembroke to Rosslare (B&I Line), as well as a variety of services to Northern Ireland.

From France there are services from Roscoff to Cork, Cherbourg to Cork and Rosslare, and Le Havre to Cork and Rosslare. You can also travel to Ireland from France via Britain. The Roscoff service is operated by Britanny Ferries, while the Cherbourg and Le Havre services are operated by Irish Ferries and can be used by Eurail pass holders. Inter-Rail pass holders receive a 50% discount on Irish Ferries. Irish Ferries (☎ 661 0511) has a Dublin office at 2/4 Merrion Row, Dublin 2.

ROAD & SEA

The Bus Éireann/National Express Supabus and Slattery Coach services operate direct from London and other UK centres to Dublin and other cities. For details in London, contact the Coach Travel Centre (☎ 071-730 0202), the Irish Tourist Board (☎ 071-493 3201) or Slattery's Coaches (☎ 071-724 0741). London to Dublin takes about 13 hours and costs £40 one way or £61 return during the summer and Christmas peak periods.

BUS

Bus Éireann is the national bus line with services all over the south and to the north. Standard one-way fares from Dublin include Belfast IR£10, Cork IR£11 or Galway IR£9. These fares are much cheaper than the regular railway fares, return fares are usually only a little more expensive than one-way, and special deals are often available. Details of unlimited travel Rambler Tickets are given in the Bus & Train Discount Deals section. Busáras Bus Éireann's Central Bus Station, is just north of the Custom House and the River Liffey. Phone ☎ 30 2222 for information.

Buses to Belfast in Northern Ireland depart from the Busáras three times a day Monday to Saturday, and twice on Sunday. Services from the Glengall St Bus Station in Belfast operate on the same frequency. The trip takes about three hours and costs IR£9.50 one way or IR£12 for a return within one month.

TRAIN

Iarnród Éireann, the Irish railway system, operates trains on routes which fan out from Dublin. Connolly Station (☎ 36 3333), just north of the Liffey and the city centre, is the station for Belfast, Derry, Sligo, Wexford and other points to the north. Heuston Station (☎ 36 5421), just south of the Liffey and well west of the centre, is the station for Cork, Galway, Killarney, Limerick, Waterford and other points to the west, south and south-west.

Distances are short in Ireland, and the longest trip you can make by train from Dublin is about three hours to Galway or Killarney. Fares are high: examples of regular fares from Dublin are Belfast IR£14, Cork IR£31.50, or Galway IR£24. As with buses, special fares are often available. A same-day return to Belfast can cost as little as IR£13, a pound less than a one-way ticket! First-class tickets cost about IR£4 to IR£7 over the standard fare for a single journey. If you're aged under 26 you can get a FairCard for IR£8 which gives you a 50% discount on regular fares.

The Iarnród Éireann Travel Centre (☎ 36 6222) is at 35 Abbey St Lower. See the next section for information on unlimited travel tickets.

BUS & TRAIN DISCOUNT DEALS

The Eurail Pass is valid for bus and train travel in Ireland but not in Northern Ireland. Inter-Rail offers free train travel in the Republic of Ireland. If you buy your Inter-Rail ticket in Northern Ireland, you receive a 50% discount on train fares in Northern Ireland and 34% discount on British Rail. For IR£7, full-time students can have a Travelsave Stamp affixed to their ISIC card. This gives up to 50% discount on Irish Rail and Bus Éireann services and on B&I ferries. Enquire at a USIT office for details.

Various unlimited travel tickets are available for buses and trains in Ireland. Rambler Tickets are available for bus or train travel and cost IR£26 (three days, bus only), IR£45 (four days, rail only), IR£60 (eight days, bus or rail) or IR£90 (15 days, bus or rail). A bus and rail version costs IR£78 (eight days) or IR£115 (15 days). Children under 16 pay half-fare and bicycles can be taken along for the ride for an additional charge.

An Emerald Card gives you unlimited travel throughout Ireland on all scheduled services of Irish Rail, Northern Ireland Railways, Bus Éireann, Dublin Bus, Ulsterbus and Citybus. The card costs IR£105 (or pounds sterling equivalent) for eight days or IR£180 for 15 days.

Getting Around

AIRPORT FACILITIES

Dublin Airport (☎ 37 9900) has an exchange counter in the baggage arrivals area, a bank that keeps regular banking hours, a post office (closed for lunch, Saturday afternoons and all day Sunday), a tourist information office that also books accommodation, shops, restaurants, bars, a hairdresser, a nursery, a church and car-hire counters.

TO/FROM DUBLIN AIRPORT

Dublin Airport is 10 km north of the centre and public transport possibilities between the airport and city consist of two bus services or taxis.

Airport Bus Services

The Express Airport Coast operates to/from the Central Bus Station (Busáras) near the river in central Dublin and less frequently to/from Heuston Railway Station for IR£2.50 (children IR£1.25). It takes about half an hour. Timetables are available at the airport or in the city. Monday to Saturday city to airport services go about every 20 to 30 minutes from 7.30 am to 10.40 pm. On Sunday they operate less frequently from 7.55 am to 10.20 pm. Monday to Saturday airport to city services operate from 8.10 am to 11.15 pm. On Sunday they run from 7.30 am to 10.55 pm. The demand for seats can sometimes exceed the capacity of the bus, in which case it's worth getting a group together and sharing a taxi.

The alternative service is the slower 41A bus, which makes a number of useful stops on the way, terminates across the river on Eden Quay and costs IR£1.10. It can take up to one hour but it has longer operating hours and runs more frequently than the express bus.

There are direct buses between the airport and Belfast.

Airport Taxi Services

Taxis are subject to all sorts of additional charges for baggage, extra passengers and 'unsocial hours'. However, a taxi usually costs IR£10 or less between the airport and the centre, so between four people it's unlikely to be more expensive than the bus. There's a supplementary charge of 80p from the airport to the city, but this charge does not apply from the city to the airport. Make sure the meter is switched on, as some Dublin airport taxi drivers can be as unscrupulous as their brethren anywhere else in the world.

TO/FROM THE FERRY TERMINALS

Buses go to the Busáras from the Dublin Ferryport terminal (☎ 874 3293) after all B&I ferry arrivals from Holyhead. For the 10 am ferry departure from Dublin, buses leave the Busáras at 9 am. For the 9.45 pm departure, buses depart from the Busáras at 8.15 and 9 pm and from Heuston Station at 8.15 pm.

To travel between the Dun Laoghaire Ferryport (☎ 80 1905) and Dublin, take a No 46A bus to St Stephen's Green or the DART (see the Train section) to Pearse Station (for south Dublin) or Connolly Station (for north Dublin).

TO/FROM CONNOLLY & HEUSTON STATIONS

The 90 Rail Link Bus runs between the two stations up to four times an hour at peak periods and costs a flat 60p. Connolly Station is a short walk north of the Busáras.

BUS

The Dublin Bus company (Bus Átha Cliath) has an information office (☎ 873 4222) at 59 O'Connell St, directly opposite the tourist office. Buses cost from 55p up to a maximum of IR£1.10 for one to three stages. Ten-ride tickets are available at a small discount. One-day passes cost IR£2.80 for the bus, or IR£4 for bus and rail. Other passes include a one-week bus pass for IR£10.50, or a bus and rail pass for IR£14 (plus IR£2 for an ID photo). Late-night buses run from the College St-Westmoreland St-D'Olier St triangle until 3 am on Friday and Saturday night.

There is a left-luggage facility at the bus station (IR£1.10, backpacks IR£1.60).

TRAIN

The DART (Dublin Area Rapid Transport) provides quick rail access to the coast as far north as Howth and as far south as Bray (see map 22). Pearse Station is convenient for central Dublin south of the Liffey and

Connolly Station for north of the Liffey. Monday to Saturday there are services every 10 to 20 minutes, sometimes even more frequently, from around 6.30 am to midnight. Services are less frequent on Sunday. It takes about 30 minutes from Dublin to Bray at one extreme or Howth at the other. Dublin-Dun Laoghaire only takes about 15 to 20 minutes. There are also Suburban Rail services north as far as Dundalk, inland to Mullingar and south past Bray to Arklow.

A one-way DART ticket from Dublin costs IR£1 to Dun Laoghaire or Howth, IR£1.20 to Bray. Within the DART region, a one-day unlimited-travel ticket costs IR£3 for an adult, IR£1.50 for a child or IR£4.50 for a family. A ticket combining DART and Dublin Bus services costs IR£4, IR£2 and IR£5.50 respectively, but this ticket cannot be used during Monday to Friday peak hours (7 to 9.45 am, 4.30 to 6.30 pm). A weekly DART and bus ticket costs IR£14 but requires an ID photo. A Dublin Explorer ticket allows you four days DART and bus travel for IR£10 but cannot be used until after 9.45 am Monday to Friday.

Bicycles cannot be taken on DART services but they can be taken on the less frequent suburban train services, either in the guards' van or in a special compartment at the opposite end of the train from the engine. There is a IR£2 charge for transporting a bicycle up to 56 km.

There are left-luggage facilities at both Heuston and Connolly railway stations (IR£1, backpacks IR£2 at Connolly).

TAXI

Taxis in Dublin are expensive with a IR£1.80 flagfall and the usual rapid increase thereafter. In addition there are a number of extra charges – 40p for each extra passenger, 40p for each piece of luggage, IR£1.20 for telephone bookings and 40p for unsocial hours, which means 8 pm to 8 am and all day Sunday. Public holidays are even more unsocial and require a higher supplement.

Taxis can be hailed on the street and are found at taxi ranks around the city, including on O'Connell St in north Dublin, College Green in front of Trinity College and St Stephen's Green at the end of Grafton St. There are numerous taxi companies that will dispatch taxis by radio. Try All Sevens Taxi (☎ 677 7777), City Cabs (☎ 872 7272) or National Radio Cabs (☎ 677 2222). Phone the Garda Carriage Office on ☎ 873 2222, ext 395/406 for any complaints about taxis.

Trams

Trams disappeared from Dublin's streets in 1948-49. Prior to that time the double-decker trams were a popular means of transport both in the city and out at Howth. Trams were introduced in 1872 when the first horse-drawn tram operated from College Green to Terenure, with later extensions to Sandymount. The routes expanded rapidly and in 1881 three separate tram companies merged into the Dublin United Tramways. By this time horses were already being replaced by steam power.

In 1893 the tram operations underwent a major revolution when Imperial Tramways of Bristol took over two other tram companies, relaid lines, introduced electric trams and halved the fares. This dramatic move galvanised Dublin United Tramways into taking over other companies and electrifying their trams as well. The last horse-drawn tram was gone by 1901; at their peak there had been 186 of them working 32 miles of tram track. The electric trams at their peak numbered 330 and worked on 63 miles of track.

In the 1920s and '30s buses began to make inroads into the tram business and the death knell of the trams was sounded in 1938. The intervention of WW II gave them a brief respite but with the end of the war they soon disappeared and the last tram service ended in 1949. See the Howth section in the Seaside Suburbs chapter for information about the trams at the National Transport Museum. ■

CAR & MOTORBIKE

As in most big cities, having a car in Dublin is as much a millstone as a convenience, though it can be useful for day trips outside the city limits. If you're going farther afield, a car is a wonderful means of getting around Ireland since there are always so many interesting little diversions to be made down back roads where public transport does not venture.

As in England, driving is on the left. There are no surprises to driving in Ireland and despite frequent apologies about the roads there's really little to complain about. Back roads may sometimes be potholed and are often very narrow, but the traffic is rarely heavy except as you go through popular tourist towns. Speed limits are 70 mp/h (112 kp/h) on motorways, 60 mp/h (96 kp/h) on other roads, and 30 mp/h (48 kp/h) or as signposted in towns. As with much else in Ireland, speed limits are treated with some disdain. Petrol costs about 60p a litre for super or unleaded.

There are parking meters around central Dublin and a selection of open and sheltered car parks. You don't even have to go that far from the centre to find free roadside parking, especially in north Dublin. However, the police warn visitors that it's safer to park in a supervised car park, since cars are often broken into even in broad daylight close to major tourist attractions. Rental cars and cars with foreign number plates, which may contain valuable personal effects, are a prime target.

Car Rental

Car rental in Ireland is expensive and in the high season there can be a shortage of cars, so it's wise to book ahead. In the off season some companies simply discount all rates by about 25% and there are often special deals on offer. Some smaller companies have an extra daily charge if you go across the border, north or south.

Avis, Budget, Hertz, Thrifty and the major local operators, Murrays/Europcar and Dan Dooley, are the big rental companies. Murrays/Europcar, Avis, Budget and Hertz have desks at the airport, but numerous other operators are based close to the airport and will deliver cars for airport collection. Typical weekly high-season rental rates with insurance and unlimited mileage are IR£280 for a small car (Ford Fiesta), IR£325 for a middle-size car (Ford Escort) and IR£375 for a larger car (Ford Sierra). Insurance will add another IR£60 a week. There are many smaller local operators with lower prices.

Some of the main rental companies are listed here:

Argus Rent-a-Car
    59 Terenure Rd East, Dublin 6 (☎ 90 4444)
Avis Rent-a-Car
    108 Leeson St Upper, Dublin 2 (☎ 677 6971)
Budget Rent-a-Car
    Dublin Airport, Dublin 9 (☎ 842 0793)
Dan Dooley Car & Van Rentals
    42/43 Westland Row, Dublin 2 (☎ 677 2723)
Hertz Rent-a-Car
    149 Leeson St Upper, Dublin 2 (☎ 676 7476)
Murrays/Europcar Car Rental
    Baggot St Bridge, Dublin 4 (☎ 668 1777)
Payless Car Rental
    Dublin Airport, Dublin 9 (☎ 840 7920)
Practical Car Rental
    19 Nassau St, Dublin 2 (☎ 671 5540)
Thrifty Rent-a-Car
    14 Duke St, Dublin 2 (☎ 679 9420)
Windsor Car Rentals
    Rialto, Dublin 8 (☎ 54 0800)

BICYCLE

Dublin is a good place to get around by bicycle, as it is small enough and flat enough to make bike travel a breeze. Many visitors explore farther afield by bicycle, a popular activity in Ireland despite the often less-than-encouraging weather.

All the hostels seem to offer secure bicycle parking areas but if you're going to have a bike stolen anywhere in Ireland, Dublin is where it would happen. Lock your bike up well. Surprisingly, considering how popular bicycles are in Dublin, there's a real scarcity of suitable bicycle parking facilities. Grafton St and Temple Bar are virtually devoid of places to lock a bike. Elsewhere, there are signs on many suitable stretches of railing announcing that bikes must not be parked there.

Bicycle Rental

You can either bring your bike with you or rent in Dublin, where typical rental costs are IR£7 to IR£10 a day or IR£35 a week.

Rent-a-Bike has eight offices around the country and offers one-way rentals between its outlets for an extra IR£5. The head office of Rent-a-Bike (☎ 872 5399, 872 5931) is at 58 Gardiner St Lower, Dublin 1. It's just round the corner from Isaac's Hostel and a stone's throw from the Busáras. They don't offer daily rentals but you can extend a weekly rental by the day.

Raleigh Rent-a-Bike agencies can be found all over Ireland, north and south of the border. Contact them at Raleigh Ireland (☎ 626 1333), Raleigh House, Kylemore Rd, Dublin 10. Raleigh agencies in Dublin include:

Joe Daly
    Main St Lower, Dundrum, Dublin 14 (☎ 298 1485)
Little Sport
    3 Merville Ave, Fairview, Dublin 3 (☎ 33 2405, fax 36 6792)
C Harding
    30 Bachelor's Walk, Dublin 1 (☎ 873 2455, fax 873 3622)
T Hollingsworth
    54 Templeogue Rd, Templeogue, Dublin 6W (☎ 90 5094, 92 0026)
Hollingsworth Bikes
    1 Drummartin Rd, Stillorgan, Dublin 14 (☎ 296 0255)
McDonald's Cycles
    38 Wexford St, Dublin 2 (☎ 475 2586)
The Cycle Centre
    Unit 7, Old Bawn Shopping Centre, Firhouse Rd, Tallaght, Dublin 24 (☎ 51 8771)

Ray's Bike Shop
2 Milltown Centre, Milltown, Dublin 6 (☎ 283 0355)
Mike's Bikes
Unit 6, St George's Mall, Dun Laoghaire Shopping Centre
(☎ 280 0417)

The C Harding outlet on Bachelor's Walk is very conveniently located only a few steps off O'Connell St and right by the river. Daily, three-day and weekly rates are offered.

TOURS

Many Dublin tours operate only during the summer months but at that time you can take bus tours, walking tours and bicycle tours. You can book these tours directly with the operators or through your hotel front desk, at the various city tourist offices or with a travel agent or American Express.

Bus Tours

Gray Line Gray Line has tours around Dublin and farther afield but only in the summer. Reservations can be made through Dublin Tourism (☎ 874 4466, 878 7981, 661 2325 & 661 9666), 14 O'Connell St Upper. Different

Grand Canal (TW)

morning and afternoon tours are available, each costing IR£13, including any admission charges, and lasting 2¾ hours. The two tours can be combined for IR£25. There is a variety of half-day tours out of Dublin to Newgrange, Malahide Castle, Powerscourt Gardens or Newbridge House, each costing IR£13. Day-long tours out of Dublin cost IR£25 and include tours to Glendalough and the Wicklow Mountains, to the Boyne Valley and various combinations of the half-day tours.

Gray Lines also has nightlife tours to the Jury's Irish Cabaret (IR£17.50 with two drinks or IR£29.50 with dinner) or to Doyle's Irish Cabaret (IR£17.50 with two drinks or IR£27.90 with dinner). See the Irish Entertainment section of the Entertainment chapter for more details.

Dublin Bus Dublin Bus (☎ 872 0000) tours can be booked at their office at 59 O'Connell St Upper or directly across the road at the Bus Éireann counter in the Dublin Tourism office (☎ 874 4467), 14 O'Connell St Upper. The three-hour tour uses an open-top double-decker bus as long as the weather permits and operates three times daily in summer and twice daily for much of the rest of the year. From mid-January to early March, however, it only operates on Tuesday, Friday and Saturday, and from mid-December to mid-January it does not operate at all. The tour costs IR£7 (children IR£3.50).

There are also two tours out of the city. These operate daily during the summer months, take 2¾ hours and also cost IR£7 (children IR£3.50). The North Coast Tour does a loop via Howth, Malahide, the Casino at Marino and the Botanic Gardens. The South Coast Tour goes via Dun Laoghaire, Bray and Greystones and then returns through the mountains via Enniskerry. An evening visit to the Irish Culture & Music Centre at Monkstown lasts 3½ hours and operates on Tuesday, Wednesday and Thursday in summer. The cost is IR£10 (children IR£6), including the live show.

Heritage Trail Bus Dublin Bus also operates a hop-on hop-off Heritage Trail bus which does a city tour six times daily from mid-April to late September. There are three additional daily circuits during the peak summer months. The IR£5 (children IR£2.50) ticket lets you travel all day, getting on or off at the 10 stops.

Bus Éireann You can book Bus Éireann tours directly at the Busáras (☎ 36 6111), or through the Bus Éireann desks at the Dublin Bus office (59 O'Connell St Upper) or Dublin Tourism office (14 O'Connell St). During the summer months they operate a Monday to Saturday city tour which takes 3¾ hours and costs IR£9 (children IR£4.50), including entry to the Book of Kells exhibit.

Bus Éireann also has several day tours outside Dublin. Tours to Glendalough and Wicklow are conducted daily from June to mid-September, and daily except Friday for a couple of additional months. The cost is IR£12 (children IR£6). A full-day tour to the Boyne Valley and Newgrange operates on Sunday, Tuesday and Thursday from mid-May to late September and also costs IR£12 (children IR£6). A Sunday tour to Powerscourt is held from early-May to mid-September and costs IR£10 (children IR£5). In the summer months there are also day tours farther afield to places such as Kilkenny, the River Shannon, Waterford and Lough Erne.

Walking Tours

During summer there are various walking tours you can go on which are a great way to explore this very walkable city. A Trinity College walking tour departs frequently from Front Square just inside the college and costs IR£3.50 (concessions IR£3), including entry to the Book of Kells exhibit. See the Trinity College section in the Things to See & Do chapter for more details.

Tour Guides Ireland (☎ 679 4291) operates 1½ to two-hour walks for IR£4; that price permits an adult to bring two children as well. The tours start from Bewley's Café on Grafton St or from the Dublin Writers' Museum on Parnell Square and explore medieval Dublin, 18th century Dublin, literary Dublin, Dublin's north side, or simply entail an early evening stroll around central Dublin.

Historical Walking Tours (☎ 84 50241) are conducted by Trinity College history graduates, take two hours and depart from the front gates of Trinity College. The walks take place several times daily and in the evening on weekends.

The Dublin Literary Pub Crawl (☎ 54 0228) operates five days a week, starting at 7.30 pm from The Bailey on Duke St, just off Grafton St. The walk is great fun and costs IR£5 (student stand-by IR£4) though Guinness consumption can quickly add a few pounds to that figure. The two actors who lead the tour put on a theatrical performance appropriate to the various places and pubs along the way. The particular pubs chosen vary from night to night but could include Mulligan's on Poolbeg St, the Palace Bar on Fleet St, the Stag's Head on Dame St, Davy Byrne's on Duke St, McDaid's on Barry

St, Neary's on Chatham St, The Norseman on Eustace St, The Long Hall on George's St or O'Neill's on Suffolk St.

Bicycle Tours

City Cycle Tours (☎ 671 5606, 671 5610) at 1A Temple Lane, Temple Bar operates three daily Dublin bicycle tours Monday to Saturday, and one on Sunday. The cost is IR£10 (students or YHA members IR£8.50), including use of a bicycle and crash helmet and any admission charges. Children under 14 years of age are not permitted.

Tour Guides

Bord Fáilte approved guides can be contacted via the tourist board. The recommended fees for a full-day approved guide in Dublin are approximately IR£50 in English, rather more in a foreign language.

Things to See & Do

Central Dublin is relatively compact and reasonably uncrowded so getting around on foot is a pleasure. The majority of the attractions in this chapter are within easy reach of the centre and the walking tours take you by many of them. To travel farther out there are taxis, buses and sightseeing tours, while for the energetic bicycles are easy to hire. See the Sightseeing Discounts section in the Facts for the Visitor chapter for information about Heritage Card entry to sites administered by the Office of Public Works and the 'Passport to Dublin's Heritage' pass to other sites.

SIGHTSEEING HIGHLIGHTS

Like any great city Dublin has a number of sights which every visitor feels almost obligated to see. It's easy to spend several days seeing the centrally located highlights and several more going on excursions farther afield in the city and surrounding countryside. Trinity College, with the Book of Kells, and the superb displays of the National Museum are two of Dublin's 'must see' attractions. Also close to the centre of the city, the two medieval (but heavily renovated) cathedrals make a compact triangle with Dublin Castle and should also feature on the high-priority sightseeing list. Between the college and the cathedrals is the intriguing old Temple Bar area, currently being rejuvenated as one of the brightest and most energetic corners of the city.

Dublin is a great city for aimless wandering and an amble from the regal Georgian squares of south Dublin to their decaying counterparts in north Dublin makes a good introduction to the city. A stroll along the banks of the River Liffey will take you by the Custom House and the Four Courts, two of the city's Georgian-era masterpieces.

Farther away are the Royal Hospital Kilmainham and Kilmainham Jail to the west of the centre or the Casino at Marino to the north-east. Dun Laoghaire, with the nearby James Joyce Museum, and Howth are two ports which make good short excursions from the centre. If you have time to get right out of Dublin, the prehistoric burial site at Newgrange to the north and the ruined

Top: Sunset over the River Liffey (JM)
Bottom: Ha'penny Bridge (JM)

monastery at Glendalough to the south should be at the top of your list.

Night-time in Dublin is the time to explore the city's plentiful supply of pubs, and a Literary Pub Crawl, conducted on summer evenings, makes a fine introduction. Finally, having sampled Guinness in the pubs, a pilgrimage to the Guinness Hop Store should complete a visit to Dublin's highlights.

ALONG THE LIFFEY

The River Liffey does more than divide Dublin into northern and southern halves – there's a psychological break between north and south also. The hit 1991 movie *The Commitments* played upon this division, where run-down north Dublin was the place with 'soul'. Although Liffey water may have once been a vital constituent in Guinness, you may be relieved to hear that this is no longer the case.

Apart from the river itself, the Liffey is spanned by an interesting collection of bridges, bounded by an equally historic array of quays, and overlooked by two of Dublin's finest Georgian buildings, the Custom House and the Four Courts.

The River Liffey

The Liffey comes down to Dublin from the Wicklow Hills, passing the open expanse of Phoenix Park and flowing under 14 city bridges (one of which is pedestrian and one a railway) before reaching Dublin Harbour and Dublin Bay. In a straight line it's only about 20 km from its source to the sea but the Liffey contrives to twist and turn for over 100 km along its route and changes remarkably in that distance. Even well into the city, around Phoenix Park, the Liffey is still a very rural-looking stream and if you're waiting for a train at Heuston Station you can wander over to the riverside and watch the large fish in the remarkably clear water below.

Not dramatic, romantic, visually appealing or even very big, the Liffey is not a particularly notable river. Nor does the city make much of it. For what it is, the best views are to be had from O'Connell Bridge or, just upstream, from the pedestrian Ha'penny Bridge which leads straight into the colourful Temple Bar area.

Liffey Bridges

Although there have been bridges over the Liffey for nearly 800 years, the oldest current bridge dates from

1768. The Liffey bridges have been through a diverse series of names. Under the British many of them were named after the lord lieutenants of the time but since independence many of them have been renamed after notable republicans. Travelling downstream you will come across the following city bridges (see Map 2 on pages 80-81).

Island Bridge The first city bridge over the Liffey is just north of Kilmainham Jail and its foundation stone was laid by Sarah Fare, the wife of the Earl of Westmoreland, John Fane, who was at the time Lord Lieutenant of Ireland (1790-95). The official name of Sarah Bridge never caught on and it was generally known as either Kilmainham Bridge or Island Bridge. It was officially renamed Island Bridge in 1922. The name comes from the island formed in the Liffey at this point by the weir.

Heuston Bridge & Frank Sherwin Bridge The bridge by Heuston Station has also gone through a few name changes, starting as King's Bridge in 1821 to commemorate the visit to Ireland by King George IV. The only problem with this initial naming was that the bridge did not exist when the king dropped by – in fact it didn't open until 1828. In 1922 it was renamed Sarsfield Bridge and in 1941 it was renamed Heuston Bridge. Sean Heuston was one of the leaders of the 1916 Easter Rising and was executed nearby at Kilmainham Jail.

The Frank Sherwin Bridge, right next to Heuston Bridge, was opened in 1982 and named after a city councillor.

O'More Bridge Although the current bridge north of the St James's Gate Brewery dates from 1860, a wooden bridge was first built here in 1674 and was probably the second bridge built over the Liffey. For a time it was known as the Bloody Bridge after a riot which took place nearby in 1671. The new bridge started life as the Victoria Bridge but was generally referred to as the Barrack Bridge after the nearby Royal Barracks (now the Collins Barracks). In 1922 it was renamed after Rory O'More, ringleader of a 1641 uprising.

Liam Mellows Bridge Opened in 1768 as Queen's Bridge, this is the oldest surviving bridge on the Liffey though it replaced even earlier bridges, including the 1683 Arran Bridge. It has also been known as the Bridewell Bridge, the Ellis Bridge and the Queen Maeve

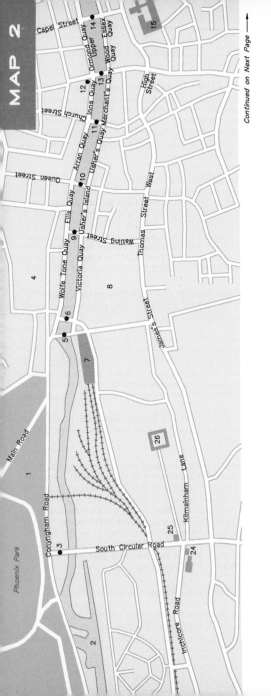

MAP 2

Continued on Next Page →

Phoenix Park

Main Road

Conyngham Road

Capel Street

Ormond Quay Upper

Essex Quay

Wood Quay

Inns Quay

Merchant's Quay

Church Street

Usher's Quay

Arran Quay

High Street

Usher's Island

Queen Street

Ellis Quay

Victoria Quay

Wolfe Tone Quay

Watling Street

Thomas Street West

James's Street

South Circular Road

Kilmainham Lane

Inchicore Road

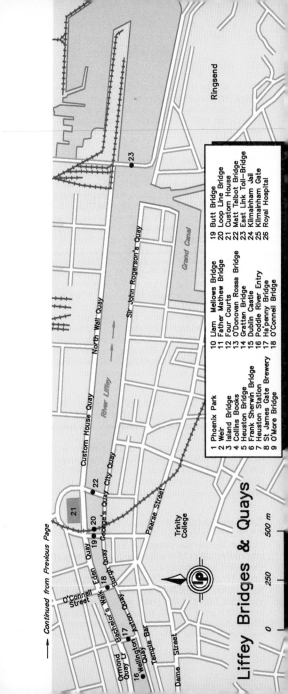

→ Continued from Previous Page

Liffey Bridges & Quays

1 Phoenix Park
2 Weir
3 Island Bridge
4 Collins Books
5 Heuston Bridge
6 Frank Sherwin Bridge
7 Heuston Station
8 St James Gate Brewery
9 O'More Bridge

10 Liam Mellows Bridge
11 Father Mathew Bridge
12 Four Courts
13 O'Donovan Rossa Bridge
14 Grattan Bridge
15 Dublin Castle
16 Poddle River Entry
17 Ha'penny Bridge
18 O'Connell Bridge

19 Butt Bridge
20 Loop Line Bridge
21 Custom House
22 Matt Talbot Bridge
23 East Link Toll-Bridge
24 Kilmainham Jail
25 Kilmainham Gate
26 Royal Hospital

Bridge and is still popularly known as the Queen St Bridge, for the simple reason that Queen St runs down to it. Liam Mellows was executed during the Civil War struggle in 1922 and his name was tagged on to the bridge in 1942.

Father Mathew Bridge The first recorded bridge over the Liffey was built in 1210 at the present site of the Father Mathew Bridge of 1818. The earlier ford of hurdles at this site, just upstream from the Four Courts, gave Dublin its Gaelic name, Baile Átha Cliath, the Town of the Hurdle Ford. Two ancient Irish roads met and crossed the river together at this point: one was known as Sligh Chualann and ran from Tara to County Wicklow, and the other was known as Sligh Midhluachara and ran all the way from Derry to Waterford. There are records of a bridge collapsing here in 1385 and being rebuilt in 1428, but until the bridge at the site of the present O'More Bridge was built in 1674 no other structure spanned the Liffey.

The new bridge, built in 1818, was first named the Charles Whitworth Bridge after the Lord Lieutenant of 1813-17. It was renamed the Dublin Bridge in 1922 and then renamed again in 1938 after Ireland's 'apostle of temperance'. On O'Connell St there's a statue of the gentleman who assayed this impossible role.

O'Donovan Rossa Bridge Republican hero and publisher of the paper *United Ireland*, Jeremiah O'Donovan Rossa died in 1915. His bridge was built in 1813 and was originally named the Richmond Bridge after the Duke of Richmond, Lord Lieutenant from 1807 to 1813. It's slightly upstream from the former Arran Bridge, which was opened in 1683 but destroyed by a storm in 1806, leading to the construction of the present bridge.

Grattan Bridge Better known as the Capel St Bridge, this bridge crosses the river from Capel St and runs through Temple Bar straight up to Dublin Castle. It was originally built in 1676 and named Essex Bridge after the then Lord Lieutenant who just happened to be Arthur Capel (Earl of Essex). The new name came with the replacement bridge built in 1874-75. The River Poddle joined the Liffey at this point, at the black pool or *dubh linn* which gave the city its name. Today the miserable Poddle runs its final five km in an underground channel and trickles into the Liffey through a grating on the south side of the river just downstream from the bridge. Note the curious sea horse motif on the bridge.

Ha'penny Bridge The cast-iron Ha'penny Bridge was constructed in 1816 as the Wellington Bridge but today is officially known as the Liffey Bridge, having been thus renamed in 1922. Earlier this century there was indeed a halfpenny toll to cross it and that's the name by which Dublin's best loved bridge is still known.

O'Connell Bridge James Gandon, Dublin's most important architect, not only designed some of the city's best buildings, including the Four Courts and the Custom House, but was also responsible for its most important bridge. Its construction in 1794-98 made O'Connell St (originally called Gardiner Mall and then Sackville St) the premier avenue in Dublin and shifted the city's axis eastward from Capel St. It was originally named Carlisle Bridge after the Lord Lieutenant in 1780-82 but was given its current name in 1882, at the same time that the statue of Daniel O'Connell, 'the liberator', was unveiled at the river end of O'Connell St. Two years earlier, in 1880, the bridge was widened, so that today it is actually wider than it is long.

Butt Bridge Just upstream from the Custom House, the 1878 Butt Bridge was named after Isaac Butt, leader of the Home Rule movement. It was rebuilt in 1932 and officially renamed the Congress Bridge but that name never caught on. The railway Loop Line Bridge which also crosses the river at this point is easily the ugliest and worst placed bridge on the river, obscuring what would otherwise be fine views of the Custom House.

Matt Talbot Bridge & East Link Toll-Bridge The 1978 Matt Talbot Bridge was named, for some reason, after a gentleman whose principal claim to fame was that, like Father Mathew, he disapproved of alcohol. The final Liffey bridge, the East Link Toll Bridge, was opened in 1985, just beyond the point where the Grand Canal enters the Liffey.

Liffey Quays

The Liffey's riverside quays have had a history almost as replete with name changes as its bridges.

Wolfe Tone & Victoria Quays The furthest quay from the sea is immediately downstream from Heuston

Station and was originally named Albert Quay after Queen Victoria's husband. It was later renamed after the Irish patriot Wolfe Tone. Queen Victoria's own quay has managed to retain its name since her 1861 visit to Dublin.

Ellis, Arran, Inns & Ormond Quays On the north side of the Liffey, Ellis Quay was built on land leased to Sir William Ellis in 1682 and has also managed to keep its name. Still on the north side, Arran Quay dates from 1683, as does the Arran Bridge, which has since been rebuilt and, on several occasions, renamed. Lord Arran was the son of the Duke of Ormonde, whose name (minus the final 'e') graces the next northside quay downstream after Inns Quay. Ormond Quay Upper and Lower stretches along both sides of Grattan Bridge and dates from 1676-78. The original plan was to build houses right down to the riverside, but Sir Humphrey Lewis, who built the quay, was persuaded to construct the quay instead and this set a pattern for other, later quays.

Usher's Island & Usher's Quay On the south side of the Liffey, Victoria Quay gives way to Usher's Island and Usher's Quay. John Ussher leased the land here in 1597 but the quay was not built until the 18th century when it adopted his name, dropping an 's' on the way.

Merchant's & Wood Quay The next south side quays, Merchant's Quay and Wood Quay, are the oldest in the city. Wood Quay was indeed built of wood, way back in the 1200s, but was rebuilt in stone in 1676. Numerous archaeological finds dating back to Dublin's Viking era were made when the land behind Wood Quay was excavated in the 1970s to construct the controversial Dublin Corporation office blocks. Merchant's Quay came a century after Wood Quay and merchant ships used to unload here until the construction of the original Custom House (see that section) slightly downstream in 1621, when the area became residential rather than commercial.

Essex & Wellington Quays Essex Quay, ending at Grattan Bridge, was yet another quay to be named after a Lord Lieutenant. This time it was Arthur Capel, who held the position from 1672 to 1677 and whose name survives on Capel St on the north side of the bridge. On the other side of the bridge, the Clarence Hotel on Wellington Quay in Temple Bar was built on the site of the original Custom House (1621-1791), which was demolished after Gandon's classic Custom House was built farther downstream. The name changed from Custom House Quay in 1817, two years after Lord Wellington's defeat of Napoleon at Waterloo.

Bachelor's Walk & Aston Quay Bachelor's Walk, between Ha'penny and O'Connell bridges on the north side, is infamous for a clash between civilians and British troops in 1914. Following the landing of arms for the republican cause by the ship *Asgard* at Howth, a crowd gathered here and jeered the soldiers of the King's Own Scottish Borders. They in turn opened fire, killing three and injuring 38 civilians. On the south side Aston Quay was named after a mayor of Dublin who acquired the land in 1672.

Other Quays Beyond O'Connell Bridge on the north side are Eden and Custom House quays and finally North Wall Quay, built by the Dublin Corporation in 1729. On the south side is Burgh Quay, which was built in 1808. Which burgh it was named after remains uncertain though it may be the architect Thomas Burgh. It's followed by George's Quay, named after King George I, then by City Quay. Finally, there's Sir John Rogerson's Quay. This was named after the member of parliament and mayor of Dublin who acquired the marshy land here in 1713, though it took him until 1728 to reclaim it.

Dublin Harbour

In medieval times the River Liffey spread out into a broad estuary as it flowed into the bay. Today the low-lying estuary land has long been reclaimed (Trinity College has stood on it for 400 years) and the Liffey is embanked right to the sea.

Dublin Harbour first came into existence in 1714, when the Liffey embankments were built. North Wall Quay was then built and, later, a five km breakwater known as the South Wall was added, followed by the North and South Bull Walls. The South Wall starts at Ringsend, where Cromwell first set fateful foot on Ireland in 1649. From here it runs out to the Pigeon House Fort, built from 1748 and now used as a power station, and from there continues a farther two km out to the 1762 Poolbeg Lighthouse at the end of the breakwater. It's a pleasant, though surprisingly long, stroll out to the lighthouse.

Ferry services to Holyhead in Britain run from the Dublin Harbour ferry terminal as well as from the Dun Laoghaire Harbour, at the southern end of the bay.

Custom House

James Gandon was 18th century Dublin's pre-eminent architect, with the Custom House, the Four Courts building farther up the river, the King's Inns and some elements of the parliament building (now the Bank of Ireland) featuring among his masterpieces.

The Custom House, his first great building, was constructed between 1781 and 1791 just past Eden Quay, in spite of vociferous local opposition. The original Custom House and its attendant docks and warehouses were farther up river and the city merchants and dockworkers were not at all enthusiastic about its new and less convenient location. Nor were local residents too happy about this commercial intrusion, and on occasion Gandon appeared on site wielding a sword! He was strongly supported by the era's property developer extraordinaire, Luke Gardiner, who saw the new Custom House as a major part of his scheme to shift the city's axis eastward from medieval Capel St to Gardiner's Mall (now O'Connell St), which was soon to be connected to south Dublin by a Gandon-designed bridge.

In 1921, during the independence struggle, the Custom House was set alight and completely gutted in a fire that burned for five days. A similar fate befell the Four Courts a year later but both were totally rebuilt. The interior of the Custom House, however, was extensively redesigned and a further major renovation took place between 1986 and 1988.

The building stretches for 114 metres along the Liffey and the best complete view is obtained from across the river, though a close-up inspection of its many fine details is also worthwhile. Arcades, each with seven arches, join the central part to the end pavilions and all the columns along the front have harps carved in their capitals. Various motifs allude to transportation and trade, including the four rooftop statues of Neptune, Mercury, Plenty and Industry, which were destroyed in the 1921 fire and not replaced until 1991. Below the frieze are heads representing the gods of Ireland's 13 principal rivers. The sole female head above the main door represents the River Liffey. The cattle heads honour Dublin's beef trade and the statues behind the building represent Africa, America, Asia and Europe. The building is topped by a copper dome with four clocks and, above that, a five-metre-high statue of Hope.

Four Courts

On Inns Quay beside the river the extensive Four Courts with its 130-metre-long façade was another of James Gandon's masterpieces. Construction of the building, which began in 1786 and soon engulfed the Public Offices (built a short time before at the western end of the same site), continued through to 1802. By then it included a Corinthian-columned central block connected to flanking wings with enclosed quadrangles. The ensemble is topped by a diverse collection of statuary.

There are fine views over the city from the upper rotunda of the central building. The original four courts – Exchequer, Common Pleas, King's Bench and Chancery – branched off this circular central building. The 1224 Dominican Convent of St Saviour formerly stood on the site but was replaced first by the King's Inns and then by the present building. The last parliament of James II was held here in 1689.

The Four Courts played a brief role in the 1916 Easter Rising, without suffering any damage, but the events of 1922 were not so kind. When antitreaty republicans seized the building and could not be persuaded to leave, Michael Collins finally decided to use force. Despite not having suitable armament for such short-range bombardment, he shelled the building from across the river; as the republican forces retreated, the building was set on fire and a great many irreplaceable early records were reduced to ashes. This event sparked off the Civil War and the building was not restored until 1932.

SOUTH OF THE LIFFEY

South Dublin is the affluent and touristy Dublin. Here you will find the fanciest shops, almost all the restaurants of note and a majority of the hotels. You'll also find most of the reminders of Dublin's early history and the finest Georgian squares and houses. South Dublin is certainly not all there is to Dublin, but it's a good place to start.

Trinity College & Book of Kells

Ireland's premier university was founded by Queen Elizabeth I in 1592 on grounds that had been confiscated from a monastery. By providing an alternative to education on the Continent, the queen hoped that the students would avoid being 'infected with popery'. The college is right in the centre of Dublin though at the time of its

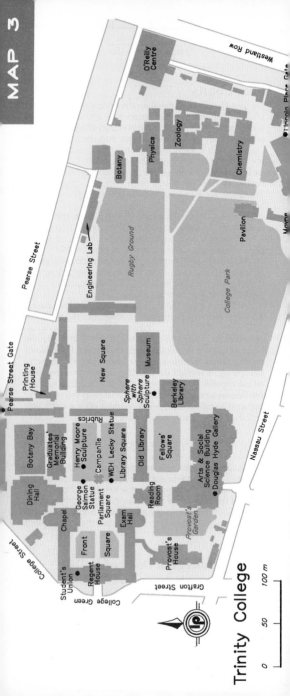

MAP 3

Trinity College

0   50   100 m

Top: Main door, Custom House (TW)
Bottom: Custom House (TW)

foundations it was outside the city walls. Archbishop Ussher, whose scientific feats included the precise dating of the act of creation to 4004 BC, was one of the college's founders. Later, one of his pupils dated the act even more precisely to 9 am on 24 October in that year.

Officially, the university's name is the University of Dublin, but Trinity College just happens to be the institution's sole college. Until 1793 Trinity College remained completely Protestant apart from one short break. Even when the Protestants allowed Catholics in, the Catholic Church forbade it, a restriction which was not completely lifted until 1970. To this day Trinity College is still somewhat a centre of British and Protestant influence although the majority of its 7000 students are Catholic. Women were first admitted to the college in 1903, an earlier date than at most British universities.

The college grounds cover 16 hectares (40 acres). The college has no admission charge or restrictions on entry apart from a ban on dogs and a request not to ride bicycles in the Library Square area. Should the rain stop and a sudden heatwave give you the urge to toss off your clothing and work on your suntan, another sign requests that you restrict that activity to College Park.

During the summer months walking tours depart regularly from the main gate on College Green, Monday to Saturday from 9.30 am to 4.30 pm, Sunday from noon to 4 pm. The IR£3.50 cost of the walking tour is good value since it includes the fee to see the Book of Kells (see that section).

Main Entrance Much of the college today dates from Dublin's wealthy 18th century heyday. From College Green (the street in front of the college), the 'Front Gate' or Regent House entrance to the college's grounds was built in 1752-59 and is guarded by statues of the poet Oliver Goldsmith (1730-74) and the orator Edmund Burke (1729-97).

Around the Campanile The open area reached from Regent House is divided into Front Square, Parliament Square and Library Square. The area is dominated by the 30-metre Campanile, designed by Edward Lanyon and erected in 1852-53 on what was believed to be the centre of the monastery that preceded the college. Earlier there had been a bell tower, designed by the noted architect Richard Castle, on the same spot. To the left of the Campanile is a statue of George Salmon, the College Provost from 1886 to 1904, who fought bitterly to keep women out of the college. He carried out his threat to permit them 'over his dead body' by promptly dropping dead when the worst came to pass. The statue to the right of the Campanile is of the historian W E H Lecky (1838-1903). On the grassy expanse of Library Square is a 1969 sculpture by British sculptor Henry Moore (1898-1986) and two very large Oregon maples.

Chapel & Dining Hall Clockwise around the Front Square from the entrance gate, the first building is the Chapel, built from 1798 by the architect Sir William Chambers (1723-96) and since 1972 open to all denominations. The chapel is noted for its extremely fine plasterwork by Michael Stapleton, its Ionic columns and its painted, not stained, glass windows. The main one is dedicated to Archbishop Ussher, the college's founder, who so precisely dated the act of creation.

Next to the chapel is the Dining Hall, originally designed in 1743 by Richard Castle but dismantled only 15 years later because of severe problems caused by inadequate foundations. The replacement was completed in 1761 and may have retained elements of the original design. It was extensively restored after a fire in 1984. The popular Buttery Restaurant is found here.

Graduates' Memorial Building & the Rubrics The 1892 Graduates' Memorial Building forms the north side of Library Square. Behind it are the tennis courts in the open area known as Botany Bay. The popular legend behind this name is that the unruly students housed around the square were suitable candidates for the British penal colony at Botany Bay (Sydney) in Australia. At the east side of Library Square, the red-brick Rubrics Building dates from around 1690, making it the oldest building in the college. It was extensively altered in an 1894 restoration and then underwent serious structural modifications in the 1970s.

Library To the south of the square is the Library, which was built in a rather severe style by Thomas Burgh between 1712 and 1732. The Library's 65-metre Long Room contains numerous unique ancient texts and the Book of Kells is displayed in the Library Colonnades. Despite Ireland's independence, the Library Act of 1801 still entitles Trinity College Library, along with three libraries in Britain, to a free copy of every book published in the UK. Housing this bounty requires nearly another km of shelving every year and the collection amounts to around three million books. Of course these cannot all be kept at the college library, so there are now

Statue of WEH Lecky, Trinity College (JM)

additional library storage facilities dotted around
Dublin. The Long Room is mainly used for the library's
oldest volumes. Until 1892 the ground floor Colonnades
was an open arcade, but it was enclosed at that time to
increase the storage area. A previous attempt to increase
the room's storage capacity had been made in 1853,
when the Long Room ceiling was raised.

The Book of Kells For visitors, Trinity College's
prime attraction is the magnificent Book of Kells, an
illuminated manuscript dating from around 800 AD –
one of the oldest books in the world. Although the book
was brought to the college for safekeeping from the

Top: Trinity College (JM)
Bottom: Statue of George Salmon, Trinity College (JM)

monastery at Kells in County Meath in 1654, it undoubtedly predates the monastery itself. It was probably
produced by monks at St Columba's Monastery on the
remote island of Iona, off the coast of Scotland. When
repeated Viking raids made their monastery untenable,
the monks moved to the temporarily greater safety of
Ireland in 806 AD, bringing their masterpiece with them
to its new home at Kells. In 1007 the book was stolen and
then rediscovered three months later, buried in the
ground. Some time before the dissolution of the monastery, the metal shrine or *cumdach* was lost, possibly taken
by looting Vikings who would not have valued the text
itself. About 30 of the beginning and ending folios
(double-page spreads) have also disappeared.

The Book of Kells contains the four gospels of the New

Testament, written in Latin, as well as prefaces, summaries and other text. If it were merely words, the Book of Kells would simply be a very old book – it's the extensive and amazingly complex illustrations which make it so wonderful. The superbly decorated opening initials are only part of the story, for the book also has numerous smaller illustrations between the lines.

The 680-page (340-folio) book was rebound in four calfskin volumes in 1953. Two volumes are usually on display, one showing an illuminated page and the other showing text. The pages are turned over regularly but if you can't spare the time for the numerous daily visits which would be required to view the entire book, you can enquire about a reproduction copy of the book available via the Trinity College Library for a mere US$18,000. If that's too much, an information brochure and 'documentation kit' are available for US$98. If that's still too steep, the library bookshop has various lesser books, including *The Book of Kells* (Thames & Hudson paperback, London, 1980) with some attractive colour plates and text for less than IR£10.

The Book of Kells is usually on display in the East Pavilion of the library Colonnades, underneath the actual library, but the entry price allows you admission to the library's Long Room. As well as the Book of Kells, the 807 AD Book of Armagh and the even older 675 AD Book of Durrow are also on display in the East Pavilion.

You can visit the Book of Kells and the Long Room from 9.30 am to 5 pm Monday to Friday, noon to 5 pm Sunday. Entry is IR£2.50 (students and children IR£2, children under 12 free). There's a very busy book and souvenir shop in the Colonnades.

The Library Long Room The Trinity College Library Long Room is lined with shelves housing 200,000 of the library's oldest books and manuscripts. Also on display is the so-called Brian Ború's harp, which was definitely not in use when this early Irish hero defeated the Danes at the Battle of Clontarf in 1014 AD. It does, however, date from around 1400, making it one of the oldest harps in Ireland.

Other exhibits in the Long Room include a rare copy of the Proclamation of the Irish Republic, which was read out by Patrick Pearse at the beginning of the Easter Rising in 1916. The collection of marble busts around the walls dates from the 18th and 19th centuries and features Jonathan Swift, Edmund Burke and Wolfe Tone, all of whom were former members of Trinity College.

Reading Room, Exam Hall & Provost's House
Continuing clockwise around the Campanile there's the
Reading Room and the Public Theatre or Exam Hall,
which dates from 1779-91. Like the Chapel building
which it faces and closely resembles, it was the work of
William Chambers and also has plasterwork by Michael
Stapleton. The Exam Hall has an oak chandelier rescued
from the Houses of Parliament (now the Bank of Ireland)
across College Green and an organ said to have been
salvaged from a Spanish ship in 1702, though evidence
indicates otherwise. Portraits of Swift, Ussher, Berkeley,
Queen Elizabeth I and other personages connected with
the college's history are hung in the Exam Hall.

Behind the Exam Hall is the 1760 Provost's House, a
particularly fine Georgian house where the provost or
college head still resides. The house and its adjacent
garden are not open to the public.

Berkeley Library To one side of the old library is the
new one – Paul Koralek's 1967 Berkeley Library. This
solid square brutalist-style building has been hailed as
the best example of modern architecture in Ireland,
though it has to be admitted the competition is not great.
It's fronted by Arnaldo Pomodoro's 1982-83 sculpture
Sphere with Sphere.

George Berkeley was born in Kilkenny in 1685,
studied at Trinity when he was only 15 years old and
went on to a distinguished career in many fields but
particularly in philosophy. His influence spread to the
new English colonies in North America where, among
other things, he helped to found the University of Penn-
sylvania. Berkeley in California, and its namesake
university, are named after him.

**Arts & Social Science Building & Douglas
Hyde Gallery** South of the old library is the 1978 Arts
& Social Science Building, which backs on to Nassau St
and forms the alternative main entrance to the college.
Like the Berkeley Library it was designed by Paul
Koralek; it also houses the Douglas Hyde Gallery of
Modern Art (☎ 70 2116). Fellows Square is surrounded
on three sides by the two library buildings and the Arts
& Social Science Building.

The Dublin Experience After the Book of Kells the
college's other big tourist attraction is the Dublin Experience, a 45-minute audiovisual introduction to the city.
It is shown every hour from 10 am to 5 pm daily from
late May to early October. Entry is IR£2.75 (students or

children IR£2.25). Combined tickets to the Book of Kells and the Dublin Experience are available.

Around New Square Behind the Rubrics Building, at the eastern end of Library Square, is New Square. In the highly ornate 1853-57 Museum Building exhibits include the skeletons of two enormous giant Irish deer just inside the entrance and the Geological Museum upstairs. The 1734 Printing House, designed by Richard Castle to resemble a Doric Temple and now used for the integrated circuits fabrication laboratory of the engineering department, is at the north-west corner of New Square. One of Dublin's best early architects, Castle was responsible for a number of buildings at Trinity College, but apart from this building little trace of his work here has survived.

At the eastern end of the college grounds are the rugby ground and College Park, where cricket games are often played. There are a number of science buildings at the eastern end of the grounds. The Lincoln Place Gate at this end is usually open and makes a good entrance or exit from the college, especially if you are on a bicycle.

Bank of Ireland

The imposing Bank of Ireland building (☎ 677 6801), on College Green directly opposite Trinity College, was originally begun in 1729 to house the Irish Parliament. When the parliament voted itself out of existence by the Act of Union in 1800, it became a building without a role. It was sold with instructions that the interior be altered to prevent it from being used as a debating chamber in the future. Consequently, the large central House of Commons was remodelled but the smaller chamber of the House of Lords survived. For some reason after independence the Irish government chose to make Leinster House the new parliamentary building and ignored the possibility of restoring this fine building to its original use.

The building involved a string of architects over a long period of time yet somehow manages to avoid looking like a hotchpotch of styles. Edward Lovett Pearce designed the original central part of the building which was constructed between 1729 and 1739. The curving windowless Ionic portico has statues of Hibernia (the Roman name for Ireland), Fidelity and Commerce, while the east front, which was designed by James Gandon in 1785, has Corinthian columns and statues of Wisdom (or Fortitude), Justice and Liberty. Other architects involved in its construction were Robert

Top: Berkeley Library and *Sphere with Sphere* (TW)
Middle: *Sphere with Sphere* (TW)
Bottom: Bank of Ireland (JM)

Park and Francis Johnston, who converted it from a parliament building to a bank after it was sold in 1803.

The Irish Parliament first sat in 1661, moved to its new home in 1731 and was wound up in 1800, a move which had disastrous economic consequences for Dublin. Throughout its history the parliament was essentially a government of the aristocracy and Jonathan Swift penned some appropriately acerbic words about their wisdom:

As I stroll the city, oft I
Spy a building large and lofty
Not a bow-shot from the college
Half the globe from sense and knowledge.

The compliment was returned when Swift's *Drapier's Letters*, an anonymous diatribe against an act of parliamentary corruption, were burnt on College Green outside the parliament building.

Inside, the banking mall occupies what was once the House of Commons but offers little hint of its former role. The Irish House of Lords is much more interesting with its Irish oak woodwork and late 18th century Waterford crystal chandelier. The tapestries date from the 1730s and depict the Siege of Derry in 1689 and the Battle of the Boyne in 1690, the two great Protestant victories over Catholic Ireland. In the niches are busts of George III, George IV, Lord Nelson and the Duke of Wellington. The mace on display was made for the House of Commons and retained by the Speaker of the House when the parliament was dissolved. It was later sold by his descendants and bought back from Christies in London by the Bank of Ireland in 1937.

The building can be visited during banking hours, Monday to Friday from 10 am to 3 pm, on Thursday to 5 pm. Guided tours take place on Tuesdays at 10.30 am, 11.30 am and 1.45 pm. The building's alternative role as a tourist attraction is not pushed very hard. You'll probably have to ask somebody if you want to find your way to the House of Lords.

Around the Bank of Ireland

Several places of interest lie within a stone's throw of the bank. The area between the bank and Trinity College, today a constant tangle of traffic and pedestrians, was once a green swathe and is still known as College Green. In front of the bank on College Green is a statue of Henry Grattan (1746-1820), a distinguished parliamentary orator. Farther up Dame St is a modern memorial to the patriot Thomas Davis (1814-45). In true Irish fashion there have been other statues here which have failed to stand the test of time or explosives – William of Orange, for instance, was dispatched by a land mine in 1929.

The traffic island where College Green, Westmoreland St and College St meet houses public toilets (no longer in use) and a statue of the poet and composer Thomas Moore (1779-1852), renowned for James Joyce's comment in *Ulysses* that standing atop a public urinal was not a bad place for the man who penned the poem 'The Meeting of the Waters'. At the other end of College St, where it meets Pearse St, another traffic island is topped by a 1986 sculpture known as *Steyne*. It's a copy of the *steyne*, the Viking word for stone, erected on the riverbank in the 9th century to stop ships from grounding. It was not removed until 1720.

Temple Bar

West of College Green and the Bank of Ireland the maze of streets that make up Temple Bar are sandwiched between Dame St and the river. It's one of the oldest areas of Dublin and was heading rapidly downhill towards total redevelopment as a bus station until it was officially recognised that local energy was already rehabilitating it as a sort of Dublin Left Bank. It will be some time before the project is complete but already Temple Bar has become a Dublin delight, with numerous interesting little restaurants and pubs and a growing collection of trendy shops (see Map 13 at the back of this book).

Dame St, which forms the southern boundary of the Temple Bar area, is the cord that links new Dublin (centred around Trinity College and Grafton St) and old (stretching from Dublin Castle to encompass the two cathedrals). Along its route Dame St changes name to become Cork Hill, Lord Edward St and Christ Church Place.

Information For information specifically on Temple Bar, the Temple Bar Information Centre (☎ 671 5717) is on Eustace St. They publish a *Temple Bar Guide*. The notice board in the Resource Centre/Well Fed Café on Crow St offers a useful collection of local goings-on. Morrigan Books' *Heritage Guide to Temple Bar* is an interesting map and description of the area.

Temple Bar has one popular hostel (Kinlay House), a middle-price hotel (Clarence Hotel, owned by the rock band U2) and an upper bracket hotel (Bloom's). See the Places to Stay chapter for more information. Bloom's is

Temple Bar (TW)

built on the site of the original Jury's Hotel, which started life here in 1839 but moved to its suburban location in 1973. The restaurant population of Temple Bar has increased dramatically in the past few years and is still growing (see the Places to Eat chapter for more information). Pubs are also well represented in Temple Bar and on summer evenings an international outdoor drinking party takes place every evening along Essex St East from the Norseman to the Temple Bar pub.

Two of Dublin's best late-night music venues – the Rock Garden Café for rock music and Bad Bob's for country music – can also be found in Temple Bar along with two theatres, the 1892 Olympia Theatre and the much more modern Project Arts Centre (see the Entertainment chapter). Finally, Temple Bar is packed with all manner of colourful and peculiar shops, which are described in the Shopping chapter.

History Sir William Temple (1554-1628) acquired the land which bears his name following the dissolution of the monasteries by Henry VIII in 1537. The term 'bar' referred to a riverside walkway so this area was called Temple's Bar. This stretch of prime riverside land had been the property of Augustinian friars from 1282 until Henry VIII made his big land grab. Temple Lane was known as Hogges Lane at that time and gave access to the friars' house. During its monastic era the Temple Bar area was marshy land that had only recently been reclaimed from the river. Much of the area was outside

Sunlight Chambers, Temple Bar (TW)

the city walls and the River Poddle flowed through it, connecting the black pool with the Liffey.

The narrow lanes and alleys of Temple Bar started to take form in the early 1700s when this was a disreputable area of pubs and prostitution. Through the 1800s it developed a commercial character with many small craft and trade businesses, but in this century it went through a steady economic decline, as did most of central Dublin.

In the 1960s it was decided to demolish the whole area to build a major bus station and from 1981 Temple Bar properties were gradually bought up for this purpose. In the Irish fashion these plans took a long, long time to develop and meanwhile the acquired properties were rented out on short-term leases at low rents. Temple Bar gradually became a thriving countercultural centre and in the 1980s it was finally decided to abandon the bus station plan and encourage the development of Temple Bar as a centre for restaurants, shops and entertainment.

The decision to recognise formally what was already taking place informally accelerated the development of Temple Bar, which changed dramatically in 1991 and 1992 and will, no doubt, continue to change with equal speed. Plans for the future include public squares, apartments, a student housing centre, a Viking museum on the riverside and a second pedestrian bridge over the Liffey. Meanwhile, Temple Bar rents are heading upwards like a space shuttle.

Around Temple Bar

The western boundary of Temple Bar is formed by Fishamble St, which is the oldest street in Dublin, dating right back to Viking times. Christ Church Cathedral, originally dating from 1170, stands beside Fishamble St. There was, however, an even earlier Viking church on this site. The parliamentarian Henry Grattan (whose statue stands outside Trinity College on College Green) and the poet James Clarence Mangan (whose bust can be seen in St Stephen's Green) were both born on Fishamble St.

In 1742 Handel conducted the first performance of his *Messiah* in the Dublin Music Hall, which stood at that time behind what is now the Kinlay House Refectory. The chorus was made up of the choirs from the two cathedrals and in order to cope with the large crowd the stewards of the Charitable Music Society requested:

... the favour of ladies not to come with hoops this day to the Music Hall in Fishamble St. The gentlemen are desired to come without their swords.

Hooped skirts and swinging swords would certainly have reduced the space for paying customers. The Music Hall, which had opened a year earlier in 1741, was designed by Richard Castle but the only reminder of it today is the entrance and the original door, which stand to the left of Kennan's engineering works.

Parliament St, which runs straight up from the river to the City Hall and Dublin Castle, has Read's Cutlers at No 4. This is the oldest shop in Dublin, having operated under the same name since 1760. At the bottom of the street, beside the river, the Sunlight Chambers has a beautiful frieze around the buildings. Sunlight was a brand of soap manufactured by the Lever Brothers, who were responsible for the turn-of-the-century building. The beautiful frieze shows the Lever Brothers' view of the world and soap: men make clothes dirty, women wash them!

Eustace St is a particularly interesting street, with the popular Norseman pub at the river end. Buildings on the street include the 1715 Presbyterian Meeting House. The United Irishmen, who sought parliamentary reform and equality for Catholics, were first convened in 1791 in the Eagle Tavern, now the Friends Meeting House.

Cecilia St was named after St Cecilia, the patron saint of music, and once had a popular music hall. The Ha'penny Bridge was constructed in part to give easy access to the theatre from north Dublin. Fownes St was named after the Mayor of Dublin in 1697; a notorious wheeler-dealer, he was the type of businessman who nowadays would have been declared bankrupt and retired to his luxurious villa in Majorca or Rio de Janeiro. Fownes St also has the Boy Scout Shop, and the head-quarters of both the Irish green movement and the Irish gay movement.

Merchant's Arch leads to the Ha'penny Bridge over the Liffey. If you cross the bridge to the north side, pause to look at the statue of two stout Dublin matrons sitting on a park bench with their shopping bags. In typically irreverent Dublin fashion the sculpture has been dubbed 'the hags with the bags'. The Stock Exchange lives on Anglesea St, in a building dating from 1878. The Bank of Ireland also occupies a corner of Temple Bar.

Dublin Castle

The centre of British power in Ireland, Dublin Castle (☎ 679 3713) would more correctly be described as a palace than a castle. Although it dates back to the 13th century, when it was built on even older Viking founda-tions, the older parts have been successively built over

MAP 4

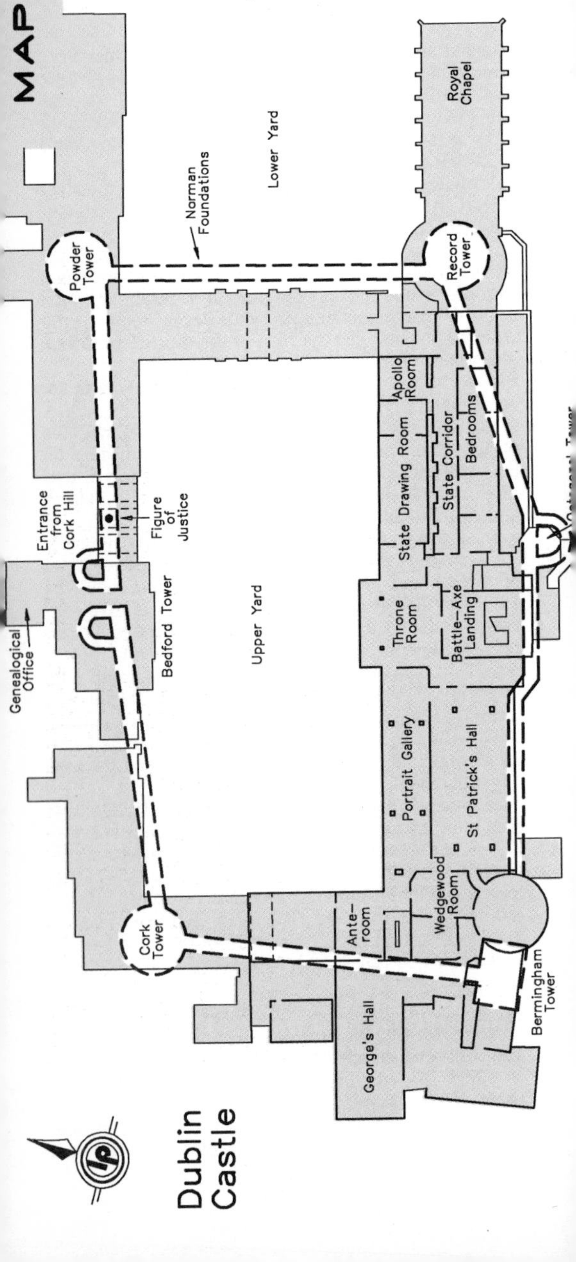

104
Things to See & Do

Dublin
Castle

Royal Chapel

Lower Yard

Norman Foundations

Powder Tower

Record Tower

Octagonal Tower

Apollo Room

State Drawing Room

State Corridor

Bedrooms

Battle-Axe Landing

Throne Room

Entrance from Cork Hill

Figure of Justice

Bedford Tower

Genealogical Office

Upper Yard

Portrait Gallery

St Patrick's Hall

Wedgewood Room

Ante-room

Cork Tower

George's Hall

Bermingham Tower

Top: Dublin Castle (TW)
Bottom: Figure of Justice above Dublin Castle yard
        entrance (TW)

through the centuries. Today only the Record Tower, built between 1202 and 1258, remains intact from the original Norman castle. The Bermingham Tower carries a faint connection with the earlier fortifications as the 14th century original was badly damaged by an explosion in 1775 and rebuilt soon after.

Underneath the more recent additions, parts of the castle's foundations still remain and a visit to the subterranean excavations, which clearly reveal the development of the castle from its original construction, is by far the most interesting part of the castle tour. The castle moats, now completely covered by more modern developments, were filled by the River Poddle, on its way to joining the Liffey at Dublin's black pool.

The original castle was built on the orders of King John in 1204 and enjoyed a relatively quiet history despite a siege by Silken Thomas Fitzgerald in 1534, a fire which destroyed much of the castle in 1684, and the events of the 1916 Easter Rising. At the time of the Easter Rising it was so lightly defended that it would probably have fallen had the insurrectionists only realised they faced such lightweight opposition. The castle was used as the official residence of the British viceroys of Ireland, up until the Viceregal Lodge was built in Phoenix Park. Earlier it had been used as prison, though not always with great success, as Red Hugh O'Donnell managed to escape from the Record Tower in 1591 and, when he was recaptured, escaped again in 1592.

The castle tops Cork Hill, behind the City Hall on Dame St, and tours are held from 10 am to 12.15 pm and 2 to 5 pm Monday to Friday, afternoons only on weekends. The tour costs IR£1 (children 50p).

Castle Tour The main Upper Yard of the castle with the entrance underneath the Throne Room is reached either directly from Cork Hill or via the Lower Yard. Starting from the main entrance, the castle tour takes you round the state chambers, which were developed during Dublin's British heyday but are still used for official state occasions. The sequence of rooms the tour takes you through may vary. From the entrance you ascend the stairs to the Battle-Axe Landing, where the viceroy's guards once stood, armed with battle-axes.

Turning left you pass through a series of drawing rooms, formerly used as bedrooms by visitors to the castle. The castle gardens, visible from the windows of these rooms, end in a high wall said to have been built for Queen Victoria's visit to block out the distressing sight of the slums on Stephen St. The wounded James Connolly was detained in the first of these rooms after the siege of the GPO in 1916. From here he was taken to Kilmainham Jail to face a firing squad, still unable to stand because of a bullet wound to his ankle. The rooms are particularly notable for the beautiful plasterwork on their ceilings. Not all of it originated in the castle – some of it was rescued from Georgian buildings facing demolition elsewhere in the city.

At the end of this series of rooms you cross the State Corridor to enter the Apollo Room or Music Room, with a 1746 ceiling that was originally in a house on Merrion Row and was installed here in the 1960s. After inspecting that room you go down the long State Corridor and enter the State Drawing Room, which suffered serious damage in a fire in 1941. It has been restored with period furniture and paintings dating from 1740. From there you enter the ornate Throne Room, which was built in 1740. It contains a large throne, said to have been presented to the castle by William of Orange (King William III), right after he defeated King James II at the Battle of the Boyne, and a brass chandelier that weighs over a ton.

The long Portrait Gallery, at one time divided into a series of smaller rooms, has portraits of some of the British viceroys. It ends at an anteroom from which you enter George's Hall, tacked on to the castle in 1911 for King George V's visit to Ireland. From these rooms you return through the anteroom to the blue Wedgewood Room (yes, the whole room does look like Wedgewood china), which in turn leads to the Bermingham Tower, originally dating from 1411 but rebuilt in 1775-77. The tower was used as a prison on a number of occasions, particularly during the independence struggle from 1918 to 1920. Leaving the tower you pass through the 25-metre-long St Patrick's Hall with its painted ceiling. The Knights of St Patrick, an order created in 1783, were invested here and their standards are displayed around the walls. Now Irish presidents are inaugurated here and it is used for receptions. Note the huge painting on the ceiling.

St Patrick's Hall ends back on the Battle-Axe Landing but the tour now takes you down to the Undercroft, the most interesting part of the castle. Remnants of the earlier Viking fort, the 13th century Powder Tower and the city wall can be seen in this excavation of the original moat, now well below street level.

Bedford Tower & Genealogical Office Other points of interest in the castle include the Bedford Tower and the 1552 Genealogical Office, directly across the Upper Yard from the main entrance. In 1907 the collection known as the Irish Crown Jewels was mysteriously stolen from this tower and was never recovered.

The entranceway to the castle yard beside the Bedford Tower is topped by a figure of justice which has always been a subject of controversy and mirth. The fact that she faces the castle and has her back to the city was taken as a sure indicator of how much justice the average Irish citizen could expect from the English. And the scales of justice had a distinct tendency to fill with rain and tilt in one direction or the other, rather than assuming an approved evenly balanced position. Eventually a hole was drilled in the bottom of each pan so the rainwater could drain out.

Royal Chapel In the Lower Yard is the Church of the Holy Trinity, previously known as the Royal Chapel, which was built in Gothic style by Francis Johnston in 1807-14. Decorating the exterior are over 90 heads of various Irish personages and assorted saints carved out of Tullamore limestone.

Record Tower Towering over the chapel is the Record Tower, which was used as a storage facility for official records from 1579 until they were transferred to the Record Office in the Four Courts building in the early 1800s. When the Four Courts was burnt out at the start of the Civil War in 1922 almost all these priceless records were destroyed. Although the tower was rebuilt in 1813 it retains much of its original appearance, including the massive five-metre thick walls.

City Hall & Municipal Buildings

Fronting Dublin Castle on Lord Edward St, the City Hall was built by Thomas Cooley in 1769-79 as the Royal Exchange and later became the offices of the Dublin Corporation. The building has a Corinthian portico with six columns, a number of statues of notable Irish citizens and a fine dome. The statue of Daniel O'Connell, at one time the Lord Mayor of Dublin, was originally intended to stand on the plinth inside the hall's balustrade but ended up inside the building.

The City Hall was built on the site of the Lucas Coffee House and the Eagle Tavern. Patrons of the tavern established Dublin's infamous Hell Fire Club in 1735 (see the section on Dublin Clubs). Parliament St (1762), which leads up from the river to the front of City Hall, was the first of Dublin's wide boulevards to be laid out by the Wide Streets Commission.

The 1781 Municipal Buildings, immediately west of

the City Hall, were built by Thomas Ivory (1720-86), who was also responsible for the Genealogical Office in Dublin Castle.

Christ Church Cathedral

Christ Church Cathedral (Church of the Holy Trinity; ☎ 677 8099) is on Christ Church Place, just south of the river and west of the city centre and the Temple Bar district. Dublin's original Viking settlement stood between the cathedral and the river. This was also the centre of medieval Dublin, with Dublin Castle nearby and the Tholsel or town hall (demolished in 1809) and the original Four Courts (demolished in 1796) both beside the cathedral. Nearby on Back Lane is the only remaining guild hall in Dublin. The 1706 Tailor's Hall was due for demolition in the 1960s but survived to become the office of An Taisce, the Irish National Trust (see the Cathedrals & Liberties Walk in the Walks chapter).

The cathedral was originally built in wood by the Danes in 1038. It was subsequently rebuilt in stone from around 1170, by Richard de Clare, the Earl of Pembroke, who is better known as the legendary Strongbow (an Anglo-Norman lord who invaded Ireland in 1170). The archbishop of Dublin at that time was Laurence (Lorcan in Irish) O'Toole, later to become St Laurence, the patron saint of Dublin. Neither lived to see the completion of

Churches

A casual glance at the Dublin skyline will illustrate what an important part churches have played in the city's history and, though you may soon feel you're getting a surfeit of them, some are well worth exploring. As in other towns in this most Catholic of countries, it's a continuing reminder of the long period of English rule that the finest and most historic churches are not Catholic. A corollary of this historically related fact is that these important, but non-Catholic, churches suffer from tiny congregations and have great difficulty in making ends meet.

In spite of Dublin's long history, little remains of any great antiquity. The exceptions are the two cathedrals, both of which date back to the Norman era and in their medieval heyday vied furiously for power and influence. Even their creation was the result of a clerical dispute. ■

the church, as Strongbow died in 1176 and Laurence O'Toole in 1180. Nor was their cathedral destined to have a long life: the foundations were essentially a peat bog so it was hardly surprising when the south wall collapsed in 1562. It was soon rebuilt, but the central tower was also a replacement for two earlier steeples which had burnt down. Most of what you see from the outside dates from a major restoration between 1871 and 1878 by the architect G E Street. Above ground level the north wall, the transepts and the western part of the choir are almost all that remain from the original. Even the flying buttresses to the north wall date from the 19th century restoration.

Through much of its history Christ Church vied for supremacy with nearby St Patrick's Cathedral but, like its neighbour, it fell on hard times in the 18th and 19th centuries and was virtually derelict when the major restoration took place. Earlier, the nave had been used as a market and the crypt had housed taverns. Today, of course, both these Church of Ireland cathedrals are outsiders in a Catholic nation.

From the south-east entrance to the churchyard (see Map 5 on the next page) you walk by the ruins of the chapter house (1), dating from 1230. The entrance (2) to the cathedral is at the south-west corner and you face the north wall as you enter. The north wall survived the collapse of its southern counterpart, but it has also suffered from subsiding foundations and from its eastern end it leans visibly. At the top it is about a half-metre out of the perpendicular.

The south side aisle has a monument (3) to the legendary Strongbow , under whom construction of the stone cathedral was begun. The armoured figure on the tomb is unlikely to be of Strongbow himself (the Earl of Drogheda is the most likely possibility), but his internal organs may indeed have been buried here and the half-figure beside the tomb may relate to that burial. A popular legend relates that this half-figure is of Strongbow's son, who was cut in two by his father when his bravery in battle was suspect.

The South Transept (4) is one of the most original parts of the cathedral and contains the superb Baroque tomb (5) of the 19th Earl of Kildare (died 1734). His grandson, Lord Edward Fitzgerald, was a member of the United Irishmen and died in the abortive 1798 rebellion. Strongbow built the cathedral for St Laurence O'Toole, the Archbishop of Dublin, who died in 1180 at Eu in Normandy. The entrance to the Chapel of St Laurence (6) is off the South Transept and contains two effigies, one of them reputed to be that of either Strongbow's wife

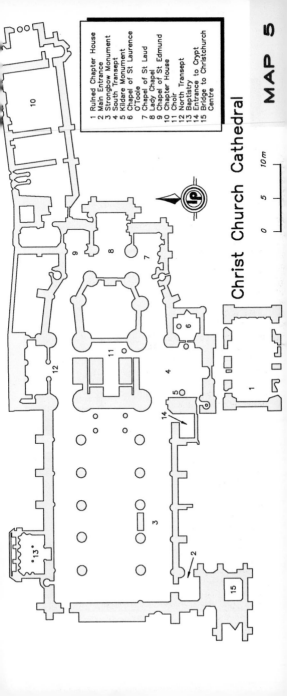

Christ Church Cathedral

1 Ruined Chapter House
2 Main Entrance
3 Strongbow Monument
4 South Transept
5 Kildare Monument
6 Chapel of St Laurence O'Toole
7 Chapel of St Laud
8 Lady Chapel
9 Chapel of St Edmund
10 Chapter House
11 Choir
12 North Transept
13 Baptistry
14 Entrance to Crypt
15 Bridge to Christchurch Centre

0   5   10m

MAP 5

Top: Christ Church Cathedral (TW)
Bottom: Strongbow Monument (TW)

or sister. Laurence O'Toole's embalmed heart was placed in the Chapel of St Laud (7).

At the east end of the cathedral is the Lady Chapel (8) or Chapel of the Blessed Virgin Mary. Also at the east end is the Chapel of St Edmund (9) and the Chapter House (10), the latter closed to visitors. Parts of the Choir (11), in the centre of the church, and the North Transept (12) are original, but the Baptistry (13) was added at the time of the 1875 restoration.

An entrance (14) by the South Transept descends to the unusually large arched crypts which date right back to the original Danish church of 1000 years ago. Curiosities in the crypt include ancient 1670 stocks that once stood in the cathedral yard. A glass display case houses a mummified cat which, until it was vandalised in 1992, used to chase a mummified mouse. From the main entrance a bridge (15), part of the 1871-78 restoration, leads to the Christchurch Centre, which was also added at that time.

The cathedral is open from 10 am to 5 pm daily and entry is 50p. As with many other fine old Church of Ireland churches in Ireland, making ends meet in an overwhelmingly Catholic country is not easy.

St Patrick's Cathedral

St Patrick himself is said to have baptised converts at a well within the cathedral grounds, so St Patrick's Cathedral (☎ 475 4817) stands on one of the earliest Christian sites in the city. Like Christ Church Cathedral it was built on distinctly unstable ground, with the subterranean River Poddle flowing under its foundations. Because of the high water table, St Patrick's does not have a crypt but, again like its rival, it has had a chequered history marked by frequent restorations, alterations and additions. Its current form dates mainly from some rather overenthusiastic restoration in 1864 which included the addition of the flying buttresses. More recently, the dismal slums that stood between the two cathedrals have been redeveloped. St Patrick's Park, the expanse of green beside the cathedral, was a crowded slum until it was cleared off and its residents were relocated in the early years of this century.

Although a church stood on the Patrick St site from as early as the 5th century, the present building dates from 1190 or 1225 – opinions differ. The stone Norman construction was rebuilt in the early 13th century in a style that has been approximated by the present form. At this time a somewhat unseemly struggle for religious supremacy was being waged between St Patrick's,

MAP 6

St Patrick's Cathedral

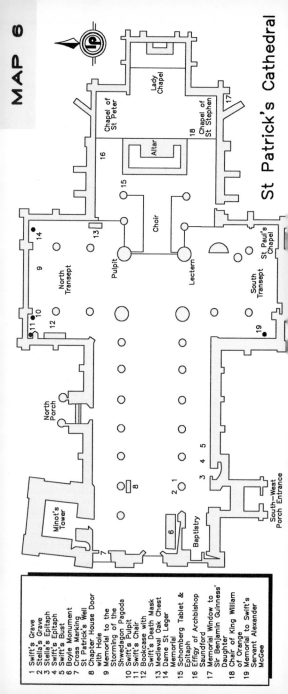

1 Swift's Grave
2 Stella's Grave
3 Stella's Epitaph
4 Swift's Epitaph
5 Swift's Bust
6 Boyle Monument
7 Cross Marking
  St Patrick's Well
8 Chapter House Door
  with Hole
9 Memorial to the
  Storming of the
  Shwedagon Pagoda
10 Swift's Pulpit
11 Swift's Chair
12 Bookcase with
   Swift's Death Mask
13 Medieval Oak Chest
14 Dame St Leger
   Memorial
15 Schomberg Tablet &
   Epitaph
16 Effigy of Archbishop
   Saundford
17 Memorial Window to
   Sir Benjamin Guinness'
   Daughter
18 Chair of King William
   of Orange
19 Memorial to Swift's
   Servant Alexander
   McGee

Minot's
Tower

North
Porch

Baptistry

South–West
Porch Entrance

North
Transept

Pulpit

Lectern

St Paul's
Chapel

South
Transept

Choir

Altar

Chapel of
St Peter

Lady
Chapel

Chapel of
St Stephen

outside the Dublin city walls, and Christ Church, within the walls. The fact that Dublin ended up with two Protestant cathedrals is a clear indication that neither church won a knockout victory. St Patrick's still bears traces of the fortifications necessitated by its unprotected position.

Like Christ Church, the building suffered a rather dramatic history. A storm brought down the spire in 1316 and soon after the building was badly damaged in a fire. Another even more disastrous fire followed in 1362. Consequently, in 1370 Archbishop Minot added the west tower which bears his name. For some reason it was constructed at a slight angle to the rest of the cathedral. In 1560 one of the first clocks in Dublin was added to the tower, and the 43-metre tower was subsequently topped by a 31-metre spire in 1749. Cromwell, during his 1649 visit to Ireland, converted St Patrick's to a stable for his army's horses, an indignity to which he subjected numerous other Irish churches. Jonathan Swift was the dean of the cathedral from 1713 to 1745, but prior to its mid-19th century restoration it was neglected and became an almost complete ruin, with a collapsed roof and individual chapels walled off as separate churches.

On entering the cathedral from the south-west porch (see Map 6 on the previous page) you come almost immediately to the graves of Swift (1) and Esther Johnson (2) or Stella, Swift's long-term companion. On the wall are the Latin epitaphs of Stella (3) and Swift (4) and a bust of Swift (5). Swift wrote Stella's epitaph and his own, which proclaims:

Here is laid the body of
Jonathan Swift, Doctor of Divinity,
Dean of this Cathedral Church,
Where fierce indignation can no longer
Rend his heart;
Go, traveller, and imitate if you can,
This earnest and dedicated
Champion of Liberty.

Also at this end of the cathedral is the huge Boyle Monument (6). Erected in 1632 by Richard Boyle, the Earl of Cork, it was decorated with numerous painted figures of members of his family. It briefly stood beside the altar until, in 1633, Dublin's Viceroy, Thomas Wentworth, the Earl of Strafford, complained that worshippers were unable to pray without 'crouching to an Earl of Cork and his lady... or to those sea nymphs his daughters, with coronets upon their heads, their hair dishevelled, down upon their shoulders'. This broadside was enough to have it shifted, but although Wentworth won this round of his bitter conflict with the Earl of Cork, the latter had the final say when he contrived to have Wentworth impeached and executed. The figure in the centre of the bottom level is of the Earl's five-year-old son, Robert Boyle (1627-91), who became a noted scientist. His contributions to physics include Boyle's Law, which relates the pressure and volume of gases.

In the north-west corner of the church is a cross on a stone slab (7), which once marked the position of St Patrick's original well. The South Transept was formerly a separate chapter house, and an old door (8) with a hole hacked through it was once the entry. It's now simply leaning against a column at the west end of the cathedral.

St Patrick's Cathedral (TW)

In 1492, the year in which Columbus was busy discovering the New World, a furious argument took place within the cathedral between the Earl of Kildare and the Earl of Ormonde. Each was supported by his armed retainers, but when strong words were about to lead to heavy blows the Earl of Ormonde retreated to the chapter house. Fortunately, a peaceful settlement was reached and a hole was chopped through the door so the earls could shake hands on the agreement. In extending his arm through the door, the Earl of Kildare added the phrase 'chancing one's arm' to the English language.

During the cathedral's decay in the 18th and 19th centuries the North Transept was virtually a separate church. It now contains various military memorials to the Royal Irish Regiments. The very first shots in the American War of Independence were fired at one of these military banners. The military monuments also include a depiction of the British forces storming the great Shwedagon Pagoda in Yangon, Myanmar (9).

The Swift corner in the North Transept features Swift's pulpit (10), his chair (11) and a book-filled glass cabinet (12) containing his death mask. At the other side of the transept is an oak chest (13) made in the mid-14th century and a difficult-to-decipher memorial (14) to one Dame St Leger (1566-1603), who outlived two earlier husbands before dying while giving birth to a child by her third husband.

The northern choir aisle has a tablet (15) marking the grave of the Duke of Schomberg, who died during the Battle of the Boyne. Swift provided the Duke's epitaph, caustically noting on it that the Duke's own relations couldn't be bothered to provide a suitable memorial. The aisle also has a marble effigy (16) of Archbishop Saundford, who built the Lady Chapel at the eastern end of the building in 1251 and died in 1271.

The Guinness family were noted contributors to the cathedral's restoration and a monument (17) to Sir Benjamin Guinness' daughter stands beneath a window bearing the words 'I was thirsty and ye gave me drink'! The chapel also has a chair (18) used by William of Orange at a service in the cathedral after his victory at the Boyne.

The South Transept, where the clash between the Earls of Ormonde and Kildare came to its conclusion, has various memorials, including one from Swift for his servant Alexander McGee (19).

The cathedral is open from 9 am to 6 pm Monday to Friday, 9 am to 5 pm Saturday (to 4 pm November to April), and 8.30 to 9 am and 10 am to 4.30 pm Sunday. Entry is 90p (children 30p). The cathedral's choir school dates back to 1432 and the choir took part in the first performance of Handel's *Messiah* in 1742. You can hear the choir every day except Wednesdays in July and August. You can get to the cathedral on bus No 50, 50A or 56A from Aston Quay or No 54 or 54A from Burgh Quay.

Marsh's Library is just outside St Patrick's Close.

Jonathan Swift

St Patrick's Cathedral is inextricably linked with its famous dean, Jonathan Swift (1667-1745), the noted satirist, author of *Gulliver's Travels* among other writings, and tireless campaigner for fair treatment for the Irish. Born at Hoey's Court, now a derelict little alley beside St Werburgh's Church and a stone's throw from either of Dublin's cathedrals. By the age of three he was said to be a fluent reader and he entered Trinity College when he was just 15 years old.

In 1689 Dublin was in turmoil, following the takeover of the British throne by William of Orange, and Swift moved to England where he worked for the wealthy diplomat Sir William Temple as a secretary. Swift's intelligence and scholarship were much appreciated by Sir William and despite various trips to Ireland Swift remained in his employ until the diplomat's unexpected death in 1699. Swift had been ordained as a priest in 1695 and he returned to Ireland to take up a variety of positions in the Irish church, first near Belfast, then near Dublin.

The publication of *The Battle of the Books* and *A Tale of a Tub* in 1704, together with a series of political pamphlets, began to cement Swift's reputation as a noted satirist and wit but also as an eccentric. He still commuted between Ireland and England, spending three years in England from 1710 to 1713, and yearned for a higher ecclesiastical position (a 'fat deanery or a lean bishopric') in the English church. His writings, however, had made him enemies and when the Whigs took over from the Tories in 1714 Swift found himself on the wrong side of the political divide. He retreated to Dublin where he had become Dean of St Patrick's Cathedral a year earlier.

Over the next 20 years Swift developed a keen social conscience and a deep concern for Irish impoverishment. He also made the transition from minor to major eccentric. His pen worked overtime righting wrongs, taking tyrants to task and attacking injustice wherever he saw it. This often took the form of anonymous tracts, such as his 1720 *Proposal for the Universal Use of Irish Manufactures*, which suggested that the Irish take their revenge on England by burning anything from that country except its coal. Swift's *Drapier's Letters* (1724-25), ostensibly written by a humble trader, tore into a corrupt German duchess and her Irish business partner who were set to make a crooked financial coup through a permit from the English king to mint coins. Their plan was to gain money by minting coins of copper instead of the standard gold or silver.

In 1729 *A Modest Proposal* modestly suggested that the children of poor Irish parents be eaten by the rich in order to reduce their parents' financial burden. First choice of the children, suggested Swift, should go to landlords who 'have already devoured their parents'. Despite this satirical defence of Irish children, it was said that Swift had absolutely no time for them, so it is a curious twist that he is remembered today primarily for what is often seen as a children's tale, *Gulliver's Travels*, which was published in 1726.

Swift's private life is full of intriguing mysteries, particularly those relating to Esther Johnson (1681-1728), better known as Stella, who was, depending on the tale, his innocent companion, his lover, his wife from a secretly conducted marriage, his niece or even his sister. He met her in England when she was just eight years old. She was the daughter of Sir William Temple's widowed house-keeper and it has been speculated that both Swift and Stella may have been the illegitimate offspring of Sir William. In 1701 he brought her to Ireland, with her chaperone, and lived with or near her until her death. At that time Swift lived in the deanery in the garden beside the cathedral (the present house is a replacement, built in 1781 after its predecessor burnt down). On the night when Stella's body lay in the church before her burial, Swift slept in a different bedroom so that he would not see the light in his cathedral. He completed *Journal to Stella* in the darkened cathedral on the nights following her death.

Swift's name is also associated with another Esther, Esther Vanhomrigh or 'Vanessa'. Swift wrote to her with the suggestion that she should come to Dublin, because: 'you will get more for your money in Dublin than in London, and St Stephen's Green has the finest walking gravel in Europe.' Vanessa duly turned up in 1714, but the Irish attraction was more probably the dean than Dublin. The two soon fell out and Vanessa retreated to her town house on Foster Place (at that time known as Turnstile Alley) off College Green where she died, so it is said, of a broken heart. Her grave is said to be somewhere nearby, but now submerged under centuries of urban development.

Jonathan Swift's cantankerous final years were unhappy ones. Hearing loss, terrible headaches and dizzy spells combined to convince him that he was heading towards insanity. It was a possibility his enemies had, no doubt, been suggesting for years. He is remembered not only for his writing and his colourful but secretive personal life, but also for the steps he made towards identifying and promoting a uniquely Irish conscience and spirit. ∎

Marsh's Library

On St Patrick's Close beside St Patrick's Cathedral is Marsh's Library (☎ 54 3511), founded in 1701 by Archbishop Narcissus Marsh (1638-1713) and opened in 1707. It was designed by Sir William Robinson, who was also responsible for the Royal Hospital Kilmainham. The oldest public library in the country, it contains 25,000 books dating from the 16th to the early 18th centuries, as well as maps, numerous manuscripts and a collection of incunabula, the technical term for a book printed before 1500. One of the oldest and finest books in the collection is a volume of Cicero's *Letters to his Friends* printed in Milan in 1472. The manuscript collection includes one in Latin dating back to 1400.

The keystone of the collection was the library of Edward Stillingfleet, Bishop of Worcester. This collection of almost 10,000 books was purchased by Narcissus Marsh in 1705 for £2500. Marsh's own extensive collection also ended up in the library, though he left his collection of Oriental manuscripts to the Bodleian Library at Oxford University in England. Marsh's interests were widespread – some of his mathematical books are extensively annotated, and a book printed in Hebrew in Italy in 1491 has a note from Marsh, in Latin, stating that it is a rare book.

Marsh's Library (TW)

The collection also includes various items from Jonathan Swift, including his own copy of the *History of the Great Rebellion*. His margin notes include a number of comments vilifying Scots, of whom the dean seemed to have a markedly low opinion. Swift also held a low opinion of Archbishop Marsh, whom he held responsible for not achieving the position in the church he felt he deserved. In 1710 Swift's barbed pen was unleashed on the archbishop in the form of an angry pamphlet. Marsh died in 1713 and was buried in St Patrick's Cathedral. Ironically, when Swift died in 1745, he was buried near his former enemy.

The three alcoves, where scholars were once locked in to peruse rare volumes, have remained virtually unchanged for three centuries. A bindery to repair and restore rare old books operates from the library. The library, hardly surprisingly, makes an appearance in Joyce's *Ulysses*.

Marsh's Library is open Monday and Wednesday to Friday from 10 am to 12.45 pm and 2 to 5 pm, Saturday from 10.30 am to 12.45 pm. An entry donation of IR£1 is requested. You can reach the library by taking bus No 50, 50A or 56A from Aston Quay or No 54 or 54A from Burgh Quay.

St Werburgh's Church

Hidden away on Werburgh St, just south of Christ Church Cathedral and tucked away beside Dublin Castle, St Werburgh's stands on ancient foundations. Its early history, however, is unknown. It was rebuilt in 1662, in 1715 and again in 1759 (with some elegance) after a fire in 1754. It is linked with the Fitzgerald family; Lord Edward Fitzgerald, who turned against England, joined the United Irishmen and was a leader of the 1798 rebellion, is interred in the vault. In what was an unfortunately frequent theme of Irish uprisings, compatriots gave him away and his death resulted from the wounds he received in being captured. Major Henry Sirr, his captor, is buried in the graveyard. A Baroque tower was added to the church in 1768 but was demolished in 1810 when Dublin Castle authorities, concerned about its use as a lookout over the castle, had it declared unsafe.

Despite its long history, fine design and interesting interior, the church is not in use today. A note at the front directs you to a house round the corner if you want to have a look inside. If you can't raise anybody there, you could try phoning ☎ 478 3710. Werburgh St was also the location of Dublin's first theatre (see the South Dublin

Theatres section for details), and Jonathan Swift was
born just off the street in Hoey's Court in 1667.

St Audoen's Churches

Lucky St Audoen has two churches to his name, both just
west of Christ Church Cathedral. The Church of Ireland
is the older and smaller building, and indeed is the only
surviving medieval parish church in the city. Its tower
and door date from the 12th century, the aisle from the
15th century and various other bits and pieces from early
times, but the church today is mainly a 19th century
restoration. The tower's bells include the three oldest
bells in Ireland, all dating from 1423. Later bells were
added in 1790, 1864 and 1880, but the newer bells were
recast in 1983, and the 1423 bells were retuned at the
same time.

The church is entered via an arch beside Cook St, to
the north of the church. Part of the old city wall, this arch
was built in 1240 and is the only surviving reminder of
the city gates. Parts of an even earlier Viking church of
St Colmcille may be included in the later constructions.

Joined onto the older Protestant St Audoen's is the
newer Catholic St Audoen's, a large church whose chief
claim to local fame is Father Flash Kavanagh, who, so
the story goes, rattled through the Mass at high speed in
order to allow his large congregation to head off to more
absorbing Sunday pursuits, such as football matches.
This St Audoen's was completed in 1846, the dome was
replaced in 1884 after it collapsed and the front with its
imposing Corinthian columns was added in 1899, after
almost 30 years in construction. Inside, the church's high
altar is flanked by reliefs of St Laurence O'Toole (see the
Christ Church Cathedral section) and St Audoen, the
latter holding a model of the church.

The Flame on the Hill is an audiovisual display on
Ireland before the arrival of the Vikings which is presented in the new St Audoen's. It is shown Monday to
Friday at 11.30 am, 2, 3 and 4 pm and costs IR£1.50
(children and students IR£1). At one time live performances relating to Viking Dublin were held in the crypts
under the church, but these have been suspended, possibly permanently.

The National Museum

The National Museum (☎ 661 8811) on Kildare St was
completed in 1890 to a design by Sir Thomas Newenham
Deane. The star attraction is the Treasury, which has two
superb collections and an accompanying audiovisual

display. One of the collections is of Bronze and Iron Age gold objects and the other is from the medieval period.

Other exhibits focus on the 1916 Easter Rising and the independence struggle between 1900 and 1921. Numerous interesting displays relate to this important period of modern Irish history. There are also displays on Irish decorative arts, ceramics, musical instruments and Japanese decorative arts. Dublin 1000 tells the story of Dublin's Viking era, with exhibits from the excavations at Wood Quay – the area between Christ Church Cathedral and the river, where, despite protests, the Dublin City Council decided to plonk its headquarters. Frequent short-term exhibits are also held.

The museum is open Tuesday to Saturday from 10 am to 5 pm and Sunday 2 to 5 pm. Entry is free but guided tours are available for IR£1.

Bronze & Iron Age Gold Objects Artisans of Ireland's early Celtic civilisation produced extraordinarily beautiful gold objects and many of the items on display in the museum are simply stunning. The Royal Irish Academy started the collection in the late 1700s and archaeological finds continue to be made. Remarkably little is known about where Ireland's gold came from, but whatever the source gold, bronze and copper were all being worked in Ireland by 2000 BC.

In the 500-year period from around 2200 BC, gold was often beaten into thin sheets to produce sun discs or the crescent-shaped ornaments known as *lunalae*. The sheet gold was decorated with patterns either from the front or by making a raised pattern from behind by the technique known as repoussé.

Five hundred years later, around 1200 to 1000 BC, much larger quantities of gold were used as gold bars or strips which were twisted to make torcs. These could be earrings, bracelets, necklaces or even waistbands. During this period gold in sheet form was also beaten into armbands.

Later still, a much wider range of highly decorated gold objects were produced by the use of gold wire or gold foil or by techniques such as casting to produce dress-fasteners and neck rings, bracelets.

Remarkably, the many gold objects found in Ireland have only very rarely been discovered during archaeological excavations. It was common for gold objects to be stashed away in remote hoards and in recent times these have been discovered in the course of ploughing land for farms, cutting peat for fuel, quarrying for building materials or excavating for railway tracks. One of the earliest recorded discoveries of a gold hoard was in 1670. The fact that so many hoards have been found in bogs suggests that these areas had some important significance to the Bronze Age Irish. During a 70-year period in the 1700s numerous hoards were found in the County Tipperary Bog of Cullen but, unfortunately, almost all of the gold was melted down.

Following are descriptions of some of the museum's finest displays.

The Broighter Hoard Discovered in County Derry by a ploughman in 1896, this collection of particularly fine gold objects from the 1st century BC includes a large gold collar of a standard of artisanship unsurpassed anywhere in Europe. Among the other finds were twisted gold neck ornaments and a model of a galley complete with oars.

The Gleninsheen Gorget This magnificent gold collar dating from around 800 to 700 BC was found in County Clare in 1932.

The Mooghaun Hoard The Mooghaun Hoard from County Clare was discovered by a gang of railway workers in 1854 and, hardly surprisingly, much of their find is suspected to have disappeared and been melted down. Nevertheless, a collection of 146 objects weighing five kg was displayed by the Royal Irish Academy in that year, including sheet gold collars, gold neck rings and numerous gold bracelets. Only 29 objects from the hoard have definitely survived and replicas are displayed at the museum.

Other Displays The Ballinesker Hoard is a collection of boxes, disks and cloak-fasteners which was discovered in late 1990 in County Wexford. The Dowris Hoard of the 8th to 6th centuries BC was a huge find made in 1820. The wonderful Loughnasade bronze war trumpet dates from the 1st century BC. There are various other superb gold collars which were made in the same era as the Gleninsheen Gorget.

Medieval Objects In the long period when the Dark Ages swept across Europe, the monasteries of Ireland were a shining beacon of knowledge and scholarship. Some of the beautiful religious objects in the gallery amply reflect the strengths of that period.

The Ardagh Chalice This 8th century chalice or bowl from County Limerick was found in 1868 and is thought to have been hidden away around the 10th century AD. The elaborately constructed and decorated chalice would have been used to dispense wine during religious ceremonies. The bowl and base of the chalice are of silver, but the find also included a bronze chalice and a number of silver-gilded brooches.

The Cross of Cong The 12th century Cross of Cong was made of wood, bronze and silver to enshrine a fragment of wood said to have come from the True Cross. This holy relic was presented by Pope Calixtus II to the King of Connaught in 1123 but has since disappeared. The cross remained in Cong, County Mayo, until 1839, when it was bought by the National Museum. The sale was not greeted with total approval in Cong and an attempt was later made to steal the cross back and return it to Cong.

St Patrick's Bell & Shrine Dating from the 5th to the 8th centuries, St Patrick's Bell is said to have belonged to Ireland's patron saint himself. Around 1100 a shrine of gold wire on a silver backplate was made to house the bell. Originally from Armagh in County Armagh, the bell and shrine had a colourful history as they were once carried off by a Norman baron and were subsequently handed down from generation to generation of the Mulholland family until the late 1700s.

The Tara Brooch The 8th century Tara Brooch was found in County Meath. The elaborately decorated brooch was made with gold wire and gold strips embellished with amber and enamel. It consists of three parts – a ring, a pin and a long chain. The piece has no connection with the ancient kingdom of Tara, but it is one of the finest examples of craftswork from that time. The Tara brooch is classified as a pseudopenannular brooch. Penannular brooches were used to fasten cloaks in the late Iron Age to the early medieval period.

The National Gallery

Opened in 1864, the National Gallery looks out on to Merrion Square. Its excellent collection is particularly strong, of course, in Irish art but there are also high-quality collections of every major school of European painting.

On the lawn in front of the gallery is a statue of the Irish railways magnate William Dargan, who organised the 1853 Dublin Industrial Exhibition at this spot; the profits from the exhibit were used to found the gallery. The gallery entrance is guarded by a statue of George Bernard Shaw, who was a major benefactor of the gallery. The proceeds from *My Fair Lady* certainly helped the gallery's acquisitions.

The gallery has three wings: the original Dargan Wing, the Milltown Rooms added early this century, and the Modern Wing added in the 1960s. The Dargan Wing's ground floor has the imposing Shaw Room, lined with full-length portraits and illuminated by a series of spectacular Waterford crystal chandeliers. Upstairs the Dargan Wing has a series of rooms dedicated to the Italian Early and High Renaissance, 16th century North Italian art and 17th and 18th century Italian art. Fra Angelico, Titian and Tintoretto are among the artists represented here.

The central Milltown Rooms were added in 1899-1903 to house the art collection of Russborough House which was presented to the gallery in 1902. The ground floor displays the gallery's fine Irish collection plus a smaller British collection, with works by Reynolds, Hogarth, Gainsborough, Landseer and Turner. One of the highlights is the room at the back of the gallery displaying works by Jack B Yeats (1871-1957), the younger brother of W B Yeats. Other rooms relate to specific periods and styles of Irish art, including one room of works by Irish artists painting in France.

Upstairs the Milltown Rooms contain works from Germany, the Netherlands and Spain. There are rooms of works by Rembrandt and his circle and by Spanish artists of Seville. The Spanish collection features works by El Greco, Goya and Picasso. The Modern Wing was added in 1964-68 and houses modern works. It also has French works by Degas, Delacroix, Millet, Monet and Pissarro, but these have been moved to another part of the gallery because much of the wing has been closed for major redevelopment. It is likely to remain closed until the end of 1994. The gallery also has an Art Reference Library, a Lecture Theatre, a good bookshop and an excellent and deservedly popular restaurant. The gallery hours are from 10 am to 6 pm Monday to Saturday (to 9 pm Thursday), and 2 to 5 pm on Sunday. Entry is free and there are guided tours at 3 pm on Saturday and at 2.30, 3.15 and 4 pm on Sunday.

Leinster House – The Dáil

Ireland's parliament, the Oireachtas na hÉireann, meets in Leinster House on Kildare St. Both the lower house (Dáil) and the upper house (Seanad) meet here. The entrance to Leinster House from Kildare St is flanked by the National Library and the National Museum. The house was originally built as Kildare House in 1745-48 for the Earl of Kildare, but the name of the building was changed when he also assumed the title of Duke of Leinster in 1766. One of the members of the Fitzgerald family who held the titles was Lord Edward Fitzgerald, who died of wounds he received in the abortive 1798 rebellion.

Leinster House's Kildare St frontage was designed to look like a town house, whereas the Merrion Square frontage was made to look like a country house. Richard Castle, the house's architect, later built the Rotunda Hospital in north Dublin to a similar design. The lawn in front of the Merrion Square country-house frontage was the site for railway pioneer William Dargan's 1853 Dublin Industrial Exhibition, which in turn led to the creation of the National Gallery. There's a statue of him at the National Gallery end of the lawn. At the other end of the lawn is a statue of Prince Albert, Queen Victoria's consort. Queen Victoria herself was commemorated in massive form on the Kildare St side from 1908 until the statue was removed in 1948. The obelisk in front of the building is dedicated to Arthur Griffith, Michael Collins and Kevin O'Higgins, architects of independent Ireland.

The Dublin Society, later named the Royal Dublin Society, bought the building in 1814 but moved out in stages between 1922 and 1925, when the first government of independent Ireland decided to establish their parliament there.

The Seanad or Senate meets in the north-wing saloon, while the Dáil meets in a less interesting room that was originally a lecture theatre added to the original building in 1897. When parliament is sitting (usually between November and May) you can arrange a visit; ask at the Kildare St entrance.

Government Buildings

On Merrion St Upper, on the south side of the Natural History Museum, the domed Government Buildings were opened in 1911, in a rather heavy-handed Edwardian interpretation of the Georgian style. On Saturdays 40-minute tours are conducted from 10.30 am to 12.45 pm and 1.30 to 4.45 pm. You get to see the Taoiseach's

Top: Leinster House (JM)
Bottom: National Gallery (JM)

office, the ceremonial staircase and the cabinet room. Tickets are available on the day from the National Gallery ticket office.

Across the road at No 24 is Mornington House, thought to be the birthplace of the Duke of Wellington, who was somewhat ashamed of his Irish origins. It's possible that his actual birthplace was Trim in County Meath. The Georgian mansion is now occupied by a government department.

The National Library

Flanking the Kildare St entrance to Leinster House is the National Library, which was built in 1884-90, at the same time as the National Museum and to a similar design by Sir Thomas Newenham Deane and his son Sir Thomas Manly Deane. Leinster House, the library and museum were all part of the Royal Dublin Society (formed in 1731), which aimed to improve conditions for poor people and to promote the arts and sciences. The library's extensive collection has many valuable early manuscripts, first editions, maps and other items. Temporary displays are often held in the entrance area and the library's reading room featured in *Ulysses*. The library is open Monday to Thursday from 10 am to 9 pm, Friday 10 am to 5 pm and Saturday 10 am to 1 pm.

Heraldic Museum & Genealogical Office

On the corner of Kildare and Nassau Sts, the former home of the Kildare St Club is shared by the Heraldic Museum and Genealogical Office and the Alliance Française. It's a popular destination for visitors intent on tracing their Irish roots. The Kildare St Club was an important right-wing institution during Dublin's Anglo-Irish heyday. Note the whimsical though rather worn stone carvings of animals that decorate the building's windows.

The Heraldic Museum's displays follow the story of heraldry in Ireland and Europe. It's open Monday to Friday from 10 am to 12.30 pm and 2.30 to 4.30 pm.

Genealogy

Tracing your ancestors is a major activity in Ireland, and many visitors from Canada, the USA and Australia come to Ireland purely to track down their Irish roots. Success in this activity is more likely if you've conducted some basic research before you arrive. A good starting point is the Irish Tourist Board's *Information Sheet No 021*.

In Dublin the Genealogical Office (☎ 661 4877, 661 1626), which includes the State Heraldic Museum, is at 2 Kildare St, Dublin 2. For a small fee they offer a consultation service on how to trace your ancestry, which is a good way to begin your research if you have no other experience. The Birth, Deaths & Marriages register of Dublin City, the files of the National Library and the National Archives at the Four Courts are all potential sources of genealogical information. The National Archive Records (☎ 478 1666) in Dublin Castle are of particular interest to Australians whose ancestors may have arrived in Australia as convicts. ■

Natural History Museum

Just as the National Library and the National Museum flank the entrance to Leinster House on the Kildare St side, the National Gallery and Natural History Museum perform the same function on the Merrion St Upper/Merrion Square side.

The Natural History Museum (☎ 661 8811) is a rather musty place, scarcely changed since 1857 when Scottish explorer Dr David Livingstone delivered the opening lecture. It's hardly surprising that it's known as the 'Dead Zoo', but despite that disheartening appellation the museum is well worth a visit, for its collection is huge and surprisingly well kept. That moth-eaten look which afflicts neglected stuffed animal collections has been kept well at bay and children in particular are likely to find it fascinating.

The collection of skeletons, stuffed animals and the like covers the full range of Irish fauna and includes three skeletons of the gigantic giant deer, the Irish elk which became extinct about 10,000 years ago. Many other extinct or rare species are also on show. Among them is a Tasmanian tiger (mislabelled as a Tasmanian wolf), the probably extinct but still much-searched-for Australian marsupial. There's a giant panda from China, a number of African and Asian rhinoceroses and plenty more from the shoot 'em and stuff 'em era of museum management. Hanging from the ceiling upstairs are the skeletons of two whales that were stranded on Ireland's shores. The fin whale was found at Bantry Bay in County Cork in 1862 and the humped whale was found at Enniscrone in County Sligo in 1893.

The museum hours are 10 am to 5 pm Tuesday to Saturday, 2 to 5 pm on Sunday. Entry is free.

Grafton St

Although O'Connell St in north Dublin is the city's major avenue, it's Grafton St which is the number one address south of the Liffey (see Map 14 at the back of this book). At one time it was also the major traffic artery of south Dublin until it was turned into a pedestrian precinct in 1982. It's now Dublin's fanciest and most colourful shopping centre with plenty of street life and the city's most entertaining buskers. The street is equally alive after dark as some of Dublin's most interesting pubs are clustered around it (see the Pub Crawl and Pub Entertainment sections of the Entertainment chapter).

Apart from fine shops, such as the Switzers (opened in 1838) and Brown Thomas (opened in 1848) department stores, Grafton St also features a branch of Bewley's Oriental Café, a Dublin institution for anything from a quick cup of coffee to a filling meal. This branch of the chain has an upstairs museum relating the interesting history of Bewley's.

Back from Grafton St on William St South is the elegantly converted Powerscourt Townhouse Shopping Centre. Built between 1771 and 1774 this grand house has a balconied courtyard, and, following its conversion in 1981, now shelters three levels of modern shops and restaurants. The Powerscourt family's principal residence was Powerscourt House in County Wicklow and this city mansion was soon sold for commercial use. It survived that period in remarkably good condition and in its new incarnation it forms a convenient link from Grafton St to the South City Market on South Great George's St. The building features plasterwork by Michael Stapleton, who also worked on Belvedere House in north Dublin.

Dublin Civic Museum

The Dublin Civic Museum (☎ 667 9426) is at 58 William St South, just a stone's throw from Grafton St. Its displays relate to the history of the city, with exhibits ranging from artefacts from Viking Dublin to a model of a Howth tram and the head from the Lord Nelson statue on O'Connell St which was toppled by the IRA in 1966. A showcase houses the small wax artists' models upon which the stone heads representing Ireland's rivers on the Custom House were based. Changing exhibits might include postcards, Dublin coal-hole covers or items relating to local shipwrecks.

The museum is open Tuesday to Saturday from 10 am to 6 pm, Sunday 11 am to 2 pm, and entry is free.

Mansion House

Mansion House on Dawson St was built in 1710 by Joshua Dawson, after whom the street is named. Only five years later the house was bought as a residence for the Lord Mayor of Dublin. The building's original brick Queen Anne style has all but disappeared behind a stucco façade tacked on in the Victorian era. The building was the site for the 1919 Declaration of Independence but it is generally not open to the public. Next door is the Royal Irish Academy, also generally not open to visitors.

Top: Flower Sellers, Grafton St (JM)
Bottom: St Stephen's Green (JM)

St Stephen's Green

On warm summer days the nine hectares of St Stephen's Green provide a popular lunch-time escape for city office workers. The green was originally an expanse of open common land where public whippings and hangings used to take place. The green was enclosed by a fence in 1664 when the Dublin Corporation sold off the surrounding land for buildings. A stone wall replaced the fence in 1669 and trees and gravel paths soon followed within. By the end of that century restrictions were already in force prohibiting buildings of less than two storeys or those constructed of mud and wattle. At the same time Grafton St, the main route to the green

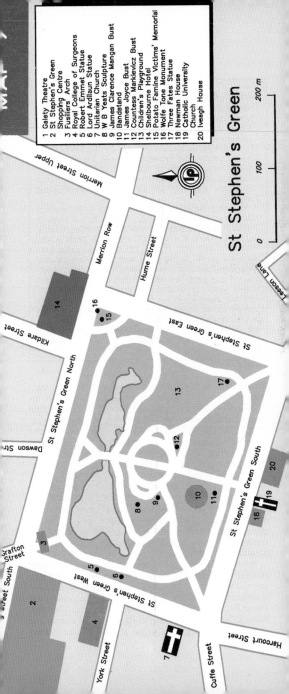

MAP

St Stephen's Green

1   Galety Theatre
2   St Stephen's Green
    Shopping Centre
3   Fusiliers Arch
4   Royal College of Surgeons
5   Robert Emmet Statue
6   Lord Ardilaun Statue
7   Unitarian Church
8   W B Yeats Sculpture
9   James Clarence Mangan Bust
10 Bandstand
11 James Joyce Bust
12 Countess Markievicz Bust
13 Children's Playground
14 Potato Famine Victims' Memorial
15 Wolfe Tone Monument
16 Shelbourne Hotel
17 Three Fates Statue
18 Newman House
19 Catholic University
    Church
20 Iveagh House

0   100   200 m

Merrion Street Upper

Merrion Row

Hume Street

Leeson Lane

Kildare Street

St Stephen's Green East

St Stephen's Green North

Dawson Str

St Stephen's Green South

St Stephen's Green West

York Street

Harcourt Street

Cuffe Street

Grafton Street

Street South

Streets & Squares

Dublin's splendid Georgian streets and squares, lined with the severe Georgian buildings whose colourful doors have become a symbol of the city, are the city's finest architectural elements. They also provide a welcome respite from the city's more hectic areas. Although St Stephen's Green, Merrion Square and Fitzwilliam Square, the city's finest squares, are all south of the Liffey, Dublin's Georgian building spree actually started north of the river and traces of that now-faded glory can still be seen at Mountjoy and Parnell squares.

The Commission for Making Wide & Convenient Streets, established in 1757, certainly had a hand in Dublin's generous supply of wide and convenient streets, the most notable of which is O'Connell St in north Dublin. Pedestrianised Grafton St is the most interesting thoroughfare south of the Liffey and is Dublin's premier shopping street. South of the Liffey, fine Georgian streetscapes can be found along Fitzwilliam St Upper and Lower, which connects Merrion and Fitzwilliam squares, and also along Ely Place. Gardiner St Upper and Lower in north Dublin would have been equally fine in its prime but is run down and decaying today. The first true Georgian street, and one of the finest though very run down, is Henrietta St in north Dublin. ■

from what was then central Dublin, was upgraded from a 'foule and out of repaire' laneway to a crown causeway.

The fine Georgian buildings around the square date mainly from Dublin's mid to late-18th century Georgian prime. At that time the north side was known as the Beaux' Walk and it is still a centre for some of Dublin society's most esteemed meeting places. Further improvements were made, with seats being put in place in 1753, but in 1814 railings and locked gates were added and an annual fee of one guinea was charged to use the green. This private use continued until 1877 when Sir Arthur Edward Guinness, later Lord Ardilaun, pushed an act through parliament which once again made the green a public place. The gardens and ponds of the central park date from 1880 and were financed by the wealthy brewer.

A variety of statues and memorials dot the green, and, since it was Guinness money that created the park you see today, it's only right that there should be an 1892 statue of Sir Arthur Edward Guinness, gazing off towards his brewery at St James's Gate from the west side of the park. Just north of the Guinness statue, but outside the railing, is a statue of Irish patriot Robert

Emmet, who was born across the road at No 124/125, though his actual birthplace has been demolished. The statue was only placed here in 1966 and is a replica of an Emmet statue in Washington DC.

Across the road from this side of the green are the 1863 Unitarian Church and the Royal College of Surgeons, which definitely has one of the finest façades around St Stephen's Green. It was built in 1806 and extended in 1825-27 to the design of William Murray. Forty years later Murray's son, William G Murray, designed the Royal College of Physicians building on Kildare St. In the 1916 Rising, the Royal College of Surgeons was occupied by the colourful Countess Markievicz (1868-1927), an Irish nationalist married to a Polish count. The countess would have handled modern media with aplomb; her first question upon taking the college was the whereabouts of the scalpels, implying they would be useful in hand-to-hand combat with British troops. The columns still bear bullet marks.

At one time the main entrance to the green was on this side but now it is through the Fusiliers' Arch at the north-west corner of the green leading from Grafton St. Modelled to look like a smaller version of the Arch of Titus in Rome, the arch commemorates the 212 soldiers of the Royal Dublin Fusiliers who died in the Boer War (1899-1902).

A path from the arch passes by the duck pond where you can see bar-headed geese, Canada geese, greylag geese, white-fronted geese, wigeons, tufted ducks, mandarin ducks, moorhens, coots and mallards. Around the fountain in the centre of the green are a number of statues, including a bust of Countess Markievicz, who played a key role in the 1916 Rising. Nearby is a bust of the poet James Clarence Mangan (1803-49) and a curious sculpture of W B Yeats by Henry Moore (1967). The centre of the park also has a garden for the blind, complete with signs in Braille and plants which can be handled.

On the eastern side of the green there's a children's play park and to the south is a fine old bandstand, erected for Queen Victoria's jubilee in 1887. Performances often take place here in the summer. Near the bandstand is a bust of James Joyce, looking across towards Newman House of University College Dublin, where he was once a student.

Just inside the green at the south-east corner, near Leeson St, is a statue of the Three Fates, presented to Dublin in 1956 by West Germany in gratitude for Irish aid immediately after WW II. The north-west corner, opposite the Shelbourne Hotel and Merrion Row, is marked by the Wolfe Tone Monument to the leader of the abortive 1796 invasion. The vertical slabs which serve as a backdrop for Wolfe Tone's statue have been dubbed 'Tonehenge'. Just inside the park at this entrance is a memorial to the victims of the mid-19th century potato famines.

Unfortunately, some of Dublin's less thoughtful architectural mistakes have taken place around St Stephen's Green. Some notable buildings still remain, however, such as the imposing old 1867 Shelbourne Hotel on the north side of the green, with statues of Nubian princesses and their ankle-fettered slave girls decorating the front. Just beyond the Shelbourne is a small Huguenot cemetery dating from 1693, when many French Huguenots fled here from persecution under Louis XIV.

Some of Dublin's most interesting streets radiate out from the green. Grafton St, the main shopping avenue of Dublin, runs from the north-west corner, while Merrion Row, with its popular pubs, runs from the north-east. At the south-east is Leeson St, the nightclub centre of Dublin. The Hotel Conrad, Dublin's Hilton Hotel, is just off the square from this corner on Earlsfort Terrace, as is the National Concert Hall.

Harcourt St, from the south-west corner, was laid out in 1775. Well-known names associated with the street include Edward Carson, who was born at No 4 in 1854. As the architect of Northern Irish 'unionism' he is an easy culprit for many of the problems caused by Ireland's division. Bram Stoker, author of *Dracula*, lived at No 16 and George Bernard Shaw at No 61. For 99 years from 1859 to 1958 the Dublin-Bray railway line used to terminate at Harcourt St Station, which was once at the bottom of this road.

Iveagh House At No 80/81 on the south side of the green is Iveagh House, where the Guinness family was once domiciled; today the Department of Foreign Affairs lives there. Designed by Richard Castle in 1730, this was his first project in Dublin. He went on to create many more buildings, including Leinster House and the Rotunda Hospital.

Newman House At No 85/86 on the south side of the green is Newman House, which has had an interesting history and is now part of University College Dublin. The main campus is now out at Belfield in Donnybrook, between Dublin and Dun Laoghaire.

These buildings have some of the finest plasterwork in the city. No 85 was built between 1736 and 1738 by

Richard Castle for the parliamentarian Hugh Montgomery. The particularly fine plasterwork was by the Swiss
stuccodores Paul and Philip Francini (also known as
Paolo and Filippo Lafranchi) and can be best appreciated in the wonderfully detailed Apollo Room on the
ground floor. The Catholic University of Ireland, predecessor of University College Dublin, acquired the
building in 1865. Some of the plasterwork was a little too
detailed for strict Catholic tastes, however, so cover-ups
were prescribed for some of the work. On the ceiling of
the upstairs Saloon the previously naked figure of Juno
was clad in what can best be described as a furry swim-
suit.

Richard Chapel Whaley had taken possession of No
85 in 1765 but decided to display his wealth by construct-
ing a much grander home next door at No 86. This was
still the southern edge of the city at the time and open
fields spread to the south. Whaley commissioned Robert
West to do the plasterwork in this house, but despite the
larger scale the work is not up to the standards set by No
85. Like Hugh Montgomery, the original owner of No
85, Whaley was a member of the Irish Parliament and
his son, Buck Whaley, contrived to become a member of
parliament while still a teenager. Buck Whaley also
found time to become one of the more notorious
members of Dublin's Hell Fire Club. He was also a noted
gambler, once walking all the way to Jerusalem to win a
bet.

After the buildings were acquired by the Catholic
University, the names of James Joyce, Gerard Manley
Hopkins and Flann O'Brien were all connected with the
university, and Newman House was named after its first
rector, John Henry Newman. Professor of Classics at the
college from 1884 until his death in 1889, Gerard Manley
Hopkins lived upstairs at No 86. It was not until some
time after his death that his rather depressive writing
gained wide appreciation. His room is now preserved as
it was during his residence. Joyce was a bachelor of arts
student of the college between 1899 and 1902, and
Patrick Pearse, leader of the 1916 Easter Rising, and
Eamon de Valera, leader of Sinn Féin, were also students
here.

The restoration of Newman House is a relatively
recent project and will continue for some time. The
house is open June to September from 10 am to 4.30 pm
Tuesday to Friday, Saturday 2 to 4.30 pm and Sunday 11
am to 2 pm. At other times of the year phone ☎ 475 1752
or ☎ 475 7255 for information. The IR£1 (concessions
75p) entry includes a video about the building and a
good guided tour.

Dublin Clubs

In its Georgian heyday Dublin had a number of colourful gentlemen's clubs where much less than gentlemanly conduct was frequently tolerated. Daly's Club at No 2/3 Dame St, opposite the Bank of Ireland near the Trinity College entrance, was founded around 1750 in Patrick Daly's coffee house. It is said that members of the club used to use the statue of St Andrew in St Andrew's Church on Suffolk St for target practice. Forty years later the club had become so popular among Dublin's socialites of the era that a new clubhouse had to be built. By the early 1820s, however, it had retreated into exclusiveness and folded up.

By this time the Kildare St Club was the prestige Dublin club, having moved to its site on the corner of Kildare and Leinster Sts, beside Trinity College, in 1782. The 1861 Venetian-style building they later erected on this site has been described as one of the most distinguished Dublin constructions of the period. The comical stone animals which decorate the windows are one of the building's more appealing touches. It's now occupied by the Alliance Française, and the Kildare St Club has amalgamated with the University Club and can be found beside St Stephen's Green.

The most colourful of the Dublin clubs was undoubtedly the Hell Fire Club, which was founded in 1735 and whose members used to meet in the Eagle Tavern on Cork Hill, in front of Dublin Castle. The members liked to play up to their colourful image and it is said they once burnt the building down in an attempt to create an ambience more akin to the real place. On at least one occasion the devil is said to have made a personal appearance at a club function, but there's no evidence that debauchery, black magic or other such lurid activities really took place.

The club's founder, Richard Parsons, Earl of Rosse, is said to have been 'fond of all the vices which the beau monde call pleasures, and by those means first impaired his fortune as much as he possibly could do; and finally, his health beyond repair.' Buck Whaley (see the section on Newman House, St Stephen's Green) was another notorious Hell Fire Club member. The club's out-of-town premises on top of Montpelier Hill in the Dublin Mountains still stands. To get there, go to Rathfarnham, about six km south-west of central Dublin, and then follow the road through Ballyboden and Woodtown to the summit. ■

Catholic University Church Next to Newman House is the Catholic University Church or Newman Chapel, built in 1854-56 with a colourful neo-Byzantine interior that attracted much criticism at the time. There's much coloured marble, much gold leaf, and all in all the effect is very pleasant. Around the walls are coloured plaques illustrating the stations of the Cross, and a bust of Cardinal Newman can be seen on the right side. Today this is one of the most fashionable churches in Dublin for weddings.

Merrion Square

Merrion Square, with its well-kept central park, dates back to 1762 and has the National Gallery on its west side, while the other three sides are lined with elegant Georgian buildings. Around this square you can find all the hallmarks of the best Georgian Dublin entrances – there are elegant doors and fanlights, ornate door knockers and more than a few foot scrapers where gentlemen would remove mud from their shoes before venturing indoors. Merrion Square residents have included, at 1 Merrion Square North, the surgeon Sir William Wilde and the poet Lady 'Speranza' Wilde, parents of the even more famous Oscar Wilde, who was born in 1854 at the now near-derelict 21 Westland Row, just north of the square.

Other Merrion Square identities were W B Yeats (1865-1939), who lived first at 52 Merrion Square East and later, from 1922 to 1928, at 82 Merrion Square South. Others along Merrion Square South included George (Æ) Russell (1867-1935), the 'poet, mystic, painter and co-operator', who worked at No 84. Daniel O'Connell (1775-1847) was a resident of No 58 in his later years. The Austrian Erwin Schrödinger (1887-1961), co winner of the 1933 Nobel Prize for physics, lived at No 65 between 1940 and 1956. Dublin seemed to attract authors of horror stories and Joseph Sheridan Le Fanu (1814-73), who penned the vampire classic *Carmilla*, was a former resident of No 70. The UK Embassy used to be at 39 Merrion Square East until it was burnt out in 1972 in protest against events in Derry, Northern Ireland, when 13 civilians were shot down by the British army.

Damage to fine Dublin buildings has not always been the prerogative of vandals, terrorists or protesters. Merrion Square East once continued into Fitzwilliam St Lower in the longest unbroken series of Georgian houses anywhere in Europe. Despite this, in 1961 the Electricity Supply Board knocked down 26 of them to build an office block. The Architectural Association, however, does live in a real Georgian House. It's at No 8 Merrion Square North, a few doors down from the Wilde residence. The house at No 12 is open to the public on Saturday and Sunday afternoons from noon to 4 pm.

The Leinster Lawn at the western end of the square has the fine 1791 Rutland Fountain and an 18-metre obelisk honouring the founders of independent Ireland. On the south side of the square there's a statue of Michael Collins (1890-1932), one of the architects of Ireland's independence, who was killed during the ensuing Civil War. Merrion Square has not always been merely graceful and affluent, however. During the 1845-51 potato famines, soup kitchens were set up in the gardens, which were crowded with starving rural refugees.

Number 29 Fitzwilliam St Lower At the southeast corner of Merrion Square the Electricity Supply Board, having demolished most of Fitzwilliam St Lower to construct a new office block, had the decency to preserve one of the fine old Georgian houses. It has been restored to give a good impression of genteel home life in Dublin between 1790 and 1820. Originally built in 1794, the first occupants were Mrs Olivia Beatty, the widow of a wealthy wine merchant, and her children. Property speculation was obviously a consideration even in that era as she paid £320 for it in 1794 but sold it 12 years later for £700.

The house is open from 10 am to 5 pm Tuesday to Saturday and 2 to 5 pm on Sunday. Entry is free and includes an audiovisual display on the house's history followed by a guided tour.

Merrion St Upper & Ely Place

Merrion St Upper runs south from Merrion Square towards St Stephen's Green. The Duke of Wellington, who often tried to downplay his Irish origins, was born at the now rather run-down 24 Merrion St Upper. On the other side of Baggot St, Merrion St becomes Ely (pronounced 'e-lie') Place. Built around 1770 this classic Georgian street has many interesting historical associations. John Philpot Curran (1750-1817), a great advocate of Irish liberty, once lived at No 4, as did the novelist George Moore (1852-1933). The house at No 6 was the residence of the Earl of Clare. Better known as Black Jack Fitzgibbon (1749-1802), he was a bitter opponent of Irish political aspirations and in 1794 a mob attempted to storm the house. Ely House at No 8 is one of the best examples of a Georgian mansion in the city. The plasterwork is by Michael Stapleton and the staircase which illustrates the Labours of Hercules is one of the finest in the city. At one time the surgeon Sir Thornley Stoker (whose brother Bram Stoker wrote *Dracula*) lived here. Oliver St John Gogarty (1878-1957) lived for a time at No 25, but the art gallery of the Royal Hibernian Academy now occupies that position.

Fitzwilliam Square

South of Merrion Square and east of St Stephen's Green is Fitzwilliam Square. Built between 1791 and 1825, it was the smallest and the last of Dublin's great Georgian squares. It is also the only square where the central garden is still the private domain of residents of the square, because in the other squares the central gardens have been turned into public parks. The very original and well-kept square is a centre for the Dublin medical profession. William Dargan, the railway pioneer and founder of the National Gallery, lived at No 2, and Jack B Yeats lived at No 18.

Fitzwilliam Square (TW)

Other South Dublin Churches

St Andrew's Church The Protestant St Andrew's Church is on St Andrew's St near Trinity College, the Bank of Ireland and Grafton St. Designed by Charles Lanyon, the Gothic-style church was built in 1860-73 on the site of an ancient nunnery. Across the street, on the corner of Church Lane and Suffolk St, there once stood a huge Viking ceremonial mound or *thingmote*. It was levelled in 1661 and used to raise the level of Nassau St, which had previously been subject to flooding. There is also a Catholic St Andrew's Church behind Trinity College on Westland Row, beside Pearse Station.

Whitefriars Carmelite Church Next to the popular Avalon House backpackers hostel on Aungier St, the Carmelite Church stands on the former site of the Whitefriars Carmelite monastery. The monastery was founded in 1278 but, like other monasteries, was suppressed by King Henry VIII in 1537 and all its lands and wealth were seized by the crown. Eventually the Carmelites returned to their former church and re-established it, dedicating the new building in 1827.

On display in the north-east corner of the church is a 16th century Flemish oak statue of the Virgin and child. It is popularly believed that this is the only known wooden statue to have escaped destruction during the Reformation and that it formerly belonged to St Mary's Abbey in north Dublin. The church's altar contains the remains of St Valentine, of St Valentine's Day fame. The relics were donated to the church in 1836 by the pope.

St Ann's Church St Ann's on Dawson St near Mansion House was built in 1720 but is now lost behind an 1868 neo-Romanesque façade. It makes a fine view down Anne St South from Grafton St and is noted for its lunch-time recitals.

St Stephen's Church Built in 1825 in Greek Revival style, St Stephen's, complete with cupola, is at the far end of Mount St Upper from Merrion Square. Because of its appearance, it has been nicknamed the 'Pepper Canister Church'.

South Dublin Theatres

Dublin's most famous theatre, the Abbey Theatre, is north of the Liffey, but the city's first theatre opened in 1637 on Werburgh St, near Dublin Castle and the two cathedrals. Although that venue is long gone, there are theatres south of the Liffey, including the Gaiety on King St South, just off Grafton St. Built in 1871 this is Dublin's oldest theatre and now hosts a variety of performances.

The 1892 Olympia Theatre on Dame St in Temple Bar is the city's largest and second-oldest theatre and is a venue for popular performances. It was previously known as the Palace Theatre and Dan Lowry's Music Hall. Also south of the Liffey is the Tivoli Theatre on Francis St in the Liberties. A number of other Dublin theatres are listed under Other Theatres in the Other Sights section of this chapter.

NORTH OF THE LIFFEY

Though south Dublin is noticeably more affluent than north Dublin and has the lion's share of the city's tourist attractions, there are still many reasons to head across the Liffey, starting with Dublin's grandest avenue.

O'Connell St

O'Connell St is the major thoroughfare of north Dublin and probably qualifies as the most important and imposing street in the whole city even though it's a faded shadow of its earlier glory. It started life in the early 1700s as Drogheda St, named after Viscount Henry Moore, the Earl of Drogheda. There are still a Henry St, a Moore St and an Earl St nearby. The earl even managed to squeeze in an Of Lane! At that time Capel St, farther to the west, was the main artery in the city and Drogheda St, lacking a bridge to connect it with south Dublin, was of little importance.

In the 1740s Luke Gardiner, later Viscount Mountjoy, widened the street to 45 metres to turn it into an elongated promenade bearing his name. However, it was the completion of the Carlisle Bridge across the Liffey in 1794 which quickly made it the city's most important street. In 1880 the Carlisle Bridge was replaced by the much wider O'Connell Bridge which stands today.

Gardiner's Mall soon became Sackville St but it was renamed again in 1924 after Daniel O'Connell, the Irish nationalist leader whose statue surveys the avenue from the river end. The 1854 bronze statue features four winged figures which are not, despite their appearance, angels. In fact they are the four Victories and are supposed to illustrate O'Connell's courage, eloquence, fidelity and patriotism. If you inspect them closely you'll notice that a couple of them are bullet marked, a legacy of the upheavals of the 1916 Easter Rising and the Civil

1	Gate Theatre	12	Kylemore Café
2	Rotunda Hospital	13	Site of Nelson's Column
3	Parnell Statue	14	James Joyce Statue
4	Aer Lingus Office	15	GPO
5	Telecom Centre	16	Jim Larkin Statue
6	Father Mathew Statue	17	Clery's & Co
7	Gresham Hotel	18	Eason Bookshop
8	Dublin Bus Office	19	Sir John Gray Statue
9	Tourist Office	20	William Smith O'Brien Statue
10	St Mary's Pro-Cathedral	21	Abbey Theatre
11	Anna Livia Statue	22	O'Connell Statue

Anna Livia Statue - *The Floozie in the Jacuzzi* (TW)

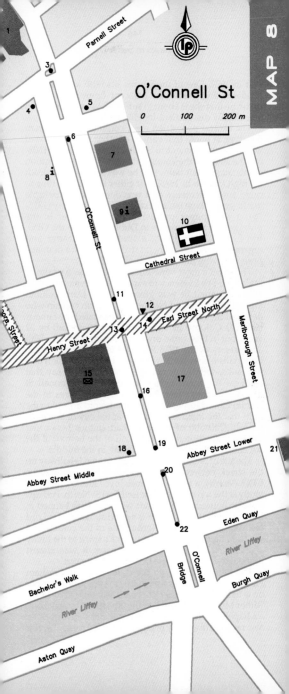

O'Connell St

MAP 8

Parnell Street

O'Connell St

O'Connell Street

Cathedral Street

Earl Street North

Henry Street

Marlborough Street

Store Street

Abbey Street Lower

Abbey Street Middle

Abbey Street Middle

Eden Quay

O'Connell Bridge

Burgh Quay

River Liffey

Bachelor's Walk

River Liffey

Aston Quay

0   100   200 m

War in 1922. One of the figures sits with an extremely obedient dog, while the adjacent figure is blissfully unaware that she is about to suffer a fatal snakebite from a decidedly disobedient-looking reptile.

The central pedestrian area, continuing north from the river, is home to a variety of other statuary, one of which is a monument to William Smith O'Brien (1803-64), the leader of the Young Ireland Party. The inscription on his monument notes that he was sentenced to death for high treason in 1848, so it either took a long time to carry out the sentence or it was done with remarkable inefficiency. There is also a statue of Sir John Gray (1815-75), a newspaper publisher and a pioneer in the provision of mains water in Dublin. Outside the GPO, Jim Larkin (1876-1947), a trade union leader and organiser of the 1913 general strike, is seen in a dramatic pose, throwing his arms up in the air.

The street's most famous monument was a victim of O'Connell St's tendency to explosive redevelopment. In 1815 O'Connell St was graced with a Doric column topped by a statue of Nelson, the English captain who defeated the French at Trafalgar. It predated the famous Nelson's Column in Trafalgar Square (London) by 32 years, but in 1966, as an unofficial celebration of the 50th anniversary of the 1916 Rising, this symbol of English imperialism was badly damaged by an explosion and was subsequently demolished. Some would say that some of the more recent additions to O'Connell St deserve a similar fate. Nelson's head survives in the Dublin Civic Museum but his demise put an end to the quip that the main street of the capital city of this most piously Catholic of countries had statues honouring three noted adulterers: O'Connell at the bottom of the street, Parnell at the top and Nelson in the middle.

The site of Nelson's demolished column is halfway up the street, between Henry and Earl Sts, opposite the GPO. Nearby, a figure of James Joyce lounges nonchalantly at the top of pedestrianised Earl St North. Perhaps a statue honouring an author who was long banned in Ireland for his 'dirty books' is a good substitute for Lord Nelson. Just beyond the former site of the column is a fountain figure of Anna Livia, Joyce's spirit of the Liffey – a 1988 addition to the streetscape. It was almost immediately dubbed 'the floozie in the jacuzzi'.

The tourist office is to the right, as is the Gresham Hotel, one of Dublin's best places to stay. A little farther on is the figure of Father Theobald Mathew (1790-1856). Father Mathew was dubbed the 'apostle of temperance' – a hopeless role in Ireland. This quixotic task, however, also resulted in a Liffey bridge bearing his name. The top of the street is completed by the imposing statue of Charles Stewart Parnell (1846-91), Home Rule advocate and victim of Irish morality. Despite his demise at the hands of Irish intolerance, it's Parnell who gets the most stirring monument, complete with a golden inscription proclaiming:

No man has a right to fix the boundary to the march of a nation.
No man has a right to say to his country,
Thus far shalt thou go and no further...

O'Connell St has certainly had its share of dramatic Dublin events; its rapid redevelopment began during the 1916 Rising when the GPO building became the starting point for, and main centre of, the abortive revolt. (See the next section for more information about this building.) The fighting badly damaged the GPO and destroyed most of that side of the street. Only six years later in 1922 the unfortunate avenue suffered another bout of destruction when it became the scene of a Civil War clash that burnt down most of the eastern side of the street.

Poor O'Connell St was to suffer even more damage in the 1960s and '70s when Dublin went through a period of rampant development under extremely lax government controls. During that time developers seemed to have open slather to tear anything down and sling anything up so long as there was a quid in it. The fast food and cheap office block atmosphere of O'Connell St today is a reminder of that era.

Among the attractions close to O'Connell St is an energetic and colourful open-air market area just to the west on Moore St. The Abbey Theatre and the Catholic St Mary's Pro-Cathedral are to the east. At the top of O'Connell St in Parnell Square are the notable Rotunda Hospital and the Gate Theatre. The Municipal Gallery of Modern Art and the Dublin Writers' Museum are on the north side of the square.

General Post Office

The GPO building on O'Connell St is an important landmark physically and historically. The huge building was designed by Francis Johnston and opened in 1818. It was the focus for the 1916 Easter Rising during which the building was totally destroyed except for the façade. In 1916 Patrick Pearse, James Connolly and the other leaders of the Easter Rising read their proclamation from the steps of the GPO. In the subsequent siege the building was completely burnt out. The façade with its Ionic portico is still pockmarked from the 1916 clash and from further damage wrought at the start of the Civil War in 1922. The GPO was not reopened until 1929. Inside the main hall of the GPO the *Death of Cuchulainn* statue commemorates the event. (Cuchulainn was the greatest of the Knights of the Red Branch, who were loyal to the king of the Ulaids (Ulster). He defended Ulster against the forces of Maeve, queen of Connaught, but is said to have been slain at the age of 27 after being tricked into an unfair fight.) The GPO's seminal role in the history of independent Ireland has made it a prime site for everything from official parades to protest rallies.

Abbey Theatre

Opened in 1904 the Abbey Theatre (☎ 878 7222) is just north of the Liffey on the corner of Marlborough St and Abbey St Lower. The Irish National Theatre Society soon made a name not only for playwrights like J M Synge and Sean O'Casey but also for Irish acting ability and theatrical presentation. The theatre became renowned as much for the uproar it provoked as for artistic appreciation. The use of the word 'shift' (petticoat) at the 1907 premiere of J M Synge's *The Playboy of the Western World* brought a storm of protest from theatregoers and Sean O'Casey's *The Plough & the Stars* prompted a similar reaction from the audience in 1926. On the latter occasion W B Yeats himself came on stage after the performance to tick the audience off!

The original theatre burnt down in 1951 and it was 15 years before the replacement was completed. Unfortunately, that long interval was not long enough to engender any artistic inspiration and the dull building is in no way equal to its famous name or continuing reputation. The smaller Peacock Theatre at the same location presents new and experimental works.

St Mary's Pro-Cathedral

On the corner of Marlborough and Cathedral Sts, just east of O'Connell St, is Dublin's most important Catholic church, built between 1816 and 1825. The Pro-Cathedral was originally intended to be built on O'Connell St, but fears that such a prominent position would provoke anti-Catholic English attitudes led to its comparatively hidden site. Unfortunately, the cramped Marlborough St location makes it all but impossible to stand back far enough to admire the front with its six Doric columns, modelled after the Temple of Theseus in Athens.

There are a number of intriguing questions connected with the Pro-Cathedral's design and even its name. The 1814 competition for the church's design was won by John Sweetman, a former owner of Sweetman's Brewery. Who organised the competition? Why William Sweetman, John Sweetman's brother. And did John Sweetman design it himself? Well possibly not, he was living in Paris at the time and may have bought the plans from the French architect who designed the remarkably similar Notre Dame de Lorette in northern France. And what does the 'pro' mean? Well, it's not very clear, but Pro-Cathedral seems to imply something along the lines of 'unofficial cathedral'.

Tyrone House

On Marlborough St, opposite the Pro-Cathedral, Tyrone House is now occupied by the Department of Education. The sombre building, built in 1740-41, was designed by Richard Castle and features plasterwork by the Francini brothers. On the lawn is a marble *Pietà* (statue of the Virgin Mary cradling the dead body of Jesus Christ) sculpted in 1930 and given to Ireland by the Italian government in 1948 in thanks for Irish assistance immediately after the war.

Nighttown

The area near St Mary's Pro-Cathedral was Joyce's 'Nighttown' in *Ulysses*, a busy red-light district known as 'Monto'. When British troops left in 1922 and Dublin regained its independence, the brothel business disappeared as well. There are still a number of popular and colourful pubs in the vicinity, but much of the area has been extensively and very unimaginatively flattened and rebuilt. Today it's an area of soul-destroying public housing and, despite the absence of brothels, it's still not a place to linger at night.

Although it's a dull thoroughfare today, Railway St, off Gardiner St, in this area has had an interesting history. It was originally known as Great Martin's Lane before being renamed Mecklenburgh St in 1733 when the Dublin Society had a botanic garden here. In 1887 it was renamed again, this time as Tyrone St after the Earl of Tyrone, whose house is opposite the Pro-Cathedral. This was the heart of the red-light district, and Bella Cohen's brothel on Tyrone St Lower featured in *Ulysses*. When the brothels departed, the street's name was still so indelibly associated with its unseemly activities that it had to be changed to Railway St. ■

Parnell Square

The principal squares of north Dublin are impoverished relations of the great squares south of the Liffey. Parnell Square was originally known as Rutland Square and has a varied collection of points of interest. The north side of the square, Parnell Square North, was built on lands acquired in the mid-18th century by Dr Bartholomew Mosse (see the next section) and was originally named Palace Row. The terrace was laid out in 1755 and Lord Charlemont bought the land for his home at No 22 in 1762. Charlemont's home was designed by Sir William Chambers, who also designed Lord Charlemont's extraordinary Casino at Marino (see that section for details). Today the building is home to the Municipal Gallery of Modern Art. The street was completed in 1769 and the gardens were renamed Rutland Square in 1786, before acquiring their current name.

Next to the gallery on the north side of the square is the Dublin Writers' Museum, and overlooking the square from the north-east corner is the Abbey Presbyterian Church. In 1966 the northern slice of the square was turned into a Garden of Remembrance for the 50th anniversary of the 1916 Rising. Its centrepiece is a sculpture by Oisin Kelly depicting the myth of the Children of Lir, who were transformed into swans for 900 years. The square also contains the Gate Theatre, the Ambassador Cinema and the Rotunda Hospital.

There are some fine, though generally rather run-down, Georgian houses on the east side of the square. Oliver St John Gogarty, immortalised as Buck Mulligan in Joyce's *Ulysses*, was born at No 5 in 1878. The founder of the Rotunda Hospital, Dr Bartholomew Mosse, was once a resident of No 9, and the Earls of Ormonde used No 11 as a town house. On the other side of the square, at No 44 Parnell Square West, you can find the Sinn Féin Bookshop.

Rotunda Hospital

Dr Bartholomew Mosse, who originally acquired the land on which Parnell Square is built, opened the Rotunda Hospital in 1757. This was the first maternity hospital in the British Isles, built at a time when Dublin's burgeoning urban population was leading to horrific infant mortality figures. The hospital shares its basic design with Leinster House because Richard Castle designed both and reused the Leinster House floorplan as an economy measure.

To his Leinster House design Castle added a three-

The Children of Lir

The children of Lir were the daughter and four sons of the ancient King Lir. As is almost a prerequisite for fairy-tales involving ill-treated children, a wicked stepmother played a key part in the legend. The king's new wife, Aoife, developed an insane jealousy over the children but, lacking the resolve to drown them, she merely enticed them into a lake to bathe and then cast a spell on them, turning them into swans.

They were forced to spend 900 years on the waters of Ireland (300 years each on Lough Derravaragh, the Sea of Moyle and the Bay of Erris). Feeling remorseful about what she had done Aoife, then allowed them to keep their human voices, so it was not long before the king discovered a group of talking swans and proclaimed that no swan should ever be killed in Ireland. King Dearg, Aoife's father, punished his dastardly daughter by turning her into a demon, but the unfortunate children still had to live out their 900 years as swans.

Christianity had just arrived in Ireland when the time span was up, so the reincarnated children, by now old and careworn, were able to be baptised when they once again took on human form but they died soon after. Swans remain a protected species in Ireland. ■

storey tower which Mosse had intended to use as a lookout to raise funds for the hospital's operation. The Rotunda Assembly Hall, now occupied by the Ambassador Cinema, was built as an adjunct to the hospital as another means of providing operating funds. At one time the hospital had an adjacent pleasure garden and this too was conceived as a money-raising venture. Over the main entrance of the hospital is the Rotunda Chapel, built in 1758 with superb coloured plasterwork by Bartholomew Cramillion.

The Rotunda Hospital still functions as a maternity hospital to this day. The Patrick Conway pub opposite the hospital dates from 1745 and has been hosting waiting fathers since the day the hospital opened.

Gate Theatre

At the top end of O'Connell St, in the south-east corner of Parnell Square, is the Gate Theatre, opened in 1929 by Micheál MacLiammóir and Hilton Edwards. MacLiammóir continued to act at his theatre until 1975, when he retired at the age of 76 after making his 1384th performance of the one-man show *The Importance of Being Oscar* (Oscar being Oscar Wilde, of course). The Gate Theatre was also the stage for Orson Welles' first professional appearance. The building dates from 1784-86 when it was built as part of the Rotunda complex of the Rotunda Maternity Hospital.

Hugh Lane Municipal Gallery of Modern Art

The Municipal Gallery of Modern Art or Hugh Lane Gallery (☎ 874 1903) at 22 Parnell Square North in north Dublin has a fine collection of work by the French Impressionists and 20th century Irish art. The exhibits include sculptures by Rodin and Degas, works by Corot, Courbet, Manet and Monet from the Lane Bequest and numerous works by Irish artists, including Jack B Yeats.

The gallery was founded in 1908 and moved to its present location in Charlemont House, formerly the Earl of Charlemont's town house, in 1933. The gallery was established by wealthy Sir Hugh Lane, who died in the 1915 sinking of the *Lusitania*, which was torpedoed off the southern coast of Ireland by a German U-boat. The Lane Bequest Pictures, which formed the nucleus of the gallery, were the subject of a dispute over Lane's will between the gallery and the National Gallery in London. A settlement was finally reached in 1959, over 40 years after Lane's death, and modified in 1979 so that 30 of the 39 paintings are now in Dublin, eight are in London and the final one goes back and forth between the two galleries.

The gallery includes a shop and the Gallery Restaurant. The gallery is open Tuesday to Friday from 9.30 am to 6 pm, Saturday 9.30 am to 5 pm, Sunday 11 am to 5 pm. Entry is free. Numerous bus services operate by Parnell Square.

Dublin Writers' Museum

The Dublin Writers' Museum (☎ 872 2077) opened in 1991 and is at 18 Parnell Square North, next to the Hugh Lane Gallery. It celebrates the city's long and continuing history as a literary centre. On display downstairs are letters, photographs, first editions and other memorabilia of a number of Ireland's best known writers. Upstairs is the Gallery of Writers, with portraits and busts of some of Ireland's most famous writers. The one serious omission in this otherwise fascinating museum is an almost complete lack of material about more recent writers. One could almost believe that the writing spark faded after WW II, which is far from the truth.

The museum also has a bookshop and the Chapter

Hugh Lane

If wealthy Sir Hugh Lane (1875-1915) became more than a little miffed by the Irish and decided to give his paintings to some other nation, it was scarcely surprising, as he was treated with less respect than he felt he deserved in his own land. Born in County Cork he began to work in London art galleries from 1893 and five years later set up his own gallery. He had a true art dealer's nose for the directions in which art would be heading and built up a superb collection, particularly of the Impressionists.

Unfortunately for Ireland, neither his talents nor his collection were much appreciated and in exasperation he turned his attention to opportunities in London and South Africa. Irish rejection led him to rewrite his will and bequeath some of the finest works in his collection to the National Gallery in London. Later he relented and added a rider to his will leaving the collection to Dublin but failed to have it witnessed, thus causing a long legal squabble over which gallery had rightful ownership. Lane was born in 1875 and was only 40 years old when he went down with the ill-fated *Lusitania* in 1915 after it was torpedoed off the southern coast of Ireland by a German U-boat. ■

One restaurant. Next door at No 19 the Irish Writers' Centre provides a meeting and working place for contemporary writers.

The building that now houses the Writers' Museum was probably first owned by Lord Farnham, who died in 1800 and passed it on to his son. After his death George Jameson, of the whiskey-distilling Jameson family, bought the house and was responsible for the large upstairs salon which houses the Gallery of Writers.

Entry is IR£2.25 (students IR£1.50, children 70p) and it's open from 10 am to 5 pm Tuesday to Saturday, 1 to 5 pm Sunday. In July and August it's also open 10 am to 5 pm on Monday. From October to March it only opens Friday, Saturday and Sunday.

National Wax Museum

Every city worth its tourist traps has a wax museum. Dublin's National Wax Museum (☎ 872 6340) is on Granby Row, just north of Parnell Square in north Dublin. Along with the usual fantasy and fairy-tale offerings, the inevitable Chamber of Horrors and a rock music 'megastars' area, there are also figures of Irish heroes like Wolfe Tone, Robert Emmet and Charles Parnell, the leaders of the 1916 Rising, and the Taoiseachs (prime ministers). There are also models of Irish cultural figures and numerous Irish TV and sporting personalities who are presumably so well known they don't even require labelling – not that it would make much difference to the average non-Irish visitor.

The museum is open Monday to Saturday from 10 am to 5.30 pm, Sunday 1 to 5.30 pm. Entry is IR£2.50 (children IR£1.50).

Abbey Presbyterian Church

The slim, soaring spire of the Abbey Presbyterian Church at the corner of Frederick St and Parnell Square North, overlooking Parnell Square, is a convenient landmark. Dating from 1864 the church was financed by the Scottish grocery and brewery magnate Alex Findlater and is often referred to as Findlater's Church.

Great Denmark St

From the north-east corner of Parnell Square, Great Denmark St runs east to Mountjoy Square, passing by Belvedere House. Building of the house began in 1775 and it has been used as the Jesuit Belvedere College since 1841. James Joyce was a student there between 1893 and 1898 and describes it in *A Portrait of the Artist as a Young Man*. The building is renowned for its magnificent plasterwork by the master stuccodore Michael Stapleton and for its fireplaces by the Venetian artisan Bossi.

Mountjoy Square

Built between 1792 and 1818, Mountjoy Square was a fashionable and affluent centre at the height of the British 'Ascendancy' but today it's just a run-down symbol of north Dublin urban decay. Lots of money and some sensitivity, however, could work wonders on what are still very fine buildings. Viscount Mountjoy, after whom the square was named, was that energetic developer Luke Gardiner, who briefly gave his name to Gardiner Mall before it became Sackville St and then O'Connell St. The square was in fact named after him twice, as it started life as Gardiner Square.

Legends relate that this was the site where Brian Ború pitched his tent at the Battle of Clontarf in 1014. It was originally intended that nearby St George's Church be located in the square but the plan was abandoned. Residents of the square included Sean O'Casey, who set his play *The Shadow of a Gunman* here, though he referred to it as Hilljoy Square. As a child James Joyce lived just off the square at 14 Fitzgibbon St.

St Francis Xavier Church

Built in 1829-32 on Gardiner St Upper, the Catholic St Francis Xavier Church has a superb Italian altar and coffered ceiling. It was originally intended that the church be built on Great Charles St, behind Mountjoy Square.

St George's Church

St George's Church is on Hardwicke Place off Temple St, even though it was originally intended to be built in Mountjoy Square. It was built by Francis Johnston from 1802 in a Greek Ionic style and has a 60-metre-high steeple modelled after that of St Martin-in-the-Fields in London. The church's bells were added in 1836 and originally hung in a bell tower in Francis Johnston's own back garden in nearby Eccles St. Not surprisingly, neighbours complained about the noise and Johnston eventually willed them to the church. Although this was one of Johnston's finest works and the Duke of Wellington was married here, the church is no longer in use.

St Mary's Abbey

Despite the intriguing history of St Mary's Abbey, there is actually little to see, the opening hours are very restricted and even finding the abbey is rather difficult. It is just west of Capel St in Meetinghouse Lane, which runs off a street named Mary's Abbey, in north Dublin. When the abbey was founded in 1139 the city of Dublin was on the other side of the river, so this was a rural location, far away from the temptations of city life. In 1147, soon after its foundation by the Benedictine monks, it was taken over by the Cistercians. Until its suppression in the mid-1500s this was the most important monastery within English-controlled Ireland. It also performed numerous important civic functions. The abbey was in use as council chambers in 1534 when Silken Thomas Fitzgerald announced his rejection of English sovereignty and launched his short-lived rebellion against Henry VIII.

In 1537 Henry VIII, having broken away from the Catholic church, ordered the dissolution of all of Ireland's monasteries. On the surface this move may have been religious, but its inspiration was in large part a simple desire to grab the country's monastic wealth. St

Mary's Abbey was certainly wealthy, as the Cistercians were notable farmers and builders and the abbey controlled huge areas of land, farms, equipment, fishing boats and even a complete village. When the confiscated property was valued, St Mary's Abbey was the richest in all of Ireland, having a total value of £537 (and 17 shillings and 10 pence if you want to-the-penny accuracy). Mellifont Abbey to the north of Dublin (see the Excursions chapter) came in second at £352 but no other monastery in the whole country was worth over £100.

The abbey was virtually derelict when the next century rolled around, although at that time Dublin had not yet started to sprawl north of the river. Most of the

Abbey Presbyterian (Findlater's) Church (TW)

buildings were still there in the late 1600s, but records indicate that in 1676 stones from the abbey were used to construct the Essex Bridge. Using the abbey as a quarry soon removed all visible traces and it was not until comparatively recently that the remaining fragments were rediscovered.

The chapter house, where the monks used to gather after morning mass, is the only surviving part of the abbey, which in its prime encompassed land stretching as far east as Ballybough. The floor level in the abbey is two metres below street level – a clear indication of the changes wrought over eight centuries. Exhibits in the abbey tell of the destruction of the Reformation in 1540 and the story of the statue from St Mary's which is now in the Whitefriars Carmelite Church on Aungier St in south Dublin (see the Whitefriars Carmelite Church section).

Opening times are very restricted: it is only open from mid-June to September and even then only on Wednesdays from noon to 6 pm. Entry is IR£1 for adults, 40p for students or children.

St Mary's Church

On Mary St, between Capel and O'Connell Sts north of the Liffey, St Mary's was designed in 1697 by Sir William Robinson, who was also responsible for the Royal Hospital Kilmainham. Just as that was the most important construction in Dublin during the 17th century, this is the most important church to survive from that century. The church was completed in 1702 and a roll call of famous Dubliners were baptised there. It was in this church that John Wesley, the founder of Methodism, preached for the first time in Ireland in 1747. Nevertheless, like so many other fine old Dublin churches, it is no longer in use. Irish patriot Wolfe Tone was born on the adjacent Wolfe Tone St.

St Michan's Church

Named after a Danish saint, St Michan's Church on Church St Lower to the north of the river dates from its Danish foundation in 1095, though there's barely a trace of that original church to be seen. The battlement tower dates from the 15th century but otherwise was rebuilt in the late 1600s and considerably restored in the early 1800s and again after the Civil War, during which it was damaged.

The church contains the organ which, it is claimed, Handel played for the first-ever performance of his

Messiah, but the main attraction is the mummified human remains in the subterranean crypts. With more than a little Irish blarney your guide will insist that the vault's special atmosphere accounts for their perfect preservation. In fact they're as dried, shrivelled and crumbling as you might expect after the odd few centuries.

Tours are conducted regularly from 10 am to 12.45 pm and 2 to 4.45 pm Monday to Friday, and on Saturday mornings only. The cost is IR£1.20 (children 50p).

Irish Whiskey Corner

Just north of St Michan's Church, the Irish Whiskey Corner (☎ 872 5566) is in an old warehouse on Bow St, Dublin 7, and the admission charge of IR£2 includes entry to the museum, a short film and a sample of Irish whiskey.

King's Inns & Henrietta St

North of the river on Constitution Hill and Henrietta St is King's Inns, home for the Dublin legal fraternity. This classical building is another James Gandon creation though it suffered many delays between its design in 1795, the start of construction in 1802 and its final completion in 1817. Along the way a number of other architects lent a hand, including Francis Johnston, who added the cupola late in the piece. The building is normally open only to members of the Inns.

The Inns have certainly made their way around Dublin. The city's original law courts stood just to the west of Christ Church Cathedral, south of the Liffey. Collett's Inn, the first gathering place for lawyers, was later established in Exchequer St and was in turn followed by Preston Inn, which stood on Cork Hill where the City Hall stands today. In 1541 when Henry VIII claimed to be King of Ireland as well as of England, the lawyers' society took the title of King's Inns. It moved to a new site on land confiscated from the Dominican Convent of St Saviour, but when that site was taken over to become the Four Courts building by the Liffey the King's Inns was moved to its present home.

Henrietta St, leading up to the south side of the building, was Dublin's first Georgian street and has buildings dating from 1720. Unfortunately, this is another of north Dublin's run-down areas and is now in a state of extreme disrepair. These early Georgian mansions were both larger and more varied in style than their later counterparts. For a time Henrietta St rejoiced in the name

'Primate's Hill', as the Archbishop of Armagh and other high church officials lived there. Luke Gardiner, who was responsible for so much of the early development of Georgian north Dublin, lived at No 10 Henrietta St.

OTHER SIGHTS

Having worked your way down the River Liffey and then explored south and north Dublin, you will have made a reasonable inroad into the city's attractions, but there's still much more. To the west are the Guinness Brewery in the colourful Liberties area, Kilmainham Jail and Phoenix Park. To the north and north-east is the Royal Canal, Prospect Cemetery, the Botanic Gardens, the Casino at Marino and Clontarf. To the south and south-east are the Grand Canal, Ballsbridge, the Royal Dublin Showground and the Chester Beatty Library. There are also more galleries and museums apart from those already covered in south and north Dublin.

St Catherine's Church

Westward from St Audoen's Church, towards that more recent Dublin shrine, the Guinness Brewery, is St Catherine's Church, whose huge front faces on to Thomas St. The church was built on the site of St Thomas Abbey, which King Henry II built in honour of Thomas à Becket, the Archbishop of Canterbury. Perhaps coincidentally the archbishop was murdered on the orders of Henry II.

Completed in 1769, St Catherine's would have been demolished during Dublin's 1960s redevelopment mania were it not for the efforts of the Irish Georgian Society. The building is now used as a community centre.

After being hanged, the corpse of patriot Robert Emmet was put to the further indignity of being beheaded outside the church in 1803. Prior to this his supporters had murdered the Lord Chief Justice Kilwarden nearby.

Guinness Brewery

Heading westward from central south Dublin, past St Audoen's Churches, Thomas St metamorphoses into James's St in the area of Dublin known as the Liberties. Along James's St stretches the historic St James's Gate Guinness Brewery (☎ 53 6700, ext 5155). From its foundation by Arthur Guinness in 1759, on the site of the earlier Rainsford Brewery, the Guinness operation has expanded all the way down to the Liffey and across both

Top: King's Inns (TW)
Bottom: Detail, King's Inns (TW)

Top: Royal Hospital Kilmainham (TW)
Bottom: Kilmainham Jail (TW)

sides of the street. In all it covers 26 hectares and for a time was the largest brewery in the world. The oldest parts of the site are south of James's St; at one time there was a gate spanning the entire street.

The Guinness Hop Store on Crane St is the historic brewery's old storehouse for hops (the main ingredient in beer-making) where visitors can watch a Guinness audiovisual display and inspect an extensive Guinness museum. It is not a tour of the brewery but it is an interesting visit and your entry fee includes a glass of the black stuff. Children pay less and don't get a drink! It is frequently claimed that Guinness tastes exactly as it should only at its original source, and you can't get any closer to the source than here. Guinness aficionados claim the Guinness 'pulled' in the hop store is better than that provided by even the most traditional of Dublin's pubs.

In its early years Guinness was only one of dozens of Dublin breweries but it outgrew and outlasted all of them. At one time a Grand Canal tributary was cut into the brewery to enable special Guinness barges to carry consignments out onto the Irish canal system or to the Dublin port. When the brewery extensions reached the Liffey in 1872, the fleet of Guinness barges became a familiar sight. There was also a Guinness railway on the brewery site, complete with a corkscrew tunnel. Guinness still operates its own ships to convey the vital fluid to the British market. Over 50% of all the beer consumed in Ireland is brewed here.

The Guinness family became noted philanthropists. Sir Benjamin Lee Guinness, grandson of the brewery founder, Arthur Guinness, restored St Patrick's Cathedral. Sir Benjamin's son, Lord Ardilaun, opened St Stephen's Green to the public and converted it into a park, and his brother Lord Iveagh helped to build a wing of the Rotunda Hospital.

Hours are 10 am to 4.30 pm (last audiovisual display at 3.30 pm) Monday to Friday. Entry is IR£2 (children 50p). To get there take bus No 21A, 78 or 78A from Fleet St. The upper floors of the building house temporary art exhibits.

IMMA & Royal Hospital Kilmainham

The IMMA or Irish Museum of Modern Art (☎ 671 8666) at the old Royal Hospital Kilmainham is close to Kilmainham Jail. The gallery only opened in 1991 and the exhibits look puny in comparison with their luxurious surroundings, but perhaps it will improve with time. There are regular temporary exhibits as well as the permanent collection.

The Royal Hospital Kilmainham was built in 1680-87 but not, as its name would suggest, as a hospital. It was in fact a home for retired soldiers and continued to fill that role until after Irish independence. It preceded the well-known Chelsea Hospital in London, which fulfilled a similar role. Royal Hospital inmates were often referred to as 'Chelsea Pensioners' although there was no connection. At the time of its construction it was one of the finest buildings in Ireland and there was considerable muttering that it was altogether too good a place for its residents. The building was designed by William Robinson, whose work included Marsh's Library.

Kilmainham Gate was designed by Francis Johnston in 1812 and originally stood, as the Richmond Tower, at Watling St Bridge near the Guinness Brewery. It was moved to its current position opposite the jail in 1846 as it obstructed the increasingly heavy traffic to the new railway station (Kingsbridge Station, now known as Heuston Station). The railway company paid for its dismantlement and reassembly.

The museum's excellent restaurant is hidden away in the basement at the back of the building. The IMMA is open from 10 am to 5.30 pm Tuesday to Saturday and noon to 5.30 pm on Sunday. Entry is free and there are guided tours on Sunday. You can get there on bus No 24, 79 or 90 from Aston Quay outside the Virgin Megastore.

Kilmainham Jail

Built in 1792-95, Kilmainham Jail (☎ 53 5984) on Inchicore Rd is a solid grey threatening old building which played a key role in Ireland's struggle for independence and was the site of the executions that followed the 1916 Easter Rising. It played an equally fateful part during the Civil War but, interestingly, this chapter in the saga is conspicuously played down when you visit the jail. Even the passing comment that the final prisoner to be released from Kilmainham was Ireland's future president, Eamon de Valera, doesn't allude to the fact that he had been imprisoned by his fellow Irish citizens.

During each act of Ireland's long and painful path to independence from neighbouring England, at least one part of the performance took place at the jail. The uprisings of 1799, 1803, 1848, 1867 and 1916 all ended with the leaders being confined in Kilmainham. Robert Emmet, Thomas Francis Meagher, Charles Stewart Parnell and the 1916 Easter Rising leaders were all visitors, but it was

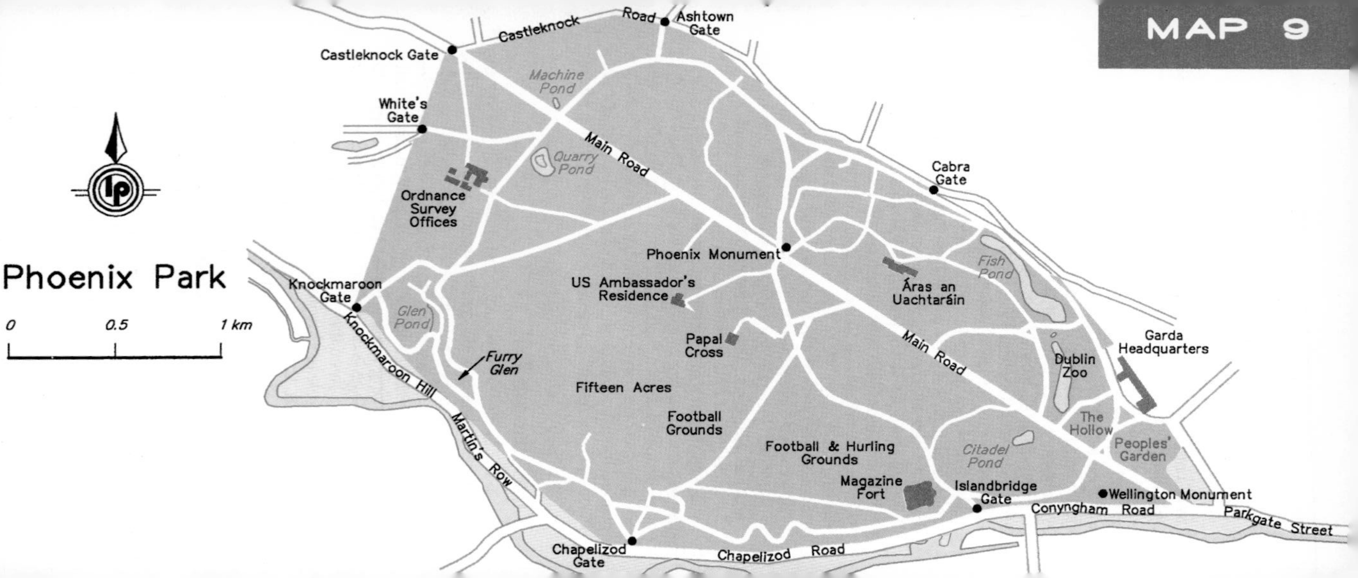

MAP 9

Phoenix Park

0   0.5   1 km

Garda Headquarters

Padgate Street

Wellington Monument

Conyngham Road

Peoples Garden

The Hollow

Islandbridge Gate

Dublin Zoo

Citadel Pond

Fish Pond

Cabra Gate

Áras an Uachtaráin

Main Road

Magazine Fort

Chapelizod Road

Football & Hurling Grounds

Ashtown Gate

Road

Phoenix Monument

Papal Cross

Football Grounds

Chapelizod Gate

Castleknock

Main Road

US Ambassador's Residence

Fifteen Acres

Machine Pond

Quarry Pond

Furry Glen

White's Gate

Castleknock Gate

Ordnance Survey Offices

Glen Pond

Knockmaroon Gate

Knockmaroon Hill

Martin's Row

the executions in 1916 which most deeply etched the jail's name into the Irish consciousness. Of the 16 executions that took place between 3 and 12 May after the Easter Rising, 14 were conducted here. As a finale prisoners from the Civil War struggles were held here from 1922, but it was finally closed for good in 1924.

A visit to the jail starts with an excellent audiovisual introduction to the old building, followed by a tour. Incongruously sitting outside in the yard is the *Asgard*, the ship which successfully ran the British blockade to deliver arms to nationalist forces in 1914. The tour finishes in the gloomy yard where the 1916 executions took place. You almost brace yourself to see the gates swing back and for a wounded James Connolly to be brought in to face the firing squad. Opening hours are 11 am to 6 pm daily from July to September, and 1 to 4 pm Monday to Friday and 1 to 6 pm on Sunday from October to May. Phone ☎ 53 5984 for further details. Entry is IR£1.50 (children 60p) and you can get there by bus No 23, 51, 51A, 78 or 79 from the city centre.

Phoenix Park

The 700-plus hectares of Phoenix Park makes it one of the world's largest city parks, dwarfing Central Park in New York (a mere 337 hectares) or any of the London parks – Hyde Park is 138 hectares, Regent's Park is 190 hectares and even Hampstead Heath is only 324 hectares. The park has gardens and lakes, a host of sporting facilities (including a motor racing track), the second-oldest public zoo in Europe, various government offices, the Garda (police) Headquarters, the residences of the US ambassador and the Irish president, and even a herd of deer.

Phoenix Park owes its origins to Lord Ormonde, who in 1671 chose to turn this land into a park; however, it was not opened to the public until 1747 by Lord Chesterfield. The land had been confiscated from the Kilmainham priory of St John in order to create a royal deer park, but was then given as a grant by Charles II. The name Phoenix is actually a corruption of the Gaelic words for clear water, *fionn uisce*. The park played a crucial role in Irish history, as Lord Cavendish, the British Chief Secretary for Ireland, and his assistant were murdered in 1882 by an Irish nationalist secret society called the National Invincibles. Lord Cavendish's home is now Deerfield, the US ambassador's residence, and the murder took place outside the viceroy's residence, now occupied by the Irish president.

Near the Parkgate St entrance to the park is the 63-

metre-high Wellington Monument obelisk. This was a long-term project, taking from 1817 to 1861 to be built, mainly because the Duke of Wellington fell out of public favour during its construction. At this south-east corner of the park are the People's Garden, dating from 1864, and the bandstand in the Hollow. Just north of the Hollow is the zoo (see the Dublin Zoo section). Main Rd separates the Hollow and the zoo from the Phoenix Park Cricket Club of 1830 and from Citadel Pond, usually referred to as the Dog Pond. Behind the zoo, on the edge of the park, the Garda Siochána Headquarters (police headquarters) has a small police museum.

Going north-west along Main Rd, which runs right through the park, you will see the Irish President's residence (see the Áras an Uachtaráin section) on the right. In the centre of the park the Phoenix Monument, erected by Lord Chesterfield in 1747, looks very unphoenix-like. In fact it's often referred to as the Eagle Monument. The southern part of the park is given over to a large number of football and hurling fields, and, though they occupy about 80 hectares (200 acres), the area is known as the Fifteen Acres.

White's Gate, the park exit from its north-west side, leads to Castleknock College and Castleknock Castle. Near White's Gate and Quarry Pond at the north-west end of the park are the offices of the Ordnance Survey, the government mapping department. This building was originally built in 1728 by Luke Gardiner, who was also responsible for O'Connell St and Mountjoy Square in north Dublin. South of this building is the attractive rural-looking Furry Glen and Glen Pond corner of the park.

Looping back towards the Parkgate entrance, you'll see Magazine Fort, which stands on Thomas' Hill. Like the nearby Wellington Monument, the fort was definitely no quick construction, the process taking from 1734 to 1801. It was a target for the 1916 Easter Rising but the fort's utter uselessness had much earlier prompted a verse from that master of sarcasm, Jonathan Swift:

Behold a proof of Irish sense!
Here Irish wit is seen!
When nothing's left that's worth defence,
We build a magazine.

Dublin Zoo Its establishment in 1830 makes it one of the oldest public zoos in the world, but the Dublin Zoo (☎ 677 1425) is merely OK – a place to take the kids.

There's a pets' corner which particularly appeals to them. The zoo is especially well known for its lion-breeding programme, which dates back to 1857 and includes among its offspring the lion that roars at the start of MGM films. Entry is IR£4.20 (children IR£1.80) and it's open from 9.30 am to 6 pm Monday to Saturday, and from 11 am on Sunday. The 12-hectare zoo is in the south-east corner of extensive Phoenix Park and can be reached by a No 10 bus from O'Connell St or a No 25 or 26 bus from Abbey St Middle.

Áras an Uachtaráin The residence of the Irish president was built in 1751, enlarged in 1782 and again in 1816, on the latter occasion by the noted Irish architect Francis Johnston, who added the Ionic portico. From 1782 until 1922 it was the residence of the British viceroys or lord lieutenants. After independence it became the home of Ireland's governor-general until Ireland cut the final ties with the British crown and created the office of president in 1937.

The Royal Canal

Two canals encircle central Dublin: the older Grand Canal to the south, and the newer Royal Canal to the north. Constructed from 1790, by which time the Grand Canal was already past its prime, the Royal Canal may have been a commercial failure but its story is certainly a colourful one. It was founded by Long John Binns, a director of the Grand Canal operating company who quit the board because of a supposed insult over his occupation as a shoemaker. He established the Royal Canal with the principal aim of revenge, but since it merely duplicated the purpose of the earlier canal it never made money. It also became known as the Shoemaker's Canal. The Duke of Leinster became a major backer for the canal on the condition that it be routed by his mansion near Maynooth. In 1840 the canal was sold to a railway company who considered its route convenient for a railway line. Tracks still run alongside much of the disused canal's route through the city.

Like the path along the southern Grand Canal, the Royal Canal towpath makes for a relaxing walk through the heart of the city. You can join it beside Newcomen Bridge at Strand Rd North, just north of Connolly Station, and follow it to the suburb of Clonsilla and beyond, over 10 km away. The walk is particularly pleasant beyond Binns Bridge in Drumcondra. At the top of Blessington St, near the Dublin Youth Hostel, is a large pond which was used as a filter bed when the canal also supplied drinking water to the city. It now attracts swans and other waterbirds.

Prospect Cemetery

Immediately next to the Botanic Gardens is Prospect or Glasnevin Cemetery, the largest in Ireland. It was established in 1832 as a cemetery for Roman Catholics, who faced opposition when they conducted burials in the city's Protestant cemeteries. Many of the cemetery's monuments and memorials have staunchly patriotic overtones with numerous high crosses, shamrocks, harps and other Irish symbols. The cemetery's most imposing memorial is the colossal monument to Cardinal McCabe (1837-1921), the Archbishop of Dublin and Primate of Ireland.

A modern replica of a round tower acts as a handy landmark for locating the tomb of Daniel O'Connell, who died in 1847 but was reinterred here in 1869, when the tower was completed. Charles Stewart Parnell's tomb is topped with a huge granite rock. Other notable people buried here include Sir Roger Casement, who was executed for treason by the British in 1916 and whose remains were not returned until 1964; Michael Collins, a leading figure in Ireland's final struggle for independence; Jim Larkin, a prime force in the 1913 general strike; and Gerard Manley Hopkins the poet.

The most interesting parts of the cemetery are at the south-eastern Prospect Square end. The cemetery wall still has watch towers that were once used to keep watch for body snatchers. Naturally, in its Dublin wanderings *Ulysses* pauses at the cemetery and there are a number of clues for Joyce enthusiasts to track down among the tombstones.

National Botanic Gardens

Founded in 1795 the National Botanic Gardens, directly north of the centre on Botanic Rd in Glasnevin, function both as a scientific resource and as a popular public park. In fact the area was used as a garden long before 1795 but only the Yew Walk, also known as Addison's Walk, has trees dating back to the first half of the 18th century. Unfortunately, much of the gardens are rather like a rather dull garden allotment, so that you start to wonder where the potato beds are.

The gardens cover 19 hectares and are flanked to the

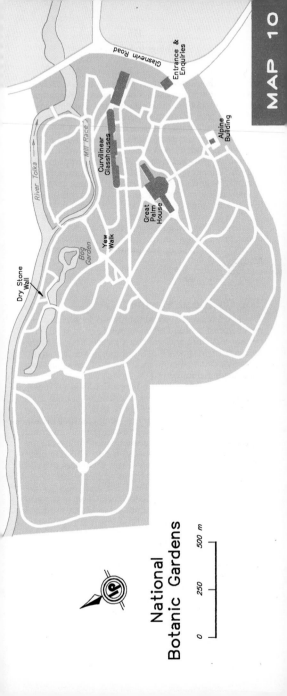

MAP 10

River Tolka →

Mill Race

Glasnevin Road

Entrance & Enquiries

Curvilinear Glasshouses

Dry Stone Wall

Bog Garden

Yew Walk

Grest Palm House

Alpine Building

National Botanic Gardens

0   250   500 m

north by the River Tolka. Apart from a variety of gardens, there is also a series of curvilinear glasshouses dating from 1843-69. The glasshouses' Dublin creator, Richard Turner, was also responsible for the glasshouse at the Belfast Botanic Gardens and the Palm House in London's Kew Gardens. Dublin's gardens also have a palm house, built in 1884. Among the pioneering botanical work conducted here was the first attempt to raise orchids from seed, back in 1844. Pampas grass and the giant lily were first grown in Europe in these gardens.

The gardens are open Monday to Saturday from 9 am to 6 pm in summer and 10 am to 4.30 pm in winter, Sundays 11 am to 6 pm in summer and 11 am to 4.30 pm in winter. The conservatories have shorter opening hours. Entry is free. You can get there on bus No 13 or 19 from O'Connell St or No 34 or 34A from Abbey St Middle.

The Casino at Marino

The Marino Casino on Malahide Rd in Marino, just north-east of central Dublin, is not a casino at all. This curious structure was built as a pleasure house in the grounds of Marino House. Although Marino House itself was demolished in the 1920s the Casino survives as a wonderful folly.

The somewhat eccentric James Caulfield (1728-99), later to become the Earl of Charlemont, set out on a European grand tour at the age of 18 in 1746. The visit was to last nine years, including a four-year spell in Italy, and he returned to Ireland with a huge art collection and a burning ambition to bring elements of Italian culture and style to the estate he acquired in 1756. He commissioned the architect Sir William Chambers to build the casino, a process which started in the late 1750s, continued right through the 1760s and much of the 1770s, and never really came to a conclusion. In part this was because Lord Charlemont's extravagances had frittered away his fortune.

Externally the building, with its 12 Tuscan columns forming a temple-like façade and its huge entrance doorway, creates the expectation that inside it will be a simple single open space. It's only when you enter the building that you realise what a wonderful extravagance it is. The interior is a convoluted maze that was originally intended as a bachelor's retreat but eventually put to a quite different use. The flights of fancy include chimneys for the central heating which are disguised as roof urns, downpipes hidden in columns, carved draperies, ornate fireplaces, beautiful parquet floors constructed of rare woods and a spacious wine cellar. A variety of statuary adorns the outside but it's the amusing fakes which are most enjoyable. The towering front door is a sham, and a much smaller panel opens to reveal the secret interior. Similarly, the windows have blacked-out panels to hide the reality that the interior is a complex of rooms, not a single chamber.

When Lord Charlemont married, the Casino became a garden retreat rather than a bachelor's quarters. It's said that Charlemont never got on with his in-laws and a visit from his mother-in-law would send him scuttling down a 400-metre-long underground tunnel that joined the main house to the casino. The casino was designed to accompany another building where he intended to house the art and antiquities he had acquired during his European tour, so it's perhaps fitting that his town house on Parnell Square, also designed by Sir William Chambers, is now the Municipal Gallery of Modern Art.

Despite his wealth Charlemont was a comparatively liberal and free-thinking aristocrat. He never fenced in his demesne and allowed the public to use it as an open park. Nor was he the only eccentric at the time. In 1792 a painter named Folliot took a dislike to the lord and built Marino Crescent at the bottom of Malahide Rd purely to block his view of the sea. The vampire writer Bram Stoker (1847-1912) was born at 15 Marino Crescent.

After Charlemont's death his estate, crippled by his debts, quickly began to collapse. The art collection was soon dispersed and in 1870 the town house was sold to the government. The Marino estate followed in 1881 and the Casino in 1930, though it was in decrepit condition when the government finally acquired it. It was not until the mid-1970s that serious restoration commenced, and it is still continuing. Although the Casino grounds are only a tiny fragment of the once park-like Marino estate, trees and planting around the building will help to hide the fact that it is now surrounded by a housing estate.

The Marino Casino is open daily from 9.30 am to 6.30 pm from mid-June to September. At other times of the year call ☎ 33 1618 or the Office of Public Works (☎ 661 3111, ext 2386) for details of opening hours. You can visit the building only on a guided tour; entry is IR£1 (children 40p). The Casino is just off Malahide Rd, north of the junction with Howth Rd in Clontarf. Bus No 20A, 20B, 27, 27A, 27B, 32A, 42 or 42B will take you there from the centre.

Clontarf & North Bull Island

Clontarf is a bayside suburb about five km north-east of the centre, with a number of popular cheaper B&Bs. It takes its name from *cluain tarbh*, the bull's meadow. It was here on Good Friday 1014 that the high king Brian Ború defeated the Danes at the Battle of Clontarf, though in the struggle the Irish hero was killed, along with his son and grandson. The Normans later erected a castle here which was handed on to the Knights Templar in 1179, rebuilt in 1835 and later converted into a hotel.

The North Bull Wall runs out from Clontarf about a km into Dublin Bay. The wall was built in 1820 at the suggestion of Captain William Bligh of HMS *Bounty* mutiny fame, in order to stop Dublin Harbour from silting up. The marshes and dunes of North Bull Island which formed behind the wall are a popular reserve for sea birds and are also home to the Royal Dublin and St Anne's Golf Courses. Many birds migrate here from the Arctic in winter, and at times the bird population can reach 40,000. There's an interpretive centre reached by the northern causeway to the island.

The Grand Canal

Built from 1756 to connect Dublin with the River Shannon, which flows down the middle of Ireland, the Grand Canal makes a graceful six-km loop around south Dublin. At its eastern end the canal forms a harbour connected with the Liffey at Ringsend. The later Royal Canal, constructed from 1790, performs a similar loop through north Dublin. True Dubliners, it is said, are born within the confines of the canals.

For more information on the canal, look for the book

1	The Locks Restaurant	10	Patrick Kavanagh Bench
2	The Lower Deck	11	Irish Tourist Board
3	Institute of Education		(Bord Fáilte)
	Business College	12	Parson's Bookshop
	(formerly Portobello	13	Macartney Bridge
	House)	14	Mount St Bridge
4	The Portobello	15	McKenny Bridge
5	An Béal Bocht	16	Waterways Visitors'
	(The Poor Mouth)		Centre
6	The Barge	17	Grand Canal Dock
7	Portobello Bridge	18	Surf Dock Windsurfing
8	Eustace Bridge		Shop
9	Patrick Kavanagh		
	Statue		

MAP 11

Grand Canal

0   250   500 m

Hanover Quay
17
Charlotte Quay
18
Ringsend Rd
South Dock St
Gordon St
Barrow St
Grand Canal Quay
16
Pearse St
Macken St
Grand Canal St Lower
Grand Canal St Upper
Northumberland Rd
Pembroke Rd
Baggot Lane
St Mary's Rd
Mount St Lower
Warrington Place
15
Haddington Rd
Percy Place
14
Baggot St Upper
Herbert Place
Mount St Upper
13
12
Baggot St Lower
11
10
Lad Lane
9
Mespil Rd
Fitzwilliam Place East
Wilton Terrace
Leeson St Lower
8
Charlemont Pl
Adelaide Road
Grand Parade
Charlemont St
5
Charlemont Place
6
Charlemont Mall
Canal Rd
Harrington St
Richmond St
4
3
2
Grove Rd
Portobello Rd
1

The Grand Canal by Conaghan, Gleeson & Maddock (Office of Public Works). The Waterways Visitors' Centre, opened in 1993, also provides a great deal of information about the canal. The canal has not been used commercially since 1960 but some stretches are very attractive and enjoyable to stroll along. It's about two km from the Mount St Bridge to Richmond St along a particularly beautiful part of the canal, with a cluster of pubs providing refreshment at the Richmond St end. The canalside path also makes a fine bicycle ride.

History An Act of Parliament to build the canal was first proposed in 1715 but work did not commence until 1756. Only 20 km had been built by 1763 when the Dublin Corporation took over the project from private interests. As the canal was also intended to bring water to the city, the corporation was concerned about the slow rate of progress. They handed it back in 1772, and in 1775 a visitor to Ireland commented that progress on the canal's construction was moving ahead at such a pace that 'it bids fair for being completed in three or four centuries'.

Nevertheless, in 1779 the first cargo barges started to operate between Dublin and Sallins, about 35 km west of Dublin. Passenger services commenced a year later, but at that time the terminus of the canal was the James's St Harbour, near the Guinness Brewery. By 1784 the canal had been extended a farther 10 km to Robertstown and the construction of the Circular Line, completed in 1791, extended the canal right around the south of Dublin to meet the River Liffey at Ringsend. The locks between the Grand Canal Docks and the Liffey were opened in 1796, making the completed canal the longest in Britain or Ireland. In all, the Grand Canal system extended for 550 km, of which about 250 km was along the Rivers Shannon and Barrow.

The Grand Canal Company operated five hotels along the canal route from Dublin to Shannon (on Ireland's west coast). The Portobello Hotel in Dublin, opened in 1807, was the city terminus and soon became a busy scene as passengers arrived and departed. Canal travel was never very speedy but it quickly became a popular alternative to the hardships of travel by road. Horses towed the barges along the canals at a steady five or six km/h clip. Passenger boats, divided into 1st and 2nd class, carried 80 passengers. In 1834 lightweight flyboats pulled by four horses were introduced and these could reach up to 15 km/h.

Railways started to spread across Ireland from the mid-1800s and the canal quickly went into a terminal decline. Passenger services ended in 1852 and soon the canal was used only for cargo services. During this era Guinness deliveries were often made by barge, departing from the harbour right at the brewery. By the end of the century steam power was starting to supplant horses. The barges were pulled by horse from Dublin to Robertstown from where a steam tug would tow up to six barges the 40 km to Ballycommon. From there horses would again take over for the final stretch to the River Shannon. In 1911 diesel engines started to replace horses and by 1924 all the Grand Canal Company barges were diesel powered. Horse-drawn barges continued to be operated by other 'traders' right through the canal's life. The decline continued, however, and though WW II proved a temporary respite the private canal company folded in 1950 and the last barge carried a cargo of Guinness from Dublin in 1960.

The canal fell into disrepair and in the early 1970s the St James's St Harbour and the stretch of canal back from there to the Circular Line were filled in. Recently the canal has enjoyed a modest revival as a tourist attraction. Despite the very limited number of boats that now ply the canal, all the locks are kept in working order.

Along the Circular Line to Ringsend The Grand Canal enters the Liffey at Ringsend, through locks that were built in 1796. The large Grand Canal Dock, flanked by Hanover and Charlotte quays, is now used by windsurfers. Surf Dock offers windsurfing tuition and sells windsurfing equipment from a barge moored in the dock.

At the north-west corner of the dock is Misery Hill, once the site for the public execution of criminals. Even more macabre was the practice of bringing the corpses of those already hung at Gallows Hill, near Baggot St Upper, to this spot to be strung up for public display for anything from six to 12 months.

Waterways Visitors' Centre Just upstream from the Grand Canal Dock is the new visitors' centre, built by the Public Works Department as an exhibition and interpretation centre on the construction and operation of Irish canals and waterways. The centre opened in 1993.

Mount St to Leeson St A memorial to the events of the 1916 Rising can be seen on the Mount St Bridge. A little farther along, Baggot St crosses the canal on the 1791 Macartney Bridge. The main office of the Irish

Tourist Board or Bord Fáilte is on the north side of the
canal and Bridge House and Parson's Bookshop are on
the south side.

This lovely stretch of the canal with its grassy, tree-
lined banks was a favourite haunt of the poet Patrick
Kavanagh. Among his compositions is the hauntingly
beautiful *On Raglan Road*, a popular song which Van
Morrison fans can find on the album *Irish Heartbeat* with
the Chieftans. Another Kavanagh poem requested that
he be commemorated by 'a canal bank seat for passers-
by' and Kavanagh's friends obliged with a seat beside
the lock on the south side of the canal. A little farther
along on the north side you can sit down by Kavanagh
himself, or at least a bronze replica of him, comfortably
lounging on a bench to watch his beloved canal.

Canalside Pubs The next stretch of the canal has
some fine pubs, such as *The Barge* and *The Portobello*, both
right by the canal. The Portobello is a fine old-fashioned
place with music on weekend evenings and Sunday
mornings. *The Lower Deck* on Richmond St and *An Béal
Bocht* (The Poor Mouth) on Charlemont St are also near
the canal. You could also pause for a meal at *The Locks
Restaurant*. The Institute of Education Business College
by The Portobello was built in 1807 as Portobello House;

Patrick Kavanagh Statue, Grand Canal (TW)

as the Grand Canal Hotel, it was the Dublin terminus for passenger traffic on the canal. The artist Jack B Yeats lived here for the last seven years of his life until his death in 1957.

Farther west from here the Circular Line is not so interesting and is better appreciated by bicycle rather than on foot. The spur running off the Circular Line alongside Grand Canal Bank to the old St James's St Harbour has been filled in and is now a park and bicycle path.

Ballsbridge & Donnybrook

Just south-east of central Dublin, the suburb of Ballsbridge was principally laid out between 1830 and 1860 and many of the streets have British names with a distinctly military bearing. Many embassies, including the US Embassy, are located in Ballsbridge. It also has some middle-bracket B&Bs and several upper bracket hotels. If you're not staying in Ballsbridge, the main reasons for a visit are the Royal Dublin Showground, the Chester Beatty Library and the Lansdowne Rd rugby stadium.

Adjoining Ballsbridge to the south is Donnybrook, at one time a village on the banks of the River Dodder. For centuries it was famous for the Donnybrook Fair which was first held in 1204. By the 19th century it had expanded to become a 15-day event centred around horse dealing, but it had become such a scene of drunken brawling and sexual debauchery that the residents of Donnybrook, by now becoming a sedate residential area, had the fair stopped in 1855.

Royal Dublin Society Showground On Merrion Rd in Ballsbridge, south of the centre, the Royal Dublin Society Showground is used for various exhibitions through the year, but the two major events reflect the society's agricultural background. The society was founded in 1731 and had its headquarters in a number of well-known Dublin buildings, including, from 1814 until 1925, after Irish independence, Leinster House. The society was involved in the foundation of the National Museum, Library, Gallery and Botanic Gardens. The two most important annual events at the showground are the May Spring Show and the August Dublin Horse Show. The Spring Show is dedicated to farming and agricultural pursuits, while the Horse Show includes an international showjumping contest and attracts the horsey set from all over Ireland and Britain.

Tickets can be booked in advance for the Spring or

Horse shows by contacting the Ticket Office (☎ 668 0645), Royal Dublin Society, PO Box 121, Ballsbridge, Dublin 4.

Chester Beatty Library & Gallery of Oriental Art

This library and gallery (☎ 669 2386) houses the collection of the mining engineer Sir Alfred Chester Beatty (1875-1968). It includes over 20,000 manuscripts, numerous rare books, miniature paintings, clay tablets, costumes and other objects, predominantly from the Middle East and the Far East. There are various ancient bibles and the Arabic collection includes over 270 Korans. There is also a range of texts and books from Tibet, Myanmar, Thailand and Mongolia and a large collection of Japanese prints. The European collection includes fine examples of early books and numerous maps and prints.

The gallery includes a reference library and a bookshop, but unfortunately the collection is far larger than the exhibit space so only a tiny fraction of the total can be shown at any one time. If you have specific interests you can easily come away disappointed, so a visit here is a rather hit-or-miss operation.

The gallery is south of the centre at 20 Shrewsbury Rd, Dublin 4. This is just beyond Ballsbridge en route to Dun Laoghaire. Bus No 5, 6, 6A, 7A or 8 from Eden Quay, No 46 or 46A from College St or No 10 from O'Connell St will take you there. Alternatively, take the DART to Sandymount Station, Sydney Parade. Opening hours are 10 am to 5 pm Tuesday to Friday, 2 to 5 pm on Saturday. Entry is free and there are guided tours on Wednesday and Saturday at 2.30 pm.

Pearse Museum

Patrick (or Padráig in the Irish he worked so hard to promote) Pearse was a leader of the 1916 Rising and one of the first batch to be executed by firing squad at Kilmainham Jail. St Enda's, the school he established with his brother Willie to further his ideas of Irish language and culture, is now maintained as a museum (☎ 93 4208) and memorial to the brothers.

The Pearse Museum is at the junction of Grange Rd and Taylor's Lane in Rathfarnham, south-west of the city centre. It's open every day from 10 am to 12.30 pm and from 2 pm to 4.30 pm (February, November), to 5.30 pm (March, April, September, October), to 6 pm (May to August) and to 3.30 pm (December, January). Entry is free and you can get there on a No 16 bus from the city centre.

Marlay Park

This park area south of the centre at Rathfarnham in Dublin 16 has numerous attractions, including a model railway with rides for children on Saturday afternoons. The park is the northern starting point for the Wicklow Way walking track.

Other Museums

Apart from the museums described in the north and south Dublin sections, there are a number of other smaller museums or museums of specialist interest.

George Bernard Shaw House This museum (☎ 872 2077) at 33 Synge St, Dublin 2, is open from 10 am to 5 pm Monday to Saturday, 2 to 6 pm Sunday and holidays, May to September. Entry is IR£1.75 (students IR£1.40, children 90p).

Irish Traditional Music Archive At 63 Merrion Square South, this archive (☎ 661 9699) collects, preserves and organises traditional Irish music. It's open to the public by appointment.

Geological Survey of Ireland The Geological Survey of Ireland (☎ 660 9511) at Haddington Rd, Dublin 4, has exhibits on the geology and mineral resources of Ireland. It's open Monday to Friday from 2.30 to 4.30 pm.

Irish Jewish Museum The Irish Jewish Museum (☎ 53 4754) at 3/4 Walworth Rd, off Victoria St, Portobello, Dublin 8, is housed in what was once a synagogue and relates the history of Ireland's Jewish community. It's open Sunday, Tuesday and Thursday from 11 am to 3.30 pm.

Museum of Childhood The Museum of Childhood (☎ 97 3223) is at The Palms, 20 Palmerston Park, Rathmines, Dublin 6, south of the centre. Its main display is a collection of dolls, some of them nearly 300 years old. The museum is open Sunday from 2 to 5.30 pm and may be open longer hours during the summer months. Entry is IR£1 (children 75p).

Irish Architectural Archive & Architecture Centre The Irish Architectural Archive at 73 Merrion Square South, Dublin 2, traces Dublin's architectural history from 1560 to the current day. The archive is housed in a fine 1793 town house. The Royal Institute of the Architects of Ireland has its headquarters across the square at 8 Merrion Square North and exhibits and displays are also held there.

Plunkett Museum of Irish Education The Plunkett Museum of Irish Education (☎ 97 0033) is at the Church of Ireland College of Education, Rathmines Rd Upper, Dublin 6, and is open on Wednesday from 2.30 to 5 pm.

Other Galleries

Apart from the National Gallery and the IMMA south of the river and the Hugh Lane Municipal Gallery of Modern Art north of the river, there are also a great many private galleries, arts centres and corporate exhibition areas.

The Douglas Hyde Gallery (☎ 70 2116) is in the Arts Building in Trinity College, and the entrance is on Nassau St. The City Arts Centre (☎ 677 0643) at 23/25 Moss St has changing exhibitions in its Gallery 1 and Gallery 2. The galleries are open Monday to Saturday from 11 am to 5 pm and entry is free. In the Bank of Ireland building on Baggot St Lower, just past Fitz-william St towards the tourist office and Ballsbridge, there are changing displays of contemporary Irish art. Other Dublin galleries include:

Andrew's Lane Theatre Gallery
  9/17 Andrew's Lane, Exchequer St, Dublin 2 (☎ 679 5720)
Apollo Gallery
  17 Duke St, Dublin 2 (☎ 671 2609)
Arts Council
  70 Merrion Square, Dublin 2 (☎ 661 1840)
Basement Art Gallery
  14 Bachelor's Walk, Dublin 1 (☎ 672 3370)
Duke St Gallery of Art
  17 Duke St, Dublin 2 (☎ 671 2609)
ENFO
  17 St Andrew's St, Dublin 3 (☎ 679 3144)
European Modern Art
  5 Clare St, Dublin 2 (☎ 676 5371)
Gallery of Photography
  37/39 Wellington Quay, Dublin 2 (☎ 671 4654)
Graphic Studio
  Dublin Cope St, Dublin 2 (☎ 679 8021)
Gutter Gallery
  above Cellary Restaurant, Fownes St Lower, Dublin 2
Irish Life Mall
  Abbey St, Dublin 1 (☎ 704 2000)

Kennedy Gallery
    12 Harcourt St, Dublin 2 (☎ 475 1749)
Kerlin Gallery
    38 Dawson St, Dublin 2 (☎ 677 9652)
Oliver Dowling Gallery
    19 Kildare St, Dublin 2 (☎ 676 6573)
Pantheon Gallery
    6 Dawson St, Dublin 2 (☎ 671 1105)
Project Arts Centre
    39 East Essex St, Dublin 2 (☎ 671 2321)
Riverrun Gallery
    82 Dame St, Dublin 2 (☎ 679 8606)
Rubicon Gallery
    11 Mount St Upper, Dublin 2 (☎ 676 2331)
Solomon Gallery
    top floor, Powerscourt Townhouse Shopping Centre,
    William St South, Dublin 2 (☎ 679 4237)
Taylor Galleries
    34 Kildare St, Dublin 2 (☎ 676 6055)
Temple Bar Gallery & Studios
    4/8 Temple Bar, Dublin 2 (☎ 671 0073)
Tom Caldwell Gallery
    31 Fitzwilliam St Upper, Dublin 2 (☎ 668 8629)
Wyvern Gallery
    26 Temple Lane, Dublin 2 (☎ 679 9589)

SPORTS & ACTIVITIES

Dublin offers plenty of sporting opportunities for both
spectators and participants.

Golf

Golf is enormously popular in Ireland and there are
many fine golf courses. Typical fees range from around
IR£10 to IR£25 a day; in Ireland fees are usually based
on a per day rather than a per round basis. Public courses
include Corballs at Donabate (24 km) and Deer Park at
Howth (15 km). There are more than 20 private nine-hole
and 18-hole club courses in and around Dublin as well
as a great many short 'Pitch & Putt' courses.

If you prefer to spectate rather than participate, the
annual Irish Open takes place in June.

Hurling

Hurling, that most Irish of sports, has a legendary beginning in the tale of Sétante, the five-year-old hurling
genius and nephew of King Conor of Ulaid (Ulster) who
later became known as Cuchulainn. Hurling encompasses elements of hockey and lacrosse and players can

hit the ball along the ground or through the air or can even carry it on the end of their hurley or *camán*.

The All Ireland Hurling Final takes place on the first Sunday in September at Dublin's Croke Park and attracts a crowd of 60,000 to 80,000 spectators. Dublin itself is not, however, a great power in hurling. The best teams are more likely to come from Kilkenny or Cork.

Gaelic Football

The most popular sport in Ireland, Gaelic football is, like hurling, a high-speed, attacking sport. It features a round ball which can be kicked along the ground as in soccer or passed between players as in rugby. Australian Rules football has many similarities with Gaelic football, and some Irish players have gone on to become major stars in Australia.

The All Ireland Football Final takes place at Dublin's Croke Park on the third Sunday in September.

Football & Rugby

The truly Gaelic sports, hurling and Gaelic football, have their greatest following in rural Ireland and it's probably true to say that football (soccer) and rugby are even more popular in Dublin itself. It's often claimed that the most popular Irish football team is Liverpool! Ireland is, however, a major power in rugby and great attention is paid to the annual Five Nations Championship, which pits Ireland against England, Wales, Scotland and France. Even more passion is likely to be roused when Ireland plays against Australia. A mecca for Irish rugby enthusiasts is the Lansdowne Rd grounds in Ballsbridge.

Horse Racing

The Irish love of horse racing can be observed at Leopardstown and Phoenix Park, Dublin's two central racecourses. There are several others within an hour's drive of the city. The Irish Grand National is held on Easter Monday at Fairyhouse, 25 km north of Dublin. Other courses are the classic Curragh course (50 km west) where many important races are held, Navan (50 km north-west) and Punchestown near Naas (40 km south-west).

Horses of a different breed can be found at the horse-trading market behind the Four Courts building in central Dublin on the first Sunday of each month.

Beaches & Swimming

Dublin is hardly the sort of place to work on your suntan and even a hot Irish summer day is unlikely to raise the water temperature above freezing. However, there are some pleasant beaches and chilly temperatures or not, many Joyce fans feel compelled to take a dip in the 40 Foot Pool at Dun Laoghaire (see the Seaside Suburbs chapter). Sandy beaches near the centre include Dollymount (six km), Sutton (11 km), Portmarnock (11 km), Malahide (11 km), Claremount (14 km) and Donabate (21 km). Although the beach at Sandymount is not so special, it is only five km from central Dublin. There are outdoor public pools at Blackrock, Clontarf and Dun Laoghaire.

Scuba Diving

The Irish Underwater Council (☎ 872 7011) is on the 2nd floor, 5/7 O'Connell St Upper, Dublin 1. They publish the quarterly magazine *Subsea*. Oceantec (☎ 280 1083) is a dive shop in Dun Laoghaire that organises local dives. See Dun Laoghaire in the Seaside Suburbs chapter for more information.

Sailing & Windsurfing

Howth and Dun Laoghaire are the major sailing centres in the Dublin area, but you can also go sailing at Clontarf, Kilbarrack, Malahide, Rush, Skerries, Sutton and Swords. See the Dun Laoghaire section in the Seaside Suburbs chapter for details of the sailing clubs there. The Irish Sailing Association (☎ 280 0239) is at 3 Park Rd, Dun Laoghaire.

Dinghy sailing courses are offered by the Irish National Sailing School (☎ 280 6654), 115 George's St Lower, Dun Laoghaire, and by the Fingall Sailing School (☎ 845 1979) Upper Strand, Broadmeadow Estuary, Malahide.

Windsurfing enthusiasts can head to the Surfdock Centre (☎ 668 3945) at the Grand Canal Dock, Dock Rd South, Ringsend, Dublin 4. This expanse of water is beside the River Liffey, where the Grand Canal connects with the Liffey, and makes a good windsurfing site right in the city. Surfdock runs windsurfing courses here costing from IR£25 for a three-hour 'taster' session to IR£50-80 for longer courses. You can also rent sailboards from IR£6 an hour.

Top & Bottom: Punters at the races (JM)

Top: Howth Harbour (JM)
Middle: Ireland versus Australia, World Cup 1992 (JM)
Bottom: Windsurfing, Dublin Bay (JM)

Fishing

Fishing tackle shops in Dublin can supply permits, equipment, bait and advice. Check the classified phone directory under Fishing Gear & Tackle. Sea fishing is popular at Howth, Dun Laoghaire and Greystones. The River Liffey has salmon fishing (only fair) and trout fishing (good). Brown trout are found between Celbridge and Millicent Bridge, near Clane, 20 km from the centre. The Dublin Trout Anglers' Association has fishing rights along parts of this stretch of the Liffey and on the River Tolka.

Gliding & Hang-Gliding

Phone ☎ 31 4551 for information on hang-gliding from the Sugar Loaf in County Wicklow. Contact the Dublin Gliding Club (☎ 282 0759, 298 3994) for information on gliding.

Other Sports

Greyhound racing takes places at Harold's Cross and Shelbourne Park. Polo matches take place in Phoenix Park on Wednesdays, Saturdays and Sundays. Car and motorcycle races are held at Mondello Park, though they have also been held in Phoenix Park, right in the city. Ireland is not a major player in the cricket world but the Irish national team can sometimes be seen playing on the green at College Park in Trinity College. The Dublin Ice Rink (☎ 53 2170) is at Dolphin's Barn, Dublin 8, and is open Monday to Friday from 2.30 to 5 pm and 7.30 to 10.30 pm. There are half a dozen 10-pin bowling centres around Dublin – check the classified phone directory. Squash and tennis courts can also be found in and around the city.

Places to Stay

Dublin has a wide range of accommodation possibilities, but in summer finding a bed can be difficult in anything from the cheapest hostel to the most expensive five-star hotel. If you can plan well ahead and book your room, it will make life easier, but the alternative is to head straight for one of the Dublin Tourism or Irish Tourist Board offices and ask them to book you a room. For a flat fee of IR£1 plus a 10% deposit on the cost of the first night, they will find you somewhere to stay, and will do so efficiently and with a smile. Sometimes this may require a great deal of phoning around so it can be a pound well spent.

The tourist offices are listed in the Facts for the Visitor chapter under Tourist Information. There are offices at Dublin Airport, beside the ferry terminal at Dun Laoghaire, and at three locations in the city. Accommodation in central Dublin can be neatly divided into areas north and south of the River Liffey. The south side is generally neater, tidier and more expensive than the north side. In compensation north-side prices are often lower for equivalent standards. Prices drop as you move away from the centre so you can go farther out for cheaper prices or for better standards at the same price.

Accommodation prices can vary between the high and low seasons and reach even greater heights at peak holiday periods or on public holidays. Prices quoted are generally those for the high season but can be expected to increase. You can usually get a bed in a hostel for IR£6 to IR£10. In a typical B&B the cost per person will be around IR£15 to IR£20. More expensive B&Bs or middle-range hotels will cost around IR£20 to IR£40 per person. Dublin's deluxe hotels will cost from IR£50 per person.

All the places listed in this chapter are in central Dublin or nearby suburbs. The seaside suburbs of Dun Laoghaire and Howth are within easy commuting distance of the centre by car or DART (Dublin Area Rapid Transit) and these possibilities are covered in the Seaside Suburbs chapter.

Camping

There's no convenient central camping ground in Dublin. *Do not* try to camp in Phoenix Park – a German cyclist camping there was murdered in 1991. The *Shankill Caravan & Camping Park* (☎ 282 0011) is 16 km south of

the centre on the N11 Wexford Rd. A site for two costs
IR£5 in summer. You can get there on a No 45 or 46 bus
from Eden Quay. Other sites are *Donabate* near Swords
and *Cromlech* just beyond Dun Laoghaire.

Hostels

Since there are no conveniently central camp sites in
Dublin, shoestring travellers usually head for one of
Dublin's numerous hostels. One is operated by An Óige,
the national youth hostel association, whereas the others
are independently run. Hostels offer the cheapest accommodation and are also great centres for meeting
other travellers and exchanging information. In summer
(late June to late September) they can be heavily booked
but then so is everything else.

Usually in a hostel you simply get a bed and this can
mean a bunk in a crowded dormitory. On the other hand
some of the hostels also offer smaller rooms or even
singles and doubles, but at a higher cost, of course. A
bunk room for four or more can be ideal for a budget-
minded family group.

The An Óige Dublin International Youth Hostel is open
to members of the International Youth Hostel Federation
(IYHF), members of An Óige (annual membership costs
IR£7.50), or to any overseas visitor for an additional nightly
charge of IR£1.25. Pay the additional charge six times (total
IR£7.50) and you become an IYHF member. To use the
hostel, you must have or hire a sleeping sheet.

Nowhere else in Europe have independent hostels
popped up as they have in Ireland and they are well
represented in Dublin. Independent hostels are usually
slightly cheaper than the An Óige ones. They emphasise
their easy-going ambience and lack of rules, and competition from them has forced the official hostels to rethink
their rule book in recent years.

North of the Liffey Despite Dublin's plentiful
supply of hostels, they can all be booked out at the height
of the summer rush. The *Dublin International Youth Hostel*
(☎ 30 1766) on Mountjoy St is a big and well-equipped
hostel in a restored and converted old building. From
Dublin Airport, bus No 41A will drop you off in Dorset
St Upper, a few minutes' walk from the hostel. It's a
longer walk from the bus and train stations but it's well
signposted. The hostel is in the run-down northern area
of the city centre, though not in the worst part of it. The
nightly cost is IR£9 and there's an overflow hostel for the
height of the summer crush.

Just round the corner from the An Óige hostel is the

middle-sized *Young Traveller Hostel* (☎ 30 5000) on St
Mary's Place, just off Dorset St Upper. All the rooms
accommodate four people and have a shower and wash-
basin but there are no kitchen facilities. The nightly cost
is IR£8.50 including breakfast.

Cardijin House Hostel (☎ 878 8484), subtitled 'Goin' My
Way', is a smaller, older hostel centrally located at 15
Talbot St, not far from O'Connell St. The nightly cost is
IR£6 plus 50p for a shower. The *Marlborough Hostel*
(☎ 878 8484) is at 81/82 Marlborough St, right behind the
Dublin Tourism office and next to the Pro-Cathedral. It
has dorms accommodating four to 10 people and the
nightly cost is IR£7.50 per person irrespective of the
dorm size. Double rooms cost IR£11 per person.

For bus and train station convenience you can't beat
the big *Dublin Tourist Hostel* (☎ 36 3877), better known as
Isaac's. It's at 2/5 Frenchman's Lane, a stone's throw
from the Busáras or Connolly Railway Station, and not
far from the popular restaurants and pubs on either side
of the Liffey. In some rooms traffic noise is the penalty
for the central location. This very well equipped hostel
is in a converted 18th century wine warehouse. It costs
IR£5.50 to IR£6.25 for dorms, IR£11.25 each for doubles
or IR£15.25 for singles. The restaurant is good value.

South of the Liffey South of the Liffey, *Kinlay House*
(☎ 679 6644) is also very centrally located but, again,
some rooms can suffer from traffic noise. It's right beside
Christ Church Cathedral at 2/12 Lord Edward St. Kinlay
House is big and well equipped and costs from IR£8.50
per person for four-bed dorms, IR£10.50 to IR£13 for the
better rooms (some with bathrooms) and IR£17 for a
single. A continental breakfast is included.

Avalon House (☎ 475 0001) at 55 Aungier St is nicely
positioned just west of St Stephen's Green. It's in an old
building that was comprehensively renovated and
opened in 1992. It is very well equipped and some of the
cleverly designed rooms have mezzanine levels, which
are great for families. The basic nightly cost is IR£7
including a continental breakfast. A bed in a room with
attached bathroom costs IR£11 in the four-bed rooms,
IR£12.50 in the two-bed rooms. The largest dorms
accommodate eight. To get there take bus No 16, 16A, 19
or 22 right to the door or No 11, 13 or 46A to nearby St
Stephen's Green. From the Dun Laoghaire ferry terminal
you can take a No 46A bus to St Stephen's Green or the
DART to Pearse Station.

Student Accommodation

In the summer months you can stay at Trinity College or University College Dublin (UCD). Trinity College sometimes has accommodation on campus in the city, but it's expensive at IR£25 per person. At *Trinity Hall* (☎ 97 1772), Dartry Rd, Rathmines, rates are IR£14 to IR£17 for singles or IR£12 to IR£15 if you share a twin. If you're under 25 and have a student card, the price may drop. There are some family rooms where children aged under 10 can stay for free with two adults. To get there, take bus No 14/14A from D'Olier St beside the O'Connell Bridge.

UCD Village (☎ 269 7696) is six km south of the centre, en route to Dun Laoghaire. Accommodation here is in apartments, with three single rooms sharing a bathroom and a kitchen/meals/living area. It's very modern and well appointed but a little far out and, at IR£16.50 (IR£96 a week), rather expensive. For a family a three-room apartment at IR£48 could be good value. If you have a car, the ease of parking may compensate for the distance; if you don't, bus No 10 departs every 10 minutes from O'Connell St/St Stephen's Green and goes direct to the campus. After 5 pm on Saturday and all day Sunday you have to switch to a No 46A from Fleet St near Trinity College and ask for the Montrose Hotel stop. Either way the fare is 95p.

Bed & Breakfasts

Throughout Ireland B&Bs are the backbone of cheap accommodation and they are well represented in Dublin. B&Bs are generally small and are often just a handful of rooms in a private house, though some places cross the line to become guesthouses. They often present opportunities to meet the Irish on less formal lines than at a regular hotel. The Irish Tourist Board offices will make bookings and direct you to a suitable choice.

In Dublin B&Bs cost around IR£15 to IR£20 per person per night, including breakfast, of course. The cheaper B&Bs usually do not have private bathrooms, but where they do the cost is often just a pound or two more. Dublin also has some more luxuriously equipped B&Bs costing from IR£25 per person, but this category is usually monopolised by the boutique hotels and guesthouses. At some places the per person costs are higher for a single room.

Since most B&Bs are very small (just two to four rooms), they can quickly fill up in summer. With so many to try there's bound to be someone with a spare room, but you may find yourself staying some distance from the centre. If you arrive when accommodation is tight and you don't like the location offered, the best advice is to take it and at the same time try to book something more conveniently located for subsequent nights. Booking just one or two days ahead can often provide a much better choice.

Breakfast at a B&B almost invariably comprises cereal followed by 'a fry', which means fried eggs, bacon and sausages. A week of B&B breakfasts exceeds every known international guideline for cholesterol intake, but if you decline fried food, you are left with cereal and toast. If your bloodstream can take it, you'll have enough food to last till dinner time, but it's a shame more places don't offer alternatives like fruit or the delicious variety of Irish breads and scones. The more expensive B&Bs usually offer a better choice at breakfast time.

There are several good hunting grounds for B&Bs in Dublin. If you want something cheap but close to the city, Gardiner St Upper and Lower in Dublin 1 on the north side of the Liffey is the place to look. It's a rather grotty and run-down area and not the prettiest part of Dublin, but it is cheap.

If you're willing to travel farther out, you can find a better price and quality combination on the coast south of the centre at Dun Laoghaire (see the Dun Laoghaire section in the Seaside Suburbs chapter) or north of the centre at Clontarf. The Ballsbridge embassy zone, just south of the centre, offers convenience and quality but you pay more for the combination. Other suburbs to try are Sandymount (immediately east of Ballsbridge) and Drumcondra (north of the centre en route to the airport).

Gardiner St Along Gardiner St there is a large collection of places on Gardiner St Lower, near the bus and railway stations, and another group on Gardiner St Upper, farther north near Mountjoy Square. This is definitely not the prettiest area of Dublin but the B&Bs are respectable if rather basic.

O'Brien's Hotel (☎ 874 5203) at 38/39 Gardiner St Lower is a more expensive place with singles from IR£22 to IR£26 and doubles from IR£40 to IR£50. There are 22 rooms in this large and rather plain place, but only a handful with attached bathrooms. At 75 Gardiner St Lower is the *Maple Guest House* (☎ 874 0225, 874 5239) which has singles/doubles for IR£27.50/40 or IR£37.50/60 with attached bathroom.

The extremely plain and rather threadbare *Harvey's Guesthouse* (☎ 874 8384) at 11 Gardiner St Upper and *Stella Maris* (☎ 874 0835) next door at No 13 are near Mountjoy Square. Singles are IR£16, doubles IR£28 to

IR£32. There are several more B&Bs in the next few buildings, such as *Flynn's B&B* (☎ 874 1702) at No 15, *Carmel House* (☎ 874 1639) at No 16 and *Fatima House* (☎ 874 5410) at No 17. Just off Gardiner St Upper from Mountjoy Square at 3/4 Gardiner Place is the *Dergvale Hotel* (☎ 874 4753, 874 3361). Regular rooms are slightly more expensive, and singles/doubles with attached bathroom cost IR£26/44.

Hardwicke St is only a short walk from these Gardiner St Upper places and has a number of popular B&Bs, such as *Waverley House* (☎ 874 6132) at No 4 or *Sinclair House* (☎ 874 6132) next door at No 3. At these places singles cost IR£16 to IR£20 and doubles IR£28 to IR£32.

Clontarf There are numerous places along Clontarf Rd, about five km from the centre. One of these is the friendly *Ferryview* (☎ 33 5893) at No 96. Farther along there's the slightly more expensive *White House* (☎ 33 3196) at No 125, *San Vista* (☎ 33 9582) at No 237, *Bayview* (☎ 33 9870) at No 265, *Sea-Front* (☎ 33 6118) at No 278 and *Sea Breeze* (☎ 33 2787) at No 312. These Clontarf Rd B&Bs typically cost IR£14 to IR£20 for singles, IR£25 to IR£35 for doubles. Bus No 30 from Abbey St will get you there for 95p.

Ballsbridge & Donnybrook Ballsbridge is not only the embassy quarter and the site for a number of upper bracket hotels but is also the locale for a number of better quality B&Bs, such as *Morehampton Townhouse* (☎ 660 2106, fax 660 2566) at 46 Morehampton Rd, Donnybrook, directly opposite the Sachs Hotel. Singles/doubles are IR£33/50. All rooms are centrally heated and have bathrooms and the excellent breakfast proves that there can be more to life than just bacon and eggs.

Mrs O'Donoghue's (☎ 668 1105) convivial but signless place at 41 Northumberland Rd costs IR£24/40. Despite its imposing Victorian presence there are only eight rooms in this fine and very traditional B&B.

Middle-Range Guesthouses & Hotels

The line dividing B&Bs, guesthouses or cheaper hotels is often a hazy one. Places in this middle-range bracket usually cost from IR£25 to IR£50 per night per person. Some of the small, centrally located, boutique-style hotels in this category are among the most enjoyable places to stay in Dublin.

These middle-range places are a big jump up from the cheaper B&Bs in facilities and price but still cost a lot less than Dublin's expensive hotels. Another advantage of many of these places, compared with either cheaper or more expensive accommodation, is that breakfast is usually provided (it usually isn't in the top-notch hotels) and it's a very good breakfast (unlike that offered by the base-level B&Bs). Many of these hotels offer fruit, a choice of cereals, croissants, scones and other morning delights. And bacon and eggs as well, of course – this is still Ireland.

These middle-range places are broken down by area: Dublin 1 is north central Dublin, Dublin 2 is south central Dublin, and everywhere else usually means the suburbs just south of the centre.

North of the Liffey – Dublin 1 Just north of the Liffey at 35/36 Abbey St Lower is *Wynn's Hotel* (☎ 874 6131, fax 677 7487). This older hotel is only a few steps away from the Abbey Theatre. It has 63 rooms, all with attached bathroom, which cost IR£45/72 for singles/doubles. Right by the river the *Ormond Hotel* (☎ 872 1811, fax 872 1909), Ormond Quay Upper, Dublin 1, has 55 rooms with attached bathroom for IR£50/76. A plaque outside notes its role in *Ulysses*.

Farther from the river is *Barry's Hotel* (☎ 874 6943, fax 874 6508) at 1/2 Great Denmark St, just off Parnell Square. It's only a few minutes' walk from O'Connell St but it's on the edge of the better part of north Dublin, before the decline sets in. The hotel's 30 recently refurbished rooms cost IR£29.75/59.50 with attached bathroom.

Across the road is the *Belvedere Hotel* (☎ 872 8522, 874 1413) opposite Belvedere College, which James Joyce attended as a boy. The 40 rooms, all with attached bathroom, cost IR£30/60 for singles/doubles.

South of the Liffey – Dublin 2 The *Fitzwilliam* (☎ 660 0448, fax 676 7488) at 41 Fitzwilliam St Upper, Dublin 2, is very centrally located, right on the corner of Baggot St Lower. Despite this location it's surprisingly quiet at night. There are 12 rooms in this recently renovated small hotel, all of which have en suite bathroom, costing IR£41/72 for singles/doubles at the height of the summer season.

Even more central is *Georgian House* (☎ 661 8832, fax 661 8834) at 20/21 Baggot St Lower, equally close to St Stephen's Green or Merrion Square. Once again this is a fine old Georgian building in excellent condition. Its 34 rooms all have attached bathrooms and cost IR£45/72 in summer. The breakfast is excellent and at night the restaurant is noted for its seafood. There's also a car park.

Also close to St Stephen's Green is the *Harcourt Hotel* (☎ 478 3677, fax 75 2013) at 60 Harcourt St. Set in a magnificent Georgian building, this hotel has 22 rooms which cost IR£35/60 or IR£55/100 for the rooms with attached bathroom. George Bernard Shaw lived here from 1874 to 1876. Closer to the green at 21/25 Harcourt St is the *Russell Court Hotel* (☎ 478 4991, fax 478 1576) with 21 rooms, all with attached bathroom and costing IR£57/82 a night.

Another place off St Stephen's Green is *Leeson Court* (☎ 676 3380, fax 661 8273) at 26/27 Leeson St Lower, at the start of Dublin's nightclub block. The 20 rooms have attached bathrooms and cost IR£55-60 for singles and IR£76-88 for doubles.

At 6/8 Wellington Quay, overlooking the River Liffey and backing on to the fascinating Temple Bar area, is the *Clarence Hotel* (☎ 677 6178, fax 677 7487), a larger old hotel. There are 67 rooms, all en suite, with nightly costs of IR£45/72. The hotel was bought by the rock band U2 in late 1992.

Elsewhere in Dublin *Ariel House* (☎ 668 5512, fax 668 5845) is at 52 Lansdowne Rd, Dublin 4, two km south-east of the centre in the Ballsbridge area. It's conveniently close to Lansdowne Rd Station and near the big Berkeley Court Hotel. There are 27 rooms, all en suite, and the nightly cost is IR£50/100 for singles/doubles, but breakfast is extra.

Continue down Lansdowne Rd and it changes names to Herbert Rd, where you will find the *Mt Herbert* (☎ 668 4321, fax 660 7077) at 7 Herbert Rd, Dublin 4, about three km from the centre. This larger hotel was once the Dublin residence of an English lord. There are 135 rooms, most of them en suite, which cost IR£53/57, but breakfast is extra.

The *Ashling Hotel* (☎ 677 2324) is on Parkgate St, Dublin 8, 2.5 km from the centre and directly across the river from Heuston Station. This well-equipped hotel has 56 rooms costing IR£48.50/70 for singles/doubles.

Expensive Hotels

Above IR£50 per person or IR£100 for a double is Dublin's top bracket. Hotels in this price range are divided into two categories: the city's best hotels, most of them categorised as A* hotels by the Irish Tourist Board and all of them costing well over IR£100 for a double; and the other expensive hotels, which fall just below the top bracket in standards and price but are still somewhat more expensive than the middle range.

Almost-but-not-quite Top Bracket At the top end of O'Connell St in north Dublin, farther up from the Gresham Hotel, is the *Royal Dublin Hotel* (☎ 873 3666, fax 873 3120). It has 117 rooms at IR£81/108 for singles/doubles.

The nicely situated new *Bloom's Hotel* (☎ 671 5622 & 671 5508, fax 671 5997) is on Anglesea St, right behind the Bank of Ireland in the colourful Temple Bar district. The hotel has 86 rooms costing IR£90/110 for singles/doubles. Just on the other side of Dame St from Temple Bar is the *Central Hotel* (☎ 679 7302, fax 679 7303) at 1/5 Exchequer St, which has 68 rooms at IR£95/140 without breakfast. It has recently been comprehensively renovated and though the rooms are rather small it's very well located.

Close to the National Museum, *Buswells* (☎ 676 4013 & 661 3888, fax 676 2090) is on Molesworth St and has singles/doubles for IR£57/90 without breakfast. The small *Longfield's* (☎ 676 1367, fax 676 1542) is at 9/10 Fitzwilliam St Lower, between Merrion and Fitzwilliam squares, and has 26 rooms at IR£85/99 for singles/doubles.

Stephen's Hall (☎ 661 0585, fax 661 0606) is just a stone's throw from the south-east corner of St Stephen's Green at 14/17 Leeson St Lower. The 37 rooms, all with attached bathroom, cost IR£90/130, including breakfast.

In Donnybrook, just beyond Ballsbridge, is the *Sachs Hotel* (☎ 668 0995, fax 668 6147) at 19/29 Morehampton Rd, Dublin 4. This is about three km south-east of the centre. This small but elegant and expensive place has 20 rooms, all en suite, costing IR£82/124.

The Top Bracket Dublin has seven hotels which have the Irish Tourist Board's A* rating. Even a single room at these hotels can cost IR£100 or more, though most guests will have probably booked through an agency or as part of a package and obtained some sort of discount from the rack (published) rates. Three of them (the Shelbourne, Conrad and Westbury) are close to the centre in the area of south Dublin which is ranked as the best part of the city. A fourth central hotel, the *Mont Clare*, only rates an A, but is up there with the best of them pricewise.

Three more of them (the Berkeley Court, Burlington and Jury's) are a couple of km south of the city centre, near the Ballsbridge embassy zone. The final one (Gresham Hotel) is just north of the River Liffey, in the less salubrious part of Dublin, but well located on O'Connell St, Dublin's premier boulevard.

The city's best known hotel is the elegant *Shelbourne*, strategically placed overlooking St Stephen's Green and indubitably the best address to meet at in Dublin. Despite the prices the rooms are a little cramped, but afternoon tea at the Shelbourne is something all Dublin visitors should experience, regardless of whether they stay there.

The *Conrad* is run, of course, by the Hilton group and is on Earlsfort Terrace, just south of St Stephen's Green. This popular business hotel is one of Dublin's newest. Also close to St Stephen's Green, the modern *Westbury* is in a small lane just off Grafton St, the pedestrianised main shopping street of south Dublin. Rooms on the upper floors offer views of the Dublin Hills. The *Mont Clare* is a classic old hotel on elegant Merrion Square, just

Shelbourne Hotel (TW)

minutes' walk from the National Gallery, Leinster House, Trinity College and other central Dublin locations. The newest top-bracket hotel in Dublin is the *Davenport Hotel*, which opened in mid-1993 opposite the Mont Clare on Westland Row. *Berkeley Court*, south-east of the centre in Ballsbridge in a quiet and relaxed location on Lansdowne Rd, offers spacious rooms. Ireland's largest hotel, the modern *Burlington* is also south of the centre, just beyond the Grand Canal on Leeson St Upper. In the same general area is *Jury's Hotel & Towers*, a large, modern hotel on Pembroke Rd. In the summer months the Irish Cabaret here is a popular attraction.

The long-established *Gresham* is on O'Connell St Upper, the imposing main street of north Dublin and indeed the best known street in the city.

Berkeley Court Hotel A*
Lansdowne Rd, Dublin 4; two km from the centre, 195 rooms, swimming pool, IR£140/156 (☎ 660 1711, fax 661 7238)
Burlington Hotel A*
Leeson St Upper, Dublin 4; two km from the centre, 451 rooms, IR£92/135 (☎ 660 5222, fax 660 8496)
Conrad Hotel A*
Earlsfort Terrace, Dublin 2; 190 rooms, IR£135/160 (☎ 676 5555, fax 676 5076)
Davenport Hotel
Westland Row, Dublin 2; 90 rooms, IR£110/140 (☎ 661 6799, fax 661 9555),
Gresham Hotel A*
O'Connell St Upper, Dublin 1; 191 rooms, IR£110/140 (☎ 874 6881, fax 878 7175)
Jury's Hotel & Towers A*
Ballsbridge, Dublin 4; 2½ km from the centre, 384 rooms, swimming pool, IR£101/119 (☎ 660 5000, fax 660 5540)
Mont Clare Hotel A
Merrion Square, Dublin 2; 74 rooms, IR£150 (☎ 661 6799, fax 661 5663)
Shelbourne Hotel A*
St Stephen's Green, Dublin 2; 142 rooms, IR£150 for singles, from IR£180 for doubles (☎ 676 6471, fax 661 6006)
Westbury Hotel A*
off Grafton St, Dublin 2; 195 rooms, IR£140/156 (☎ 679 1122, fax 679 7078)

Airport Hotels There are several hotels near Dublin Airport, including the large *Forte Crest Hotel* (☎ 844 4211, fax 842 5874), off the N1 Motorway beside the airport. There are 188 rooms costing IR£110/140 for singles/doubles.

Places to Eat

FOOD IN IRELAND

It's frequently said that Irish cooking doesn't match up to the ingredients and traditional Irish cooking tends to imitate English – that is, cook it until it's dead. Fortunately, the Irish seem to be doing a better job than the English in kicking that habit and you will find it's no problem to eat very well. Of course, if you want meat or fish cooked until it's dried and shrivelled and vegetables turned to mush there are plenty of places that can still perform this feat.

Fast food is well established, ranging from traditional fish and chips to more recent arrivals like burgers, pizzas, kebabs and tacos. You'll find branches of McDonald's and Burger Kings, plus the local pizza chain La Pizza and a great many other pizza specialists. You'll also find numerous branches of *Abrakebabra*, an Irish chain offering kebabs and other vaguely Middle Eastern fast food. It's a good alternative to the more familiar international chains.

Pubs are often good places to eat, particularly at lunch time, when a bowl of the soup of the day (usually vegetable) and some good bread can make a fine and economical meal. Seafood restaurants, long neglected in Ireland, are often very good and there are some superb vegetarian places.

Irish bread has a wonderful reputation and indeed is very good, but unfortunately there's a tendency to fall back on the infamous white-sliced bread (*pan* in Irish). B&Bs are often guilty of this crime. Irish scones are a delight, however, and tea and scones are a great snack at any time of day. Even pubs will often offer tea and scones. See Bed & Breakfasts in the Places to Stay chapter for information about the famous Irish breakfast.

DRINK

In Ireland a drink means a beer – either lager or stout. Stout usually means Guinness, the famous black beer of Dublin, though in Cork it can mean a Murphy's or a Beamish. If you don't develop a taste for stout (and you should at least try), a wide variety of lager beers are available, including Irish Harp or Smithwicks and many locally brewed 'imports' like Budweiser, Foster's or

Heineken. Simply asking for a Guinness or a Harp will get you a pint (570 ml, IR£1.70 to IR£2 in a pub). If you want a half-pint (90p to IR£1.10) ask for a 'glass' or a 'half'. Children are allowed in pubs until 7 or 8 pm at night, and in smaller towns at least this restriction is treated with customary Irish flexibility.

Another traditionally Irish drink, though of recent origin, is Irish coffee. It's essentially strong, hot, creamed coffee with a healthy shot of Irish whiskey.

SPECIALITIES & SPECIAL HOURS

If you're looking for certain types of restaurants (Irish food, seafood, vegetarian food or one of Dublin's top-bracket restaurants) or for meals at certain hours (an early breakfast or a late-night snack) some suggestions follow. The places mentioned are then covered in more detail in the Where to Eat section, which lists restaurants by area.

Irish Dishes

There are various traditional Irish dishes and several restaurants in Dublin where you can find them – see the information that follows on Gallagher's Boxty House and The Broker's Restaurant in or near Temple Bar, The Bailey off Grafton St and Paddy's Place in north Dublin. Dublin's pure and simple Irish specialist is Oisin's on Camden St Upper. Irish dishes and specialities you might like to try include:

Bacon & Cabbage
   a stew consisting simply of its two named ingredients: bacon and cabbage
Barm Brack
   an Irish cake-like bread
Boxtys
   rather like a filled pancake
Dublin Coddle
   a semi-thick stew made with sausages, bacon, onions and potatoes
Guinness Cake
   a popular fruitcake flavoured with Guinness beer
Irish Stew
   this quintessential Irish dish is a stew of mutton, potatoes and onions, flavoured with parsley and thyme and simmered slowly
Soda Bread
   Belfast is probably the place in Ireland for bread at its best, but soda bread in particular, white or brown, is found throughout the country

Seafood

The curious Irish aversion to seafood probably has, like so many other Irish curiosities, a religious connection. Ireland has always been a meat-eating country but it's also been a strictly, even bizarrely, Catholic one. Until very recently the Catholic Friday fasting restrictions were strictly adhered to, so fish became something you were forced to have on Friday and, like long-suffering schoolchildren, if you're forced to eat it you don't like it. As a result Ireland is an island with a remarkably small fishing industry, and fish is still in the process of finding a place on the Irish dining table. Try it – the trout and salmon are delicious.

Seafood specialists worth sampling include the *Ante-Room* on Baggot St Lower and *King Sitric's*, looking out over the harbour at Howth (see Howth in the Seaside Suburbs chapter). *Restaurant Mahler* in the Powerscourt Townhouse Shopping Centre also has some good seafood dishes, or you can try the *Periwinkle Seafood Bar* at the same location at lunch time. The *Lobster Pot* in Ballsbridge is solidly old-fashioned and rather expensive.

For pub food with a nautical flavour try the *Lord Edward Seafood Restaurant* in the Lord Edward Pub on Christ Church Place. For Dublin's best fish and chips turn the corner to *Leo Burdock's* on Werburgh St.

Vegetarian

Despite the locals' carnivorous tendencies (a meal isn't a meal without meat) there are some excellent places for vegetarians in Dublin, particularly at lunch time. Places to try include *Cellary* and the *Well Fed Café* in Temple Bar, *Cornucopia* in Wicklow St just off Grafton St, *Blazing Salads II* in the Powerscourt Townhouse Shopping Centre and the *Coffee Bean* on Nassau St opposite Trinity College. There are also many restaurants offering international cuisines with a strong vegetarian influence (Mexican, Lebanese or Italian for example) and these days a great many other restaurants have at least some vegetarian dishes on their menu.

Expensive Restaurants

Should you run into some rich relatives and they offer to take you out for dinner, or there's somebody you need to impress, and hang the cost, Dublin has some appropriate places.

French food tends to be expensive in Dublin whether you try *Les Frères Jacques* in Temple Bar, the nouvelle cuisine specialist *Patrick Guilbaud* off Baggot St Lower or the staunchly traditional *Le Coq Hardi* towards Ballsbridge. In Ballsbridge the *Lobster Pot* is also firmly old-fashioned and pricey. *Polo One*, on the other hand, is up-to-the-minute and close to the centre at 5/6 Molesworth Place. *La Stampa* at 35 Dawson St is Dublin's upper bracket Italian restaurant.

Late Night

After Dublin's pubs close their doors you can still get a drink – either at a stiff price or after paying an equally stiff admission charge – at a number of nightspots around the centre. See the Entertainment chapter for more details. Alternatively, there are cafés and restaurants where you can sip coffee or even get a meal until well past the witching hour.

Good old *Bewley's*, for example, stays open at its Grafton St branch until 1 am on Thursday and until 2 am on Friday and Saturday. Nearby on Anne St South the *Coffee Inn* is a good place for a late-night coffee and you can sit outside, which is very pleasant on a mild summer evening. Also on Anne St South the American diner-style *Eddie Rocket's* will even sling you a very good burger until 1 am on weeknights, until 3 am on Thursday and right through to 4 am on Friday and Saturday. If you're looking for real restaurant food until reasonably late (past midnight), you could certainly do worse than try *QV-2* on St Andrew's St.

If the Leeson St nightclubs have satisfied a late-night thirst but a late-night hunger persists, try the *Hungry Wolf* at 74 Leeson St Lower on Dublin's nightclub strip. *Break for the Border* on Stephen St Lower, west of Grafton St, doles out food and entertainment.

Breakfast

Bed and breakfast is such an Irish institution that it's hardly surprising that Dublin is not the best place for breakfast. The problem is compounded by the fact that the Irish are a long way from being early risers, so even those places that do turn out a good breakfast may not do so until a discouragingly late hour. The Irish are likely to reply that holiday-makers shouldn't be concerned about being up early in any case!

A glowing exception is *Eddie Rocket's*, which not only manages to stay open amazingly late but also manages to reopen at the amazingly early hour of 7.30 am. It's just off Grafton St in central Dublin. The various *Bewley's* cafés are also excellent places for breakfast and they too open from 7.30 am.

Cornucopia, a wholefood specialist on Wicklow St, opens from 8 am Monday to Friday, from 9 am Saturday. In Temple Bar the *Elephant & Castle* will rustle up a hearty breakfast from 8 am weekdays, from 10 am weekends. *Fitzer's* on Dawson St also opens from 8 am weekdays, from 9 am Saturday. Round the corner on Nassau St *The Kilkenny Kitchen* is open from 9 am Monday to Saturday.

On Sunday, if you can hold your breakfast appetite until lunch time, head for the *Imperial Chinese Restaurant* on Wicklow St for a dim sum brunch, a popular Chinese Sunday tradition.

Other early-morning possibilities include *Restaurant Mahler* in the Powerscourt Townhouse Shopping Centre on William St South (open from 8.30 am) and *Pasta Fresca* on Chatham St (from 8 am Monday to Saturday). *Munchies* on the corner of Exchequer St and William St South is open from 7 am Monday to Saturday. There are other *Munchies* on Baggot St Lower and Pembroke St Lower. ■

WHERE TO EAT

There are several popular zones for restaurants. This chapter is divided into four areas – North of the Liffey; Temple Bar; Around Grafton St; and Merrion Row, Baggot St & Beyond. The trendy Temple Bar enclave and Dame St along its southern boundary are packed with restaurants of all types. Apart from this there are numerous restaurants on both sides of busy Grafton St and along Merrion Row and Baggot St.

North of the Liffey

Dining possibilities north of the Liffey essentially consist of fast food, cheap eats or chains. Which is not to say that you'll eat badly here, just that the choice of restaurants is much better to the south.

Fast Food O'Connell St is the fast-food centre of Dublin, not just of north Dublin. At No 34 there's an *Abrakebabra*, at No 9 there's a *Burger King*, at Nos 14 and 52 there are branches of *La Pizza* and at No 62 there's a *McDonald's*.

Cafés *Isaac's* and the *Dublin International Youth Hostel* (see Hostels in the Places to Stay chapter) both have good cafeteria-style facilities.

At 1/2 O'Connell St the *Kylemore Café* is a big, fast-food place which is also good for a cup of tea or coffee any time of day. At 5/7 O'Connell St there's the *International Food Court* with a variety of counters, including *Beshoff's* for fish and chips.

There's a *Bewley's Café* north of the Liffey at 40 Mary St. Bewley's is a Dublin institution offering good-quality food at reasonable prices. See the Bewley's & Beshoff's section later in this chapter for more details.

If you're around the Corporation Fruit Market, between Chancery St and Mary's Lane, pop in to *Paddy's Place* (☎ 873 5130) where the food is as staunchly Irish as the name. It's open from 7.30 am to 3 pm Monday to Friday so you can go there for an early breakfast or a filling lunch-time Irish stew or Dublin coddle.

Restaurants Restaurant possibilities north of the Liffey are distinctly limited but *Chapter One* (☎ 873 2266, 873 2281) at the Dublin Writers' Museum on the north side of Parnell Square is worth a look even though the food is resolutely conservative. They serve lunch and dinner and feature a pre- and post-theatre menu for literary-minded theatregoers who might be patronising the Gate Theatre, on the other side of the square.

Closer to the river at 101 Talbot St (off O'Connell St to the east and just north of the Abbey Theatre) is *101 Talbot St* (☎ 874 5011), open for lunch Monday to Saturday, dinner Tuesday to Saturday. This is a brave attempt to bring good food north of the river. The prices are reasonable and the food moderately adventurous and very well prepared.

Temple Bar

The old, interesting and rapidly revitalising Temple Bar area is Dublin's most concentrated restaurant area. It's bounded by the river to the north, Westmoreland St to the east and Christ Church Cathedral to the west. The southern boundary is Dame St and its extension, Lord Edward St, but for convenience' sake restaurants on both the northern and southern side of Dame St are listed in this section (see Map 13 at the back of this book).

Fast Food *Abrakebabra* has a branch at the O'Connell Bridge end of Westmoreland St. Ireland's most famous purveyor of fish and chips is *Beshoff's* (☎ 677 8026) at 14 Westmoreland St, also just south of O'Connell Bridge. There's now a restaurant area with waiter service upstairs.

Cafés Backpackers staying at *Kinlay House* at the Christ Church Cathedral end of Lord Edward St (see Hostels in the Places to Stay chapter) will find good cafeteria-style facilities there. The *Well Fed Café* (☎ 677 2234) at 6 Crow St is a big and busy alternative-style place with big portions of food. It's a great place for lunch or a snack and caters particularly well to vegetarians. It's open from 10.30 am to around 8.30 pm Monday to Friday, only to 4.30 pm on Saturday.

Cellary (☎ 671 0362), at 1 Fownes St just off Wellington Quay, offers 'veg and demi-veg' food! That seems to mean vegetarian but not strictly so. Either way their soup of the day or a bread roll make a tasty lunch. There's a restaurant section upstairs which opens on Thursday to Saturday evenings.

Café Carolina (☎ 671 4005) at 66 Dame St offers dishes of the shepherd's pie, lasagne or chicken curry variety. Just beyond Dublin Castle and directly opposite Christ Church Cathedral on Lord Edward St, Kinlay House's *Refectory* is a good place for lunch-time sandwiches or a quick snack at any time of day.

Italian Restaurants Temple Bar has all sorts of restaurants but the Irish passion for pasta and pizza comes through loud and clear – Italian food is definitely the number-one option.

The very popular *Bad Ass Café* (☎ 671 2596) at 9/11 Crown Alley is a cheerful and bright warehouse-style place just south of Ha'penny Bridge. It offers pretty good pizzas from IR£3 to IR£7 in a very convivial studentish atmosphere. One of its claims to fame is that Sinéad O'Connor once worked here as a waitress. A couple of doors down is *Paddy Garibaldi's* (☎ 671 7288) at 15/16 Crown Alley. Here it's that popular variation (locally at least) on Italian food – Irish-Italian – with burgers and steaks to complement the pizza and pasta.

A couple of blocks over at 20 Temple Lane is *Fat Freddy's* (☎ 679 6769), an equally popular pizzeria although the prices are a bit higher at around IR£5 to IR£9. *Pizzeria Italia* (☎ 677 8528) at 23 Temple Bar is another simple pizzeria offering classic pizzas at standard prices. It's open from Tuesday to Saturday.

You can also find pizza at the fancier *Pizza on the Corner* (☎ 671 9308) at 38/40 Parliament St on the corner of Dame St. This spacious and bright restaurant has pizzas at IR£3.25 to IR£5.25 and a wide international selection of beers at IR£1.50 and IR£2. At 71 Dame St, right beside the Olympia Theatre, *Da Lorenzo* is a basic Italian restaurant offering pasta dishes from IR£5 to IR£8 and pizzas from IR£4 to IR£7.

La Mezza Luna (☎ 671 2840) is also on Dame St but the entrance is round the corner in Temple Lane. This slightly more up-market restaurant is enormously popular, and you may have to book a table or be prepared to wait. The pasta dishes are great value at IR£4 to IR£6. It's open Monday to Thursday from 12.30 to 11 pm,

Friday and Saturday 12.30 to 11.30 pm and Sunday 4 to 10.30 pm.

Other Restaurants Despite the plethora of trattorias, ristorantes and pizzerias, there's more to Temple Bar than pasta and pizza. The *Rock Garden Café* (☎ 679 9114) (see the Discos & Nightclubs section of the Entertainment chapter) is done up in what could be called techno-sleaze style. You can get a very respectable burger or Mexican dish for IR£6 to IR£9 and get into the show at reduced price. It's at 3A Crown Alley, directly across from The Bad Ass Café.

Burgers are a speciality at the popular and bustling *Elephant & Castle* (☎ 679 3121) at 18 Temple Bar but the menu also extends to curries, and vegetarian and pasta

The Bad Ass Café (TW)

dishes and encompasses a wide range of international influences. It's also open until reasonably late every night of the week. Right next door at 20/21 Temple Bar is the equally popular *Gallagher's Boxty House* (☎ 677 2762). A boxty is rather like a stuffed pancake and tastes like an extremely bland Indian *masala dosa*. Real Irish food is not something that's widely available in Dublin so it's worth trying. On the corner of Wellington Quay and Asdills Row is *Omar Khayyam* (☎ 677 5758), a popular and very good Middle Eastern restaurant offering all the usual Lebanese-style dishes. Count on paying around IR£15 a head. You can remain in the Arab world at *Le Restaurant Casablanca* (☎ 679 9996) at 22 Temple Bar. Here the food is Moroccan and includes such North African specialities as tahini (Arab as opposed to Irish stew) and couscous. The Casablanca is open every day.

Poco Loco (☎ 679 1950) at 32 Parliament St offers very straightforward Tex-Mex interpretations of Mexican food but they do have Corona beer (cerveza if you wish!) and their combination plates are great value at IR£5 to IR£8. It's open weekdays for lunch and every day for dinner.

Dame St's international mix of restaurants includes Chinese possibilities like *Fans Cantonese Restaurant* (☎ 679 4263, 679 4273) at No 60. *Les Frères Jacques* (☎ 679 4555) at No 74 is one of Temple Bar's fancier places with set meals for IR£20. The food is as French as the name would indicate, the mood is slightly serious, and though the final bill might not be quite as high at it would be at Patrick Guilbaud or Le Coq Hardi (Dublin's other expensive French restaurants) it can still make quite a dent in your credit card limit. It's open Monday to Friday for lunch, Monday to Saturday for dinner.

Turn off Dame St into Crow St where you'll find *Tante Zoé's* (☎ 679 4407) at No 1. It's open Monday to Saturday for lunch, Monday to Sunday for dinner and is yet more proof of how cosmopolitan Dublin dining can be, since Cajun and Creole food is the speciality. The next lane again is Fownes St Upper, where your taste buds can continue their travels to Portugal at the *Little Lisbon* (☎ 671 1274). It's open every day and Australians will feel right at home here as it has a BYO licence, allowing you to bring your own wine.

The *Broker's Restaurant* (☎ 679 3534) at 25 Dame St serves up truly traditional Irish fare – you can even have Irish stew or three-course meals for around IR£8. *Nico's* (☎ 677 3062) at 53 Dame St also offers conservative food, except that here it's Italian, though strongly under the Irish influence. It's solidly popular and open for dinner Monday to Saturday, and also for lunch on weekdays.

Around Grafton St

Pedestrianised Grafton St is the number-one shopping street in south Dublin and although it's notably deficient in restaurants and pubs there are a great many possibilities in the streets to the east and west of Grafton St (see map 14 at the back of this book). Dame St restaurants are all covered in the Temple Bar section.

Fast Food Grafton St is the fast-food centre south of the Liffey with a *McDonald's* at No 9, a *Burger King* at No 39 and *La Pizza* just round the corner at 1 St Stephen's Green North. *Captain America* (☎ 671 5266), at 44 Grafton St at the St Stephen's Green, has burgers until midnight every night of the week.

Round the corner from Dublin Castle at 2 Werburgh St is *Leo Burdock's* (☎ 54 0366), next to the Lord Edward Pub. It is frequently claimed to dole out the best fish and chips in Ireland. You can eat them down the road in the park beside St Patrick's Cathedral. It's open in the evenings from Wednesday to Saturday and on Monday.

Cafés The Grafton St area has office workers, Trinity College students and tourists to feed and there are plenty of cafés and restaurants to keep them happy at lunch time. Backpackers staying at *Avalon House* on Aungier St (see Hostels in the Places to Stay chapter) will find good cafeteria-style facilities there.

Bewley's is a huge cafeteria-style place that offers good-quality food, including breakfast, lunch-time sandwiches (IR£1.50 to IR£3) and complete meals (IR£2.50 to IR£3.50). Bewley's is equally good for a quick cup of tea or coffee and actually offers a choice of teas, a very pleasant surprise in a country where tea is usually made strictly to the British recipe – white and sweet.

There are three branches of *Bewley's* cafés around the centre. The 78 Grafton St branch is the Bewley's flagship, with the company's interesting little museum upstairs. It's open from 7.30 am to 10 pm Monday to Wednesday, to 1 am Thursday and to 2 am Friday and Saturday. On Sunday it's open from 9.30 am to 7 pm. The branch at 11/12 Westmoreland St is open from 7.30 am to 7 pm Monday to Saturday and 10 am to 6 pm Sunday. There's also a branch at 13 South Great George's St.

Subs n Salads is on Anne St South just off Grafton St and turns out filling sandwiches, baps (an Irish version of a bread roll) and rolls for IR£1.20 to IR£2, snappily and with a smile. Eat there or even better, if it's a sunny day, have a park picnic in nearby St Stephen's Green. At 6 Anne St South is *The Coffee Inn* (☎ 677 0107) with good

Bewley's & Beshoff's

In a city of institutions, Bewley's is an institution many visitors will be grateful for. At one of *Bewley's Oriental Cafés* you can be sure of getting a good meal at a reasonable price or simply a good cup of tea or coffee (neither of which is necessarily easy to find in Ireland) and a place to rest your weary feet. The Bewley family, Quakers from England, established their first tea shop in Dublin around 1840, close to where the Olympia Theatre now stands.

The Bewley business went through numerous changes in the following century before a shop was opened in Westmoreland St in 1916. The Oriental style also arrived with this coffee shop and it became a fashionable and stylish centre, complete with a door attendant to help guests from their carriages or cars. The Grafton St café followed in 1927 and today there are other branches of Bewley's on South Great George's St and Mary St in Dublin as well as in a number of other towns in Ireland and Northern Ireland.

In 1971, when the cafés were still family owned, Bewley Community Ltd was established as a pioneering example of employee ownership. Unhappily, it almost became the company's death knell as inefficient methods and a bloated workforce led to near bankruptcy. In 1986 the business was bought out and now runs profitably. Despite the introduction of self-service, Bewley's still manages to exude Dublin's easy-going charm at its best, and you can still admire the stained-glass windows at the Grafton St branch or sit in the old wooden pews at Westmoreland St. At Grafton St there's even a Bewley's museum!

At *Beshoff's* the main attraction is fish and chips rather than coffee, but there's the same old-fashioned style to the establishment. Founded by Ivan Beshoff, a survivor of the tsar-era mutiny on the Russian battleship *Potemkin* in 1905, the Victorian-looking *Beshoff's* is on Westmoreland St near Bewley's. A modern fast-food-style branch can be found on O'Connell St. ∎

coffee, outdoor tables (weather permitting) and late opening hours every night of the week. There are pizzas and pasta dishes to go with the coffee.

Munchies on the corner of Exchequer St and William St South, just west of Grafton St, claims to produce the best sandwiches in Ireland. For IR£1.70 (sandwiches) or IR£1.90 (baps) you can check if it's true. There are other branches of Munchies around Dublin. A little closer to Grafton St at 19 Wicklow St is *Cornucopia* (☎ 677 7583), a popular wholefood café turning out all sorts of healthy goodies for those trying to escape the Irish cholesterol

Top: Bewley's Oriental Café, Temple Bar (TW)
Bottom: Powerscourt Townhouse Shopping Centre (TW)

habit. It's open for lunch Monday to Saturday and until 8 pm on weekday evenings, 9 pm on Thursdays. Head the other way along Exchequer St to the new *Wed Wose Café* at No 18.

The Powerscourt Townhouse Shopping Centre, in its wonderfully restored old building between William St South and Clarendon St, has many eating places and makes a great place for lunch. They include *Blazing Salads II* (☎ 671 9552), a very popular vegetarian restaurant on the top level with a variety of salads for 60p each. It's open Monday to Saturday from 9.30 am to 6 pm. In the open central area is *Mary Rose*, a good place for lunch or a coffee. *O'Brien's* is a popular sandwich place with a daily lunch-time soup and sandwich special for IR£2.95.

There are other branches at 54 Mary St and in the St Stephen's Green Shopping Centre.

The large *Kilkenny Kitchen* (☎ 677 7066) is on the 1st floor of the Kilkenny Shop at 6 Nassau St. The generally excellent food is served cafeteria-style and at times the queues can be discouragingly long. At peak times there's a simpler food counter which can be somewhat faster. The Kilkenny Kitchen is open Monday to Saturday from 9 am to 5 pm, and to 8 pm on Thursday.

The *Coffee Bean* (☎ 679 7140) is at 4 Nassau St, also opposite Trinity College. It's popular with college students, and from the upstairs room you can gaze across the college grounds. The food comes in healthy quantities, in healthy style (plenty of vegetarian dishes) and with lots of salads. Within Trinity College is the basement *Buttery Café*, which is OK if you like everything with chips.

Fitzer's collection of slick outlets make a great place for lunch or an early evening meal on weekdays. There's a Fitzer's (☎ 677 1155) at 52 Dawson St, towards the Trinity College and Nassau St end but the best Fitzer's is in the National Gallery and is covered in the Merrion Row, Baggot St & Beyond section.

Restaurants St Andrew's St, just west of Grafton St, is packed with good restaurant possibilities. The excellent *Trocadero* (☎ 677 5545, 679 9772) at 3 St Andrew's St offers no culinary surprises and that is exactly why it is so popular. Simple food, straightforward preparation, large serves and late opening hours are the selling points. The Troc, as it's locally known, is open past midnight every night except Sunday, when it closes just a little earlier.

Across the road, *QV-2* (☎ 677 3363, 677 2246) at 14/15 St Andrew's St manages to look more expensive than it is. There are good pasta dishes for IR£5.50 to IR£6.50 and main courses for IR£8 to IR£12, but vegetables cost extra. It offers good, mildly adventurous food, pleasant surroundings and a dessert called Eton Mess (IR£1.95) which should not be missed. It's open every day for lunch and dinner until after midnight.

Still on St Andrew's St the *Cedar Tree* (☎ 677 2121) at No 11A is a Lebanese restaurant with a good selection of vegetarian dishes. If thoughts of Greek sunshine could inspire an imaginary escape from a grey Dublin day then turn the corner to *La Taverna* (☎ 677 3665) at 33 Wicklow St. It's open Monday to Saturday for lunch and every day for dinner and combines sunny Greek food with an equally sunny atmosphere. At 12A Wicklow St the *Imperial Chinese Restaurant* (☎ 677 2580) is open every day but is notable for its lunch-time dim sums. These Chinese snack dishes are especially popular on Sundays when the Imperial serves Sunday brunch Chinese-style in what is known as *yum cha*, or 'drink tea', since that is what is traditionally drunk with dim sum.

Pasta Fresca (☎ 679 2402) is at 3/4 Chatham St, just off Grafton St's southern end. This modern, cheerful restaurant proves once again that the Irish really like their Italian food. It has very authentic pasta dishes for IR£6.50 to IR£8.50 and is open from breakfast time until reasonably late Tuesday to Saturday, but on Monday it closes at 7 pm. Just off Chatham St *Pizza Stop* (☎ 679 6712) at 6 Chatham Lane is a very popular pizzeria with pizzas for IR£4 to IR£7. Alternatively, at 27 Exchequer St, off the other end of Grafton St, there's the popular *Restaurant Pasta Pasta* (☎ 679 2565) with pasta dishes for around IR£7.

There are several pubs with good food close to Grafton St. The *Stag's Head* (☎ 679 3701) is on Dame Court, and, apart from being an extremely popular drinking spot during the summer months (see the Entertainment chapter), it also turns out simple, well-prepared and very economical meals. At 37 Exchequer St on the corner of St Andrew's St is the *Old Stand*, another very popular place for pub food with meals at about IR£5.

Davy Byrne's at 21 Duke St has been famous for its food ever since Leopold Bloom dropped in for a Joycean Gorgonzola cheese sandwich with mustard. It's now a rather swish watering hole but you can still eat there. Directly across the road *The Bailey* (☎ 677 3055) at 2 Duke St also has a restaurant serving traditional Irish food like Irish stew or Dublin coddle. Farther west the *Lord Edward Seafood Restaurant* (☎ 54 2420) is in the Lord Edward Pub at 23 Christ Church Place opposite Christ Church Cathedral and has pub-style seafood. It's open Tuesday to Friday for lunch and Thursday to Saturday for dinner.

Head to Mexico at *Judge Roy Bean's* (☎ 679 7539) at 45/47 Nassau St on the corner of Grafton St for popular tacos and an equally popular bar. *Eddie Rocket's* (☎ 679 7340) at 7 Anne St South is a genuine 1950s-style American diner ready to dish out anything from breakfast at 7.30 am to an excellent late-night burger from IR£2.85. Friday and Saturday nights it's open right through to 4 am. Next door is the trendy, popular *Independent Pizza Company* (☎ 679 5266) at 8 Anne St South. These are pizzas prepared with some pizzazz.

Restaurant Mahler (☎ 679 7117) is in the Powerscourt Townhouse Shopping Centre on William St South but its

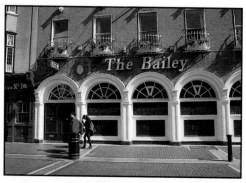

The Bailey (TW)

entrance is actually on the street. The speciality is food
presented simply but stylishly. It's open Monday to
Saturday for lunch and morning or afternoon coffee. On
Friday and Saturday it's also open for dinner and,
during the summer tourist season, it's open on the other
weekdays as well. The *Periwinkle Seafood Bar* (☎ 679 4203)
is also in the Powerscourt Townhouse Shopping Centre
and serves economically priced seafood lunches with
the accent on shellfish.

Regular visitors to India may remember Rajdoot as a
popular brand of Indian motorcycle; those in search of
Indian food in Dublin can scoot down to *Rajdoot Tandoori*
(☎ 679 4274, 679 4280) for superb north Indian tandoori
dishes. It's at 26/28 Clarendon St in the Westbury
Centre, behind the Westbury Hotel. Nearby, and with
similarly Mogul-style Indian cuisine, is the *Shalimar*
(☎ 671 0738) at 17 South Great George's St. They offer a
wide variety of delectable Indian breads.

La Stampa (☎ 677 8611) at 35 Dawson St is Dublin's
up-market Italian restaurant with a large and very
attractive Georgian dining area; when it's buzzing this
is one of the nicest places to eat in the city. It's open from
lunch time until late every day and main courses are in
the IR£8 to IR£12 range, including vegetables.

The very stylish *Polo One* (☎ 676 3362) is at 5/6
Molesworth Place, a smaller lane off Molesworth St,
tucked in behind St Ann's Church which fronts on to
Dawson St. The food is that modern international style
which combines European flavours with a hint of California. There are set menus at IR£15 for lunch or IR£22
for dinner and the wines are pricey but the food tastes
just as good as it looks.

Finally, on Stephen St Lower, behind the big St Stephen's Green Shopping Centre, the recently opened *Break for the Border* is a very big and busy restaurant, bar and entertainment complex serving Tex-Mex food until late. Look for the Western horse and rider statue out front.

Merrion Row, Baggot St & Beyond

Merrion Row, leading out south-east from St Stephen's Green, and its extension, Baggot St, is a busy boulevard for middle to upper bracket guesthouses, popular pubs and an eclectic selection of restaurants.

Merrion Square, connected to Merrion Row by Merrion St, has a restaurant well worth a detour, particularly at lunch time. The National Gallery *Fitzer's* (☎ 668 6481) is rather hidden away since you have to go through the gallery (entry is free) to find it. The artistic interlude as you walk through makes a pleasant introduction to this slightly pricier but very popular restaurant. It has the same opening hours as the gallery (Thursdays until 8.30 pm) and has meals for IR£4.25 to IR£5.25, as well as salads, sandwiches and wine. There's a *Fitzer's Take-Out* (☎ 660 0644) at 24 Baggot St Upper.

Starting from the Shelbourne Hotel on St Stephen's Green, *Galligan's Café* (☎ 676 5955) at 6 Merrion Row is a great place for breakfast from 7.30 am weekdays or from 9 am on Saturday and for lunch or afternoon snacks. Farther along, *Georgian Fare* (☎ 676 7736) at 14 Baggot St Lower has good sandwiches, while *Miller's Pizza Kitchen* (☎ 676 6098) at 9/10 Baggot St Lower is firmly in pastaland.

On the other side of the street *Istanbul Kebabs*, also labelled *Bosphorus Kebabs*, is a popular place for late-night cheap eats. It's right next to the Baggot Inn on Baggot St Lower. If the music and drinking in the busy Baggot St pubs gives you an appetite then this could be a good place to visit.

There's quite an international collection of restaurants among the colourful Baggot St pubs, one of which is *Eureka* (☎ 676 2868) at 142 Baggot St Lower. This authentically Greek restaurant is open Monday to Thursday for lunch, every day for dinner. A bit farther along is *Ayumi-ya* (☎ 662 0233, 662 0223), in the basement at 132 Baggot St Lower, a very Westernised Japanese steakhouse offering good-value set meals comprising a starter, soup, main course, dessert and tea or coffee from IR£10 to IR£13. There are no surprises here but the food is good. There's a second branch of Ayumi-ya in the suburb of Blackrock and this is a more formal place serving more traditional Japanese food.

The Ante Room (☎ 660 4716), 20 Baggot St Lower, located underneath the popular Georgian House guesthouse, is a seafood specialist with main courses for IR£8 to IR£14.50 and traditional Irish music on most nights.

Restaurant Patrick Guilbaud (☎ 676 4192) has a reputation as Dublin's best place for French food in the modern idiom and the restaurant itself is equally modern. Don't come here unless your credit card is in A1 condition. The smooth décor and service is backed up by delicious food. There's nothing overpoweringly fancy about anything, it's just good food, beautifully prepared and elegantly presented. There's a set menu for IR£25 but with drinks and service you should count on at least IR£40 per person. Patrick Guilbaud is at 46 James's Place, just off Baggot St Lower beyond Fitzwilliam St. It's open for lunch and dinner Monday to Saturday.

You can slide backwards in time by continuing along Baggot St, across the Grand Canal and on to Pembroke Rd where you will find *Le Coq Hardi* (☎ 668 4130) at No 35. This is the older counterpart of Patrick Guilbaud with heavier, more traditional French dishes and a superb wine list. The bill is likely to be a little heavier as well though. It's open for lunch Monday to Friday and for dinner Monday to Saturday.

Also out from the centre is the *Lobster Pot Restaurant* (☎ 668 0025) at 9 Ballsbridge Terrace, Dublin 4. It's a staunchly old-fashioned place offering substantial and solid dishes in an equally substantial atmosphere. As the name indicates, seafood is the speciality and the prices are reasonably high. Close by at 15/17 Ballsbridge Terrace is *Kites Chinese Restaurant* (☎ 660 7415, 660 5978), where Chinese food with style is the story and the prices are moderate to high – this is not a cheapie.

Back towards the centre at 74 Leeson St Lower, in the heart of Dublin's nightclub strip, is the *Hungry Wolf* (☎ 676 3951), open for lunch or dinner but especially noteworthy for being open until very late at night with food to satisfy the Leeson St nightclubbers.

If you're after real Irish food then *Oisin's* (☎ 475 3433) at 31 Camden St Upper is the place to go. Camden St is to the south-west of St Stephen's Green, a block over from Harcourt St. The menu offers all the traditional Irish dishes, including Irish stew and Dublin coddle and it's done well but is also expensive. Oisin's is open for dinner Tuesday to Sunday.

Finally, west of the city centre, the IMMA (Irish Museum of Modern Arts) at the Royal Hospital Kilmainham has an excellent café in the basement. If you're planning a visit to the museum, it's well worth including a lunch stop in your itinerary.

Entertainment

Dublin has theatres, cinemas, nightclubs and concert halls, but just as in every village throughout the emerald isle it's pubs which are the real centres of activity. Dublin has hundreds of pubs and they're great for anything from a quiet, contemplative pint of Guinness to a rowdy night out with the latest Irish rock band to provide the entertainment. For what's on info get the fortnightly magazine *In Dublin* or the giveaway *Dublin Event Guide*.

A Pub Crawl

See the Tours section in the Getting Around chapter for information on the excellent and highly recommended Literary Pub Crawl, which on summer nights makes a fine introduction to some of Dublin's pubs and to Ireland's literary history. Pubs must close at night by 11.30 pm, or by 11 pm during the winter months.

Since Irish life is so tied up with its historic pubs, a visit to the city should properly include a walking tour of some of the best. In a truly traditional Irish pub look for the *snugs*, partitioned-off tables where you can meet with friends in privacy. Some snugs will even have their own little serving hatches, so drinks can be passed in discreetly should the drinkers not want to be seen ordering 'just the one'.

Dublin's pub-going tradition has a long history. Even in medieval times the city was well supplied with drinking establishments and in the late 1600s a count revealed that one in every five houses in the city was involved in selling alcohol. A century later another survey counted 52 public houses along Thomas St in the Liberties. There may not be quite so many today but Dublin still has a huge selection of pubs, so there's no possibility of being unable to find a Guinness should you develop a terrible thirst.

Apart from imbibing large quantities of alcohol, the Irish have also been responsible for some important developments in the field. They were pioneers in the development of distilling whiskey (distilled three times and spelt with an 'e' as opposed to the twice-distilled Scotch whisky). The Irish adopted the dark British beer known as porter (since it was particularly popular with the porters who worked around Covent Garden market in London). Promoted by the Guinness family, it soon gained an enduring stranglehold on the Irish taste for

beer. In neighbouring Britain, Foster's and other modern lager beers have stolen the beer market from traditional British beers (flat and warm British beers the less generous might say), but in Ireland Guinness still reigns supreme.

In an Irish pub, talk is just as important an ingredient as the beer though the talk will often turn to the perfect Guinness. Proximity to the St James's Gate Brewery is one requirement for perfection, for although a Guinness in Kuala Lumpur can still be a fine thing it's frequently reiterated that a Guinness at its best can only be found in Ireland. The perfect Guinness also requires expertise in its 'pulling'. If you want a perfect pint you certainly do not simply hold the glass under the tap and slosh it in. The angle at which the glass is held, the point at which the pouring is halted, the time that then passes while the beer settles and the head subsides and the precision with which the final top-up is completed, are all crucial in ensuring satisfaction.

A Dublin pub crawl should start at *The Brazen Head* on Bridge St just south of the Liffey. This is Dublin's oldest pub, though its history is uncertain. Its own sign proclaims that it was founded in 1198, but the earliest reference to it is in 1613 and licensing laws did not come into effect until 1635. Others claim that it was founded in 1666 or 1688, but the present building is thought to date from 1754. The sunken level of the entrance courtyard is a clear indicator of how much street levels have altered since its construction. In the 1790s it was the headquarters of the United Irishmen, who, it would appear, had a tendency to talk too much after a few drinks, leading to numerous arrests being made here. At that time Robert Emmet was a regular visitor. Not surprisingly, James Joyce mentioned it in *Ulysses* with a recommendation for the food: 'you get a decent enough do in the Brazen Head'.

From The Brazen Head walk eastward along the Liffey to the trendy Temple Bar district and dive into those narrow lanes for a drink at popular pubs like *The Norseman* and *The Temple Bar*. On summer evenings young visitors to Dublin congregate for a nightly street party that stretches along Temple Bar from one pub to the other. Next door to the Clarence Hotel on Essex St East, the *Garage Bar* is owned by the rock band U2 and has an appropriately garage-like décor complete with a porcupine car.

On Fleet St in Temple Bar, *The Palace*, with its tiled floor and mirrors, is frequently pointed out as a perfect example of an old Dublin pub. It's popular with journalists from the nearby *Irish Times*. On the corner of Temple

Bar and Anglesea St is the *Auld Dubliner*, and on the opposite corner, at the junction of Fleet and Anglesea Sts, is the recently restored and renovated *Oliver St John Gogarty*.

From Temple Bar cross Dame St, itself well supplied with drinking establishments, to the intersection of Dame Court and Dame Lane, where *Dame Tavern* and the *Stag's Head* face each other from opposite corners. Here, too, a street party takes place between the pubs on summer evenings. The *Stag's Head* was built in 1770, then remodelled in 1895 and is sufficiently picturesque to have featured on a postage stamp series on Irish pubs.

Continue down Dame Lane past *The Banker's* to *O'Neill's* on Suffolk St. It's only a stone's throw from Trinity College, so this fine old traditional pub has long been a student haunt. A block over on Exchequer St is the *Old Stand*, furnished in Victorian style and renowned for its sporting connections and fine pub food. On the other corner, on Wicklow St, the *International Bar* has entertainment almost every night, including a Comedy Cellar on Wednesdays.

Emerge on to Grafton St, which, despite being Dublin's premier shopping street, is completely publess. Fear not – there are numerous interesting establishments just off the street, including two on Duke St where *The Bailey* and *Davy Byrne's* face each other across the street. *Davy Byrne's* was Bloom's 'moral pub' in *Ulysses* and he stopped there for a Gorgonzola cheese sandwich with mustard washed down with a glass of Burgundy. It also featured in *Dubliners*, but after a recent glossy refurbishment it has become something of a yuppie hang-out and Joyce would hardly recognise it. The door from 7 Eccles St in north Dublin, the Bloom home in *Ulysses*, was salvaged when the building was demolished in 1982 and can now be seen in *The Bailey*.

On Harry St, also off Grafton St, you'll find *McDaid's*, Brendan Behan's 'local' and a bit of a tourist trap. Across the road from it is the *Bruxelles*. On Anne St South there's *John Kehoe's* with its old snugs, where patrons can still savour their Guinness in privacy. Chatham St features *Neary's*, a showy Victorian era pub with a particularly fine frontage popular with actors from the nearby Gaiety Theatre.

From the end of Grafton St turn along the north side of St Stephen's Green, the 'Beaux Walk', and continue on past the Shelbourne Hotel to Merrion Row for a drink at *O'Donoghue's*. In the evening you'll probably have music to accompany your pint as this is one of Dublin's most famous music pubs and, it's proudly proclaimed, was the starting point for the folk group the Dubliners. On summer evenings a young and international crowd spills out into the courtyard beside the pub.

Merrion Row changes name to become Baggot St Lower and facing each other across the street are two very traditional old pubs – *James Toner's* and *Doheny & Nesbitt's*. Toner's, with its stone floor, is almost a country pub in the heart of the city and the shelves and drawers are reminders that it once doubled as a grocery store. Doheny & Nesbitt's is equipped with antique snugs and is a favourite place for political gossip among politicians and journalists; Leinster House is only a short stroll away. *Baggot Inn*, just beyond Toner's, is a popular pub for rock music. If you continue farther along Baggot St you'll come to *Larry Murphy's* and the *Henry Grattan*.

Backtrack a few steps to Merrion St Upper and walk north past Merrion Square to *Kenny's* on Lincoln Place, which is tucked in behind Trinity College and has long been a Trinity student haunt. It's well known for its spontaneous traditional music sessions. Continue round the edge of Trinity College towards the river where you'll come to *John Mulligan's* on Poolbeg St, another pub that has scarcely changed over the years. It featured as the local pub in the film *My Left Foot* and is popular with journalists from the nearby newspaper offices. Mulligan's was established in 1782 and has long been reputed to have the best Guinness in Ireland as well as a wonderfully varied collection of 'regulars'.

South of the centre there are some interesting pubs along the Grand Canal (see Canalside Pubs in the Grand Canal section of the Things to See & Do chapter) and the traditional old *An Béal Bocht* on Charlemont St.

No thorough pub crawl should be restricted to pubs south of the Liffey, so head north to try *Slattery's* at 129 Capel St, on the corner of Mary's Lane, and *Sean O'Casey's* at 105 Marlborough St, on the corner of Abbey St Lower. Both are busy music pubs where you'll often find traditional Irish music downstairs and loud rock upstairs. Other north Dublin pubs to sample are *The Oval* on Abbey St Middle, another journalist's hang-out, and *Abbey Mooney's* on Abbey St Lower.

Head farther north to the *Patrick Conway* on Parnell St. It has been in operation since 1745 so, no doubt, new fathers have been stopping in here for a celebratory pint from the day the Rotunda Maternity Hospital opened across the road in 1757. *Joxer Daly's* at 103/104 Dorset St Upper is a Victorian-style pub, which is conveniently close to the Young Traveller and An Óige hostels.

Pub Entertainment

There's considerable overlap between music styles at the various Dublin pubs – some specialise solely in one type of music, others switch from night to night. Others may have one band on upstairs and another, of an entirely different style, downstairs.

Rock Music Various pubs specialise in rock acts, and some of them charge an entry fee. The *Rock Garden Café* in Temple Bar (see the Discos & Nightclubs section) has rock acts on every night, often with an early and a late show. *McGonagle's* on Anne St South is another possibility. *Whelan's, The Purty Loft* and the *Baggot Inn* are other places which hold rock acts almost every night. Other pubs which often have rock music are *An Béal Bocht, Fibber McGee's, The Grattan, The International* and *Larry O'Rourke's*. During the summer months the *Olympia Theatre* has 'Midnight at the Olympia' performances on Friday and Saturday nights.

Traditional & Folk Music Traditional Irish music and folk music also have big followings in Dublin pubs. Some of these entertainment pubs may switch from rock one night to folk the next to Irish traditional the night after. They include *An Béal Bocht, The Auld Dubliner, Boss Croker's, The Brazen Head, Larry O'Rourke's, O'Donoghue's, The Purty Loft, Sir Arthur Conan Doyle's, Slattery's* and *The Wexford Inn*.

Country Music Along with all the other popular music forms in Ireland, there's a real passion for country music. It's especially popular at *Bad Bob's* in Temple Bar (see the Discos & Nightclubs section). Pubs where country music is popular include *Barry's Hotel, The Lower Deck* and *The Purty Loft*.

Jazz & Blues Jazz and blues are also played at several pubs, including *The Barge, Boss Croker's, The Grattan, Harcourt Hotel, McDaid's, Hotel Pierre* and *Slattery's. Sach's Hotel* and *Jury's Hotel* also have jazz sessions on Sundays.

Comedy Given the international fame of the Irish joke, it's surprising that there aren't more comedy venues in Dublin. Several pubs may have comedy acts from time to time, such as *The Waterfront* and *The Purty Loft*, but the *International Bar* has a regular Wednesday night Comedy Cellar – which takes place upstairs, of course.

Venues The phone numbers and locations of the music and entertainment pubs mentioned here are as follows:

An Béal Bocht
  58 Charlemont St, Dublin 2 (☎ 475 5614)
The Auld Dubliner
  17 Anglesea St, Dublin 2 (☎ 677 0527)
Bad Bob's Backstage Bar
  East Essex St, Dublin 2 (☎ 677 5482)
The Baggot Inn
  143 Baggot St, Dublin 2 (☎ 676 1430)
The Barge Inn
  42 Charlemont St, Dublin 2 (☎ 475 0005)
Barry's Hotel
  Great Denmark St, Dublin 1 (☎ 874 6943)
Boss Croker's
  39 Arran Quay, Dublin 7 (☎ 872 2400)
The Brazen Head
  Bridge St, Dublin 8 (☎ 677 9549)
Fibber Magee's
  Gate Hotel, Parnell St, Dublin 2 (☎ 874 5253)
The Grattan
  165 Capel St, Dublin 1 (☎ 873 3049)
The Harcourt Hotel
  60 Harcourt St, Dublin 2 (☎ 778 3677)
The International Bar
  23 Wicklow St, Dublin 2 (☎ 677 9250)
Jury's Hotel
  Ballsbridge, Dublin 4 (☎ 660 5000)
Larry O'Rourke's
  72 Dorset St Upper, Dublin 1 (☎ 30 6693)
The Lower Deck
  Portobello Harbour, Dublin 8 (☎ 475 1423)
McDaid's
  3 Harry St, Dublin 2 (☎ 679 4395)
McGonagle's
  Anne St South, Dublin 2 (☎ 677 4402)
The Night Train (O'Dwyer's Pub)
  8 Mount St Lower, Dublin 2 (☎ 676 1717)
O'Donoghue's
  15 Merrion Row, Dublin 2 (☎ 661 4303)
Hotel Pierre
  Seafront, Dun Laoghaire (☎ 280 0291)
The Purty Loft
  Old Dunleary Rd, Dun Laoghaire (☎ 280 1257)
The Rock Garden
  3A Crown Alley, Dublin 2 (☎ 679 9114)
Sach's Hotel
  19/29 Morehampton Rd, Dublin 4 (☎ 668 0995)
Sir Arthur Conan Doyle
  160 Phibsborough Rd, Dublin 7 (☎ 30 1441)
Slattery's
  129 Capel St, Dublin 1 (☎ 872 7971)

The Waterfront
  Sir John Rogerson's Quay, Dublin 2 (☎ 677 8466)
The Wexford Inn
  16 Wexford St, Dublin 2 (☎ 478 0391)
Whelan's
  25 Wexford St, Dublin 2 (☎ 478 0766)

Irish Entertainment

Although strictly aimed at tourists, there are several places in Dublin where you can go for an evening of Irish entertainment comprising Irish songs, Irish dancing and probably a few Irish jokes thrown in along the way.

Jury's Irish Cabaret (☎ 660 5000) at Jury's Hotel, Ballsbridge, Dublin 4, features 2½ hours of Irish music, song and dance. Not surprisingly this is a tourist favourite and has been for 30 years. You can either come for dinner and the show from 7.15 pm (IR£29.50) or just for the show from 8 pm (IR£17.50, including two drinks). It operates nightly except Mondays from the beginning of May to mid-October.

Similar performances are put on at the *Burlington Hotel* (☎ 660 5222) at Leeson St, Dublin 4. The two-hour performances take place nightly from 8 pm May to October. Dinner starts an hour earlier and the cost for dinner and the show is IR£27.90. The *Clontarf Castle* (☎ 33 2321, 33 2271) at Castle Ave, Clontarf, Dublin 3, also has shows from 7.30 pm Monday to Saturday.

Cinema

Dublin's restaurant supply is overwhelmingly located south of the river, pubs are more evenly spread between north and south, but city cinemas are more heavily concentrated on the north side.

The multiscreen first-run cinemas are the four-screen Adelphi (☎ 873 1161, 98 Abbey St Middle, Dublin 1); the four-screen Carlton (☎ 873 1609, 52 O'Connell St Upper, Dublin 1); and the five-screen Savoy (☎ 874 8487, O'Connell St Upper, Dublin 1). The three-screen Screen at College St (☎ 671 4988 & 872 3922, College St, Dublin 2) is south of river and is more art house, less big release. Ditto for The Light House (☎ 873 0438, Abbey St Middle, Dublin 1). The Irish Film Centre (☎ 679 5744) has two screens at 6 Eustace St in Temple Bar.

Entry prices are generally between IR£3 and IR£5, though there may be reduced prices for afternoon shows. Late-night shows take place from time to time, particularly at the Carlton and Savoy on Saturday nights.

Theatre

Dublin's theatre scene is small but busy. See the Theatre section in the Things to See & Do chapter for more information about the histories of some of Dublin's best known theatres. Theatre bookings can usually be made by quoting a credit card number over the phone and the tickets can then be collected just before the performance.

The famous *Abbey Theatre* (☎ 878 7222) is on Abbey St Lower, Dublin 1, near the river. This is Ireland's national theatre and it puts on new Irish works as well as a steady series of revivals of classic Irish works by W B Yeats, J M Synge, Sean O'Casey, Brendan Behan, Samuel Beckett and others. The smaller *Peacock Theatre* is part of the same complex.

Also north of the Liffey is the *Gate Theatre* (☎ 874 4045) on the south-east corner of Parnell Square, right at the top of O'Connell St. It specialises in international classics and older Irish works with a touch of comedy by play-wrights such as Oscar Wilde, George Bernard Shaw and Oliver Goldsmith. It was built between 1784 and 1786 as part of the Rotunda building but did not become the Gate Theatre until 1929.

The *Olympia Theatre* (☎ 677 8962) is on Dame St, and, apart from staging plays, it is also often used for rock concerts. The *Gaiety Theatre* (☎ 677 1717) on King St South opened in 1871 and is used for modern plays and TV shows. Over in the Liberties the *Tivoli Theatre* (☎ 54 4472) is on Francis St, Dublin 8, directly opposite the Iveagh Market.

Experimental and less commercial performances take place at the City Arts Centre (☎ 677 0643) at 23/25 Moss St, Dublin 2, and at the Project Arts Centre (☎ 671 2321), 39 Essex St East, Temple Bar, Dublin 1. Several pubs host theatrical performances. These include An Béal Bocht (☎ 475 5614), 58 Charlemont St, Dublin 2, and The International Bar (☎ 677 9250), 23 Wicklow St, Dublin 2. Puppet performances are put on at the Lambert Puppet Theatre & Museum (☎ 280 0974) in Clifton Lane, Monkstown.

Theatrical performances also take place at:

Andrew's Lane Theatre
    9/17 St Andrew's Lane (☎ 679 5720)
Focus Theatre
    6 Pembroke Place, Dublin 2 (☎ 676 3071, 689 2000)
New Eblana Theatre
    Busáras, Dublin 1 (☎ 679 8404)
Players' Theatre Trinity
    College, Dublin 2 (☎ 677 2941, ext 1239)
Riverbank Theatre
    Merchant's Quay, Dublin 2 (☎ 677 3370)

Top & Bottom: Buskers, Grafton St (JM)

Concerts

Classical concerts are performed at the *National Concert Hall* (☎ 671 1888) on Earlsfort Terrace, Dublin 2, just south of St Stephen's Green. There are often lunch-time concerts with entry prices of around IR£3 to IR£4. Classical performances may also take place at the Bank of Ireland Arts Centre on Foster Place, at the Hugh Lane Gallery on Parnell Square or at the Royal Dublin Showground Concert Hall.

Big rock concerts are held at the *Point Depot* at East Link Bridge, North Wall Quay, by the river. The building was originally constructed as a railway terminus in 1878. The Lansdowne Rd stadium, a mecca for rugby enthusiasts, is also used for big rock performances. Smaller performances often take place at the pleasantly tatty *Olympia Theatre* (☎ 677 8962) in Dame St, Temple Bar.

Bookings can be made either directly at the concert

venue or through HMV at 18 Henry St, Dublin 1 (☎ 873 2899), and 65 Grafton St, Dublin 2 (☎ 79 5332). Golden Discs (☎ 677 1025 for concert bookings) also handles concert bookings through its outlets, which are at Grafton Arcade, 8 Earl St North, St Stephen's Green Shopping Centre and St Anne's Lane.

Discos & Nightclubs

Leeson St Lower, to the south-east of St Stephen's Green, is the nightclub quarter of Dublin, with a whole string of clubs along this one busy block. They're easily pin-pointed by the black-suited bouncers lined up outside, but which clubs are in changes from one year (or even one month) to another. It's probably best just to follow the crowds – if it looks busy it's likely to be good. Leeson St clubs usually stay open until around 4 am and there are no admission charges, but the price of drinks certainly makes up for that; count on paying at least IR£15 for a bottle of very basic wine.

Other popular venues usually do have an entry charge. They include *Lillie's Bordello*, whose entrance is in an alley off Grafton St at the Trinity College end. It's usually open to 2 am. In Temple Bar the *Rock Garden Café* on Crown Alley also operates until around 2 am, with a rock act every night. Entry prices depend on the act and the day but are usually around IR£6 to IR£8. Eating in the restaurant section will give you a reduction on the entry charge. Also in Temple Bar is *Bad Bob's* on East Essex St where again there's music every night, except that here it's usually country music rather than rock. Entry is in the IR£6 to IR£8 bracket. Still in Temple Bar, *Club M* at Bloom's Hotel is very popular.

McGonagle's on Anne St South typically charges IR£4 to IR£6. *Break for the Border* on Stephen St Lower is a huge new entertainment complex combining a bar with a Tex-Mex restaurant.

Buskers

Dublin is well set up for free entertainment in the form of buskers, but contributions are always gratefully accepted. The best of the city's plentiful supply work busy Grafton St, where they are occasionally hassled by shopkeepers (for blocking access to their concerns) and by the police but are mainly left to get on with it. At the Trinity College end of Grafton St you'll usually trip over pavement artists, busily chalking their pictures around the statue of Molly Malone. Farther along the street you're likely to meet crooning folk singers, raucous rock bands, classical string quartets and oddities like the saw doctor who produces surprisingly tuneful noises from a bowed saw and sells cassettes of his recordings.

The end result of all this busking can be surprisingly varied, ranging from frenetic rock star 'wannabes' (who just might be one day) to tuneless wailers who make you wish there was a buskers' entrance exam without which they couldn't get a licence! The most fun often takes place late on summer nights when the crowds thin out and the late-night people have time to kill. Wandering down Grafton St after midnight one summer night I paused to watch a Led Zeppelin reincarnation when who should come wandering by in the opposite direction but a Robert Plant reincarnation, who proceeded to grab the microphone and put on a performance that would have shamed Page and Plant at their late 1960s peak.

Shopping

If it's made in Ireland, you can probably buy it in Dublin. Popular buys include fine Irish knitwear, such as the renowned Áran sweaters; jewellery with a Celtic influence; books of Irish interest; crystal from Waterford, Galway, Tyrone and Tipperary; Irish coats of arms; china from Belleek; and Royal Tara chinaware or linen from Donegal.

There are all sorts of weird and wonderful small shops in the Temple Bar area, including a number of interesting record shops (see the Records & Musical Instruments section), an equally varied collection of small bookshops, some of Dublin's most eclectic clothes shops (see the Clothing & Woollens section) and a variety of other unusual outlets. The latter category includes Rory's Fishing Tackle (☎ 677 2351) at 17A Temple Bar – just the place for fishing enthusiasts.

Shopping Centres & Department Stores

The wonderful Powerscourt Townhouse Shopping Centre, between William St South and Clarendon St, just to the west of Grafton St in Dublin 2, is a big, modern shopping centre in a fine old 1774 building. Among its up-market shops are an antique market, several high-fashion outlets and the Crafts Council Gallery.

The Royal Hibernian Way Centre off Dawson St in Dublin 2 is also a relatively exclusive shopping centre with a collection of small shops on the site of the old Royal Hibernian Hotel.

The St Stephen's Green Shopping Centre is a short distance south, overlooking the north-west corner of St Stephen's Green, and also has a diverse collection of shops.

Dublin's two best known Grafton St department stores are the long-running Brown Thomas (☎ 679 5666) and, right across the road from it, Switzers (☎ 677 6821). North of the River Liffey is Clery & Co (☎ 878 6000) on O'Connell St.

Markets

Dublin has some very colourful markets, such as the open-air Moore St Market with flowers, fruit and vegetables. Moore St runs from Henry to Parnell Sts, and is parallel to O'Connell St in north Dublin. The market operates from Monday to Saturday.

The Iveagh Market on Francis St, Dublin 8, in the area known as the Liberties, operates from Tuesday to Saturday. On Saturdays it extends right down Francis St as Dublin's best known flea market. Almost directly behind the Iveagh Market is the Christchurch Festival Market, tucked away on Back Lane near Christ Church Cathedral and the two St Audoen's churches. It has a colourful collection of stalls selling everything from antiques to records and is open Friday to Sunday.

The Dublin Corporation Market is on both sides of St Michan's St, between Chancery St and Mary's Lane in Dublin 7.

Irish Crafts & Souvenirs

The Trinity College Library Shop, in the library building at Trinity College, has a wide variety of books and other items of Irish interest but its best known items are, of course, reproductions from the Book of Kells.

The Kilkenny Shop (☎ 677 7066) on Nassau St, Dublin 2, has a wonderful selection of fine Irish crafts, featuring clothing, glassware, pottery, jewellery, crystal and silver. The House of Ireland (☎ 671 4543) on Nassau St, Dublin 2, is another all-purpose emporium for all types of Irish

St Stephen's Green Shopping Centre (TW)

crafts. You can also find a wide range of Irish crafts in the many individual shops in the Powerscourt Townhouse Shopping Centre.

The Tower Design Centre (☎ 677 5655) on Pearse St, Dublin 2, off Grand Canal Quay has studios for local craftspeople. They produce jewellery in both contemporary and Celtic-inspired designs, Irish pewter, ceramics, silk and other fabrics, pottery, rugs and wall hangings, cards, leather bags and various other handcrafted items.

Various smaller shops specialise in Irish crafts, among them the Irish Celtic Craftshop (☎ 667 9912) at 10/12 Lord Edward St, Dublin 2, near Christ Church Cathedral. The Crafts Council Gallery (☎ 679 7368) is in the Powerscourt Townhouse Shopping Centre on William St South, Dublin 2.

Clothing & Woollens

Clothing, particularly warm woollen sweaters, is probably the most authentically Irish purchase. The Irish also produce some high-quality outdoor activities gear as they have plenty of experience with wet weather.

Irish knitwear is justly famous though the demand for those superb heavy Aran sweaters is so great that even the most genuinely handknit sweater is unlikely to have been knitted on the islands. One of the major outlets in Dublin for woollen goods is the Dublin Woollen Company (☎ 677 5014) at 41 Ormond Quay Lower, Dublin 1, near the O'Connell Bridge. They have a large collection of sweaters, cardigans, scarves, rugs, shawls and other woollen goods.

Traditional and exciting contemporary designs in knitwear can be found at The Sweater Shop (☎ 671 3270), 9 Wicklow St, Dublin 2. This is just off Grafton St and near Trinity College. Blarney Woollen Mills (☎ 671 0068) is at 21/23 Nassau St, Dublin 2.

For less conventional clothing the Temple Bar district is the place to head for as there is a diverse collection of unusual outlets: American Classics and China Blue, both at Merchant's Arch; Damascus and Eager Beaver, both on Crown Alley; Los Desparados and Man of McLir, both on Fownes St Upper; and Purple Haze on Crown Alley are just some of the possibilities. Flip at 4 Fownes St Upper specialises in 'vintage' American clothing and DV8 on Crown Alley has unusual shoes.

Martian Clothing's amusingly designed T-shirts have a distinctively Irish flavour and can be found at Switzers, Clery's, the Great Outdoors and other outlets. For high fashion your best bet is the Powerscourt Townhouse Shopping Centre.

Camping & Backpacking Equipment

There are plenty of places with good-quality camping, walking and backpacking equipment. The Scouting Adventure Shop (☎ 671 1925) is at 7 Anglesea St in Temple Bar. A number of outlets, including surplus specialists, are to be found along Talbot St off O'Connell St and Little Mary St off Capel St, both in Dublin 1.

Records & Musical Instruments

Music plays an important role in Ireland, whether it's traditional Irish music or the contemporary music that has given Ireland a position on the cutting edge of modern rock. Dublin's biggest record store is the riverside Virgin Megastore (☎ 677 7361) at 14 Aston Quay, Dublin 2. Nearby, but far more intimate in size, is the knowledgeable little Claddagh Records (☎ 677 0262) on Cecilia St in Temple Bar, Dublin 2. Also in Temple Bar at 5 Cope St is Comet Records (☎ 671 8592), which specialises in independent label releases – metal, indie, ska and techno.

Other possibilities in Temple Bar are Attack Records in Merchant's Arch, Borderline Records at 17 Temple Bar and Ruffin Records at 8 Fownes St. Dublin outlets with a number of branches include Dolphin Discs, the Golden Disc Group and HMV.

Waltons (☎ 874 7805) at Frederick St North, Dublin 1, or at the George's St Shopping Centre in Dun Laoghaire, has traditional Irish records and music as well as bodhráns and other traditional musical instruments.

Antiques

If you're after antiques, try the antique market at Powerscourt Townhouse Shopping Centre or head for Francis St in the Liberties area, which is Dublin's premier street for antique shops. Check the Sunday edition of the *Irish Times* for information on antiques sales and auctions.

Books

See the Books & Maps section of the Facts for the Visitor chapter for details on Dublin's fine supply of good bookshops. Most of the bookshops offer an extensive choice of books on Ireland and on subjects of Irish interest, as well as Irish literature and more.

Jewellery & Crystal

There are several jewellery shops in the Powerscourt Townhouse Shopping Centre. Sleaters (☎ 677 7532) 9 Johnsons Court and Westbury Mall, Grafton St, or Lawrences (☎ 72 8688) at the ILAC Centre, Mary St, and (☎ 73 1493) at Henry St, Dublin 1, specialise in Irish and Celtic-inspired jewellery, including Claddagh rings. John Brereton has a number of outlets in Dublin including in the Powerscourt Townhouse; at 29 O'Connell St Lower, Dublin 1; at 2 Chatham St, Dublin 2, and at 108 Capel St, Dublin 1.

Waterford crystal is world-famous and a number of places stock an extensive range of it, particularly Switzers department store. Although Waterford is far and away the best known Irish crystal, there are other companies that cut crystal glass.

Designer Goods & Oddities

If you've admired those wonderful brass door knockers on fine Dublin Georgian doors, then Knobs & Knockers (☎ 671 0495) at 19 Nassau St, Dublin 2, has plenty of them for sale.

The Irish should know a good umbrella when they see one, as they have plenty of opportunity to try them out. H Johnston – The Umbrella Shop (☎ 677 1249) is at 11 Wicklow St, Dublin 2.

Thomas Read & Co (☎ 677 1487) at 4 Parliament St in Temple Bar dates back to1670 andis Dublin's oldest shop. It sells knives and cutlery.

For hi-tech design items of both Irish and foreign origin, try Presents of Mind (☎ 671 6063) at Royal Hibernian Way, Dawson St, Dublin 2.

Art

Dublin has many galleries where you can buy the works of modern Irish artists. For a list of these galleries and where to find them, see the Other Galleries section in the Things to See & Do chapter.

Dublin Walks

WALK 1: DUBLIN NORTH & SOUTH

A Walk from Mountjoy Square to St Stephen's Green

Walking from Mountjoy Square to St Stephen's Green takes you from one part of the city's Georgian heritage to another (see Map 17 at the back of this book). You start at one of Dublin's great Georgian squares, in the run-down northern part of the city, go down O'Connell St, the city's major thoroughfare, cross the Liffey and end up at another of the great Georgian squares, this time in the city's richest area. Many of the attractions passed en route are described in greater detail earlier in this book. The relevant page numbers are given in parentheses; the initial number refers to the item on the map key.

Mountjoy Square (1, pp 154-5) is one of Dublin's magnificent squares but it has now fallen on hard times. The fine buildings are still there, though, just waiting for a renaissance to sweep through north Dublin. From the north-west corner of the square walk up Gardiner St Upper and left along Dorset St Lower to No 7 Eccles St (2), the fictional home of Joyce's Leopold and Molly Bloom. Apart from a plaque and a relief face of Joyce, there's nothing to see as the house was demolished to build a nursing home in 1982. At least the hall door was saved, and is now in The Bailey pub. Real-life residents of Eccles St included the architect Francis Johnston (p 31) whose home at No 64 (3) did survive though in a rather shabby state. At one time Johnston had his own private bell tower in the back garden, until neighbours complained about the noise.

Reverse direction and cross Dorset St on to Temple St. On Hardwicke Place by Temple St is the fine, but now disused, St George's Church (4, p 155) designed by Francis Johnston, whose house we have just left. And where did the church's bells come from? Why from Johnston's back garden bell tower of course!

Turn right on to Denmark St past the Jesuit College at Belvedere House (5, p 154). James Joyce attended the school between 1893 and 1898 and was its most famous student. The tall spire of the Abbey Presbyterian Church (6, p 154) on the corner of Parnell Square North and Frederick St looms ahead. Built in 1864 it is often referred to as Findlater's Church after the grocery magnate who financed its construction.

The northern slice of the square is the Garden of Remembrance (7, p 150), opened in 1966 to commemorate the 50th anniversary of the Easter Rising. The sculpture (8) in the park illustrates the legend of the Children of Lir, who were transformed into swans by their wicked stepmother. Just outside the park is a monument (9) to the victims of a Northern Irish terrorist bomb campaign in Dublin on 17 May 1974. The writer Oliver St John Gogarty (1878-1957) was born opposite the square at 5 Parnell Square East (10).

On the northern side of the square, facing the park, are the Dublin Writers' Museum (11, pp 152-3) and the Hugh Lane Gallery of Modern Art (12, p 152). Walk around the square, noting more fine but dilapidated Georgian buildings on the west side of the square, one of them housing the Sinn Féin Bookshop (13). The southern part of Parnell Square is occupied by the 1757 Rotunda Hospital (14, pp 150-1). As you walk along the south side of the square look for the Patrick Conway pub (15), which opened in 1745 and predates the hospital. In the south-east corner of the square is the old Rotunda, now occupied by the Gate Theatre (16, pp 151-2).

O'Connell St (pp 143-7), Dublin's major boulevard, begins from this corner of the square and sweeps south to O'Connell Bridge and the River Liffey. Unfortunately, the street has had a hard time of it this century. One side was burnt out in the 1916 Easter Rising, the other side followed suit during the Civil War, and whatever was left was ripped through by a remarkably short-sighted batch of property developers in the 1960s and '70s.

Despite this O'Connell St has numerous points of interest, including a varied collection of statues down the centre, starting with the grandiose statue of Parnell (17). Continue down O'Connell St, passing the fountain statue of Anna Livia (based on the Irish name for the Liffey), known as 'the floozie in the jacuzzi' (18). The Henry St-Earl St crossing was the former position of Nelson's Column (19), blown up by the IRA in 1966. There's a notable statue of James Joyce (20) at the pedestrianised O'Connell St end of Earl St. It's ironic that a writer whose masterpiece was banned in his own country throughout his life should be so honoured.

On the other side of O'Connell St, the GPO (21, pp 147-8) towers over the street. Its role as the starting point for the 1916 Easter Rising makes this an overwhelmingly important site in the history of independent Ireland. At the river end of the street the statue of O'Connell (22) looks squarely up his street.

Cross the Liffey on O'Connell Bridge (23, p 83), the most important bridge in the city. If you look to the right you can see the pedestrian Ha'penny Bridge (24, p 83). Across the bridge you join Westmoreland St and pass two of Dublin's best known restaurant names, Beshoff's (25, p 208) and Bewley's (26, p 208). At the bottom of Westmoreland St, on the left, is a statue of the poet Thomas Moore (27), eloquently plonked in front of a public toilet.

On the right-hand side is the long, curving, window-less façade of the Bank of Ireland (28, pp 96-8), which started life not as a bank but as the Irish Houses of Parliament. When the Act of Union subsumed the Irish Parliament into the British one, the building became a bank. Perhaps surprisingly it did not become the parliament building for independent Ireland. On the left is the main entrance to Trinity College (29, pp 87-96), flanked by statues of Burke and Goldsmith looking out over College Green, once a real green but now filled with buildings, including those popular tourist destinations, the offices of American Express and Thomas Cook (30).

Your steps now take you into Grafton St, passing the popular statue of the fictional character Molly Malone (31). In the song 'In Dublin's Fair City' she 'wheeled a wheelbarrow, through streets broad and narrow', which is just what she is doing here. In typical Dublin fashion the notably well-endowed statue has been dubbed 'the tart with the cart'. In summer, pavement artists are often busy producing chalk pictures on the pavement here, a foretaste of the buskers who perform so busily farther along Grafton St.

Road traffic has to turn off into Nassau St but on foot you can enter the pedestrianised area of Grafton St (pp 130-1), Dublin's fanciest shopping street. Your credit cards can breathe a sigh of relief at the next corner: turn left off Grafton St into Duke St, where two famous pubs, Davy Byrne's (32) and The Bailey (33) face each other. Earlier on the walk we passed the site of 7 Eccles St, and though this famous literary locale is gone the front door is still on display in The Bailey. At the bottom of Duke St turn right on to Dawson St and left into Molesworth St, looking for the gabled Huguenot-style houses (34) built between 1736 and 1755 (one is actually dated 1755).

Molesworth St brings you out on Kildare St, facing the back of Leinster House (35, p 127), the new Irish parliament. It is flanked on either side by the similarly designed National Library (36, pp 128-9) and National Museum (37, pp 122-5). Turn right down Kildare St, looking for the sign at No 30 (38) which announces that Bram Stoker, the author of *Dracula*, used to live there. At

Top: Pavement Artist, Grafton St (TW)
Middle: Molly Malone – *The Tart with the Cart* (TW)
Bottom: Sweny's Chemist Shop (TW)

the bottom of the street the Shelbourne Hotel (39, p 136) stands on the corner, facing St Stephen's Green (pp 132-9). The Shelbourne is Dublin's premier hotel and commenced business in 1824 though the present building only dates back to 1867. At the front of the hotel note the statues of Nubian princesses and their ankle-fettered slave girls. Just beyond the Shelbourne is a Huguenot Cemetery (40), a reminder of the French Huguenots who came to Ireland from the late 1600s. The Shelbourne is a good place to end this stroll, because if you've timed it right you can pop in for afternoon tea and scones.

Statues

It's a tough task being a statue in Dublin. The Irish tendency to make political statements with dynamite has had disastrous consequences for many statues, most notably Nelson's Column on O'Connell St which was felled in 1966.

Equestrian statues have had a particularly bad time of it, perhaps because anyone regally riding a horse was likely to be some oppressive Englishman and fully deserved to be unseated. William of Orange, for example, was erected with his horse on College Green in front of Trinity College in 1701. Unfortunately, he was portrayed riding away from the college and for this slight (quite apart from any general Irish dislike for King Billy) the statue suffered numerous indignities over the years. Consequently, in 1765 it was raised to a much higher pedestal. This new elevated position did not prevent it from being bombed in 1836, but a new head, leg and arm put the king to rights until a more serious explosion resulted in his complete removal in 1929.

King George II was honoured with an equestrian statue in St Stephen's Green in 1758 but it was demolished by a bomb in 1937. King George I had a Dublin equestrian statue on Essex Bridge in 1722, but it was moved to Aungier St in 1753 when the bridge was rebuilt and then moved again to Mansion House in 1798. In 1937 it was sold to a British professor and left Ireland. An equestrian statue of Field-Marshal Gough was erected in Phoenix Park in 1880. In 1944 the head and sword were removed, but with a saw rather than explosives. The high explosives followed in 1956 and, with more effect, in 1957, thus eliminating the city's last equestrian statue.

Riding a horse was not, however, the sole prerequisite for explosive destruction; pedestrian statues have had the same treatment. Among these were the Earl of Carlisle (1869, Phoenix Park, blown up in 1958) and the Earl of Eglington & Winton (1866, St Stephen's Green, blown up in 1958). ■

WALK 2: ARCHITECTURE – SOME OF THE BEST, SOME OF THE WORST

A Walk from the Custom House to the Four Courts

Dublin's architecture is a curiously mixed bag and new or old it's mostly of a subdued scale – there's nothing overpowering about the Dublin skyline. Although nothing wonderful has been torn down and replaced with something colossal and awful, much has been torn down to be replaced with something mediocre. Dublin's skyline is a strong indication that architecture is not a modern Irish skill. When Dublin was in its prime, its most important architect was James Gandon, and this walk takes you by a convoluted route between his two riverside masterpieces (see Map 18 at the back of this book).

On Custom House Quay is the Custom House (1, p 86), built between 1781 and 1791. It's a building that rewards both close inspection and a distant view, so start by walking along the front to see the heads that represent the gods of Ireland's greatest rivers. The only goddess is that of the River Liffey, over the main entrance. The building, which was burnt out during the 1921 Civil War and then totally rebuilt, now houses government offices so there's nothing to see inside.

From the Custom House walk along Eden Quay past Liberty Hall (2), still Dublin's only real skyscraper. It's the headquarters of the Irish Transport & General Workers' Union and though it scrapes the Dublin sky at a height of 61 metres (197 feet) it's simply a boring 17-storey building. When it first opened in 1965, however, there was a rooftop observation level.

Turn up Marlborough St to the Abbey Theatre (3, p 148) on the corner of Abbey St Lower. Opened in 1966, this replacement for the original Abbey Theatre, which burnt down in 1951, is a dismal-looking place to carry such a famous name. Considering they spent 15 years getting around to building it, you would think they could have come up with something better.

Walk along Abbey St Lower under the elevated DART railway line to Beresford Place behind the Custom House. There you'll find the main Dublin bus station, the Busáras (4), which also houses offices and the Eblana Theatre. The latter opened in 1953 and, like the Abbey Theatre, was designed by Michael Scott. The huge Inter-

national Financial Services Centre (5), also on Beresford
Place, houses the Allied Irish Bank Building, the Bank of
Ireland and other financial institutions.

Cross the river by the Matt Talbot Bridge (6, p 83) then
stand on George's Quay to admire the view of the
Custom House from across the Liffey. This is the best
view you can get of the building since farther upriver
the railway Loop Line Bridge (7, p 83) slashes right
across the front. Walk up Moss St from the river and turn
left into Townsend St then immediately right past St
Mark's Church (8), on the corner of Pearse St. Built in
1758, the church is no longer used for worship.

Turn left along Pearse St then right at Westland Row,
behind Trinity College. Pearse Station (9), originally
known as Westland Row Station, was the city terminus
for the Dublin-Kingstown (Dun Laoghaire) line, which
commenced operation in 1834 as the first commuter
train service in the world. The line was built by the
railway engineer William Dargan, who also organised
the 1853 Dublin Industrial Exhibition.

Next door to the station is St Andrew's Church (10), a
Catholic church built in 1832-37. There is a Church of
Ireland St Andrew's on Suffolk St, at the other end of
Trinity College. On the way down Westland Row you
pass Oscar Wilde's birthplace (11) at No 21.

A left and then a right turn brings you to the north-
west corner of Merrion Square (pp 139-40), but as you
make that first left turn look on your right for Sweny's
Chemist Shop (12) at 1 Lincoln Place. This is where
Bloom pauses in *Ulysses* to buy a bar of lemon soap. Walk
along the north side of the square passing some of
Dublin's finest Georgian houses, though few of them
are private homes today. The Wildes lived at No 1 (13)
and the Irish Architectural Association is at No 8 (14).
On the east side at No 39 (15) is the former home of the
UK Embassy.

Look down Mount St Upper to the 1824 St Stephen's
Church (16, p 142), a popular landmark affectionately
known as 'the pepper canister'. On the corner of Mount
St Upper at No 29 Fitzwilliam St Lower (17) is a beautifully restored old Georgian house now open to the
public. Perhaps its restoration by the Electricity Supply
Board was an act of contrition, for Merrion Square East
and its continuation, Fitzwilliam St Lower, made up the
longest unbroken stretch of Georgian architecture in
Europe until 1965, when the board demolished 16 of the
buildings to construct a new office block (18). There were
loud protests but to no avail.

Head south, across Baggot St Lower to Fitzwilliam
Square (p 141), the last of Dublin's great Georgian

squares and one of the finest. The park in the centre of the square is still private and reserved for residents of the square. Make a circuit of the square and exit heading north up Pembroke St Lower to rejoin Baggot St Lower. Turn left onto Baggot St Lower then turn right up Merrion St Upper, glancing at the imposing Government Buildings (19, pp 127-8) on the left and passing No 24 (20) on the right where Arthur Wellesley, the Duke of Wellington, may have been born. The Iron Duke and defeater of Napoleon at Waterloo may have been born in any one of several places, but the actual one is rather uncertain. On the left you pass The Natural History Museum (21, p 130), Leinster House (22, p 127), the seat of the Irish government, and the National Gallery (23, pp 125-6). You're now back on Merrion Square. At the top corner turn left along Clare St and then Leinster St, beside Trinity College.

On the corner of Kildare and Leinster Sts, the Kildare St Club (24, p 138) is now occupied by the Heraldic Museum and National Genealogical Office and the lliance Française but at its peak the club was the very bastion of Dublin conservatism. Across Leinster St are the grounds of Trinity College. It is said that in a cricket match in College Park the great Victorian batsman W G Grace (1848-1915) once hit a magnificent six (the cricketing equivalent of a baseball home run) which soared right over Leinster St and smashed a window of the Kildare St Club. The club was founded in 1782 and moved into these Venetian-style premises in 1861. Note the now-fading carved animals which decorate the window ledges.

Continue along Nassau St with the grounds of Trinity College (pp 87-96) on your right. The Arts & Social Science Building (25, p 95) is one of the newest buildings on the campus and houses the Douglas Hyde Gallery of Modern Art. Rounding the end of the campus you turn into Grafton St, passing the statue of Molly Malone (26) and the offices of American Express and Thomas Cook (27), and then into College Green with the columned sweep of the Bank of Ireland (28, pp 96-8) across the road. This was the original Irish Parliament before the 1800 Act of Union ended not only the parliament but also Dublin's Georgian boom years.

On the left you can see the Church of Ireland St Andrew's Church (29, p 142) on Suffolk St and the site (30) of a Viking thingmote or ceremonial mound. It was levelled in 1685. On the right is the modern elevated Central Bank (31), completed in 1978. When almost finished, the building was found to be nearly 10 metres higher than shown on the plans and completely out of scale with its surroundings. An enquiry was held and the copper roof was removed to reduce the intrusion.

Continuing along Dame St you come to the ageing Olympia Theatre (32, p 143) on the right and the City Hall (33, p 108) on the left. Behind the City Hall is Dublin Castle (34, pp 103-8), an architectural conglomeration of styles which has been built and rebuilt over the centuries. Dame St becomes Lord Edward St before you turn right down Fishamble St, the oldest street in Dublin, beside Christ Church Cathedral (35, pp 109-13). The Dublin Music Hall (36, pp 102-3) once stood on Fishamble St but only its doorway remains.

On the other side of Fishamble St are the Dublin Corporation Civic Offices (37), probably the most controversial new constructions in all of Dublin. There was outrage at the city council's lack of taste and judgement when these large buildings were planned as they would clearly overshadow the cathedral. Anger turned to fury when excavations of the Wood Quay site revealed numerous remains of Dublin's earliest Viking settlement. History didn't interest the council either, so despite a huge protest march in 1978, the excavations were completed and the new offices went up.

Turn left on to Wood Quay (p 84); originally built in wood in the 1200s then rebuilt in stone in 1676, this is the oldest quay on the Liffey. On the far side of Winetavern St is St Francis' Church (38), which is usually known as Adam and Eve's Church after the pub that once stood in front of it.

Finally, cross the O'Donovan Rossa Bridge (39, p 82) to James Gandon's second riverside masterpiece, the Four Courts (40, p 87). Originally begun by Thomas Cooley in 1776, it was integrated into Gandon's grandiose plan, which was built between 1786 and 1801. Its copper dome mirrors the dome of Adam and Eve's Church across the river.

WALK 3: MEDIEVAL DUBLIN – OUTSIDE THE CITY WALLS

A Walk from the Cathedrals through the Liberties

This walk takes you from Dublin's two Church of Ireland cathedrals through the area to the west of Temple Bar known as the Liberties and ends at Heuston Station (see Map 19 at the back of this book). This area of Dublin includes Christ Church and St Patrick's cathedrals and stretches to the St James's Gate Guinness Brewery. Medieval Dublin had a number of 'liberties' – areas outside city jurisdiction where local courts were at liberty to administer the law. In the 17th century Protestants, including many French Huguenots, flocked here from the Continent to escape religious persecution at home. The weaving industries they established flourished until British trading restrictions brought about their collapse in the 18th century. The area degenerated into a squalid slum and much of the recent redevelopment has concentrated on creating depressing modern public housing.

Although this is the oldest area of Dublin, settled by the Vikings 1000 years ago, in medieval times it was the area 'without', the part of the town outside the city walls, which once enclosed Dublin Castle. In that era Christ Church was the cathedral 'within' (inside the city walls), while St Patrick's was the cathedral 'without'. The Liberties has a surprising number of twin (Catholic and Protestant) churches. There are two St Audoen's, two St Nicholas Withouts and two St Catherine's.

The walk starts from St Patrick's Cathedral (1, pp 113-19), indelibly connected with author, poet and satirist Jonathan Swift (pp 118-19). Turn into St Patrick's Close beside the cathedral with the Deanery (2) on your right. Swift once lived here but the present building is a more recent replacement. Just beyond the bend in the close is the old Marsh's Library (3, pp 120-1) on the left.

From St Patrick's Close turn left at Kevin St Upper to Kevin St Garda Station (4) on the corner of Bride St. Once the Archbishop's Palace of St Sepulchre, little remains from that medieval construction. From the corner make a short detour to the small park known as the Cabbage Garden (5). The name dates back to 1649, when Cromwell's troops grew cabbages here. From 1685 until 1858 Huguenot refugees from France used this area as a burial ground and some old headstones can be seen on one side.

Back at the junction head north up Bride St, which becomes Werburgh St, and walk past St Werburgh's Church (6, pp 121-2). This fine old church is no longer in use and is now in a rather tatty condition. Just before the church is an alley (7) with an employment exchange where Hoey's Court, the birthplace of Jonathan Swift, once stood.

At the top of Werburgh St stands Christ Church Cathedral (8, pp 109-13) on Christ Church Place. Between the cathedral and Wood Quay, excavations for the Dublin Corporation Civic Offices (9) revealed an archaeological treasure house of the city's 9th to 11th century Viking origins. A storm of protest blew up when the city council announced they would go ahead with the building despite the importance of the site. They did. Fishamble St, running down to the river beside the corporation offices, has followed this same curving route and rejoiced in the same name for 1000 years.

From the cathedral walk west along High St, turn left down Nicholas St and then right up Back Lane. On Back Lane is Tailor's Hall (10), built between 1703 and 1707, though 1770 is the date on the front door. This is Dublin's oldest surviving guildhall, dating from the time when the local weaving industry provided the material for the Liberties' tailors. Tailor's Hall was on the brink of demolition when the Irish National Trust (An Taisce) stepped in and restored it for use as their headquarters. Across the lane is Christchurch Festival Market (11), a colourful collection of stalls selling everything from antiques to records. It's open from Friday to Sunday. Back Lane emerges where High St changes into Cornmarket, and across the road is St Audoen's Church (12, p 122). Right behind this newer Catholic St Audoen's is the medieval Church of Ireland St Audoen's (13), which has one of the few remaining fragments of the old city wall.

The Cornmarket was indeed the grain market of medieval Dublin, but if you turn left from this street into Francis St you'll find a more modern market on the left side. The Iveagh Market (14), was established in 1907 by Lord Iveagh of the Guinness family. There are wonderfully expressive stone faces over the arches. Round the corner, the face giving a broad wink is said to be modelled on Lord Iveagh himself. The market operates from Tuesday to Saturday and on that last day it expands to become Dublin's best known flea market, taking over Francis St. Across the road from the market is the Tivoli Theatre (15).

Walk down Francis St, a centre for antique shops, past the 1832 Catholic church of St Nicholas Without (16), better known as St Nicholas of Myra. At the bottom of Francis St turn right into The Coombe, so named because it was once the 'coomb' or river valley of the Poddle. At its eastern end The Coombe becomes Dean St, named after the deanery of St Patrick's Cathedral, but it was previously known as Crosspoddle St, as it used to cross the Poddle here. Turn west along The Coombe, not east, and continue to the gateway of the now relocated Coombe Maternity Hospital (17). A plaque on the gate tells the sad story of the hospital's foundation in 1826, after two poor women and their newborn babies died during a snowstorm while making a dash for the Rotunda Hospital in north Dublin. The hospital was

Dublin's Seaside Suburbs

Although the centre of Dublin is set back from the bay, there are a number of seaside suburbs around the curve of Dublin Bay. Dun Laoghaire to the south and Howth to the north are historic ports and popular day trips from the city. Connected to central Dublin by the convenient DART rail service, they are both interesting alternatives to staying right in the city.

DUN LAOGHAIRE

Dun Laoghaire (pronounced 'dun leary'), only 13 km south of central Dublin, is both a busy harbour with ferry connections to Britain and a popular resort. From 1821, when King George IV departed from here after a visit to Ireland, until Irish independence in 1922, the port was known as Kingstown. There are many B&Bs in Dun Laoghaire, they're a bit cheaper than in central Dublin and the fast and frequent DART rail connections make it easy to stay out here (see Map 15 at the back of this book).

History

A coastal settlement was made at the site of Dun Laoghaire over 1000 years ago, but it was little more than a small fishing village until 1767, when the first pier was constructed. Dun Laoghaire grew more rapidly after that time and the Sandycove Martello Tower was erected in the early 1800s, as there was great fear of an invasion from Napoleonic France.

Construction of the harbour was proposed in 1815 to provide a refuge for ships unable to reach the safety of Dublin Harbour in inclement weather. Originally, a single pier was proposed, but a plan by engineer John Rennie was developed to build two massive piers enclosing a huge 100-hectare (250-acre) artificial harbour. Work commenced in 1817 and by 1823 the working force comprised 1000 men. However, despite huge expenditure the harbour was not completed until 1842, Carlisle Pier was not added until 1859, and parts of the West Pier stonework have never been finished. The total cost approached one million pounds, an astronomical figure in the mid-19th century.

Shipping services commenced to/from Liverpool and Holyhead and the completion of a rail link to Dublin in 1834 made this a state-of-the-art transport centre. The line from Dublin was the first railway anywhere in Ireland. It's only just over 100 km from Dun Laoghaire to Holyhead in Wales and a ferry service has operated across the Irish Sea on this route since the mid-1800s.

The first mail steamers took nearly six hours to make the crossing, but by 1860 the crossing time was reduced to less than four hours and on one occasion in 1887 the paddle steamer *The Ireland* made the crossing in less than three hours. Car ferries were introduced in the early 1960s. During WW I the RMS *Leinster* was torpedoed by a German U-boat 25 km from Dun Laoghaire and over 500 lives were lost.

Orientation & Information

The tourist office (☎ 280 6984) is on St Michael's Wharf, near the Dun Laoghaire ferry terminal. Pembrey's Bookshop at 78 George's St Lower, almost at the junction with Marine Rd, has a good selection of books. Across the road there's a branch of Eason, the newsagent and bookshop chain.

George's St Upper and Lower, which runs parallel to the coast, is the main shopping street through Dun Laoghaire. The huge harbour is sheltered by the encircling arms of the East and West Piers. Sandycove with the James Joyce Museum and the 40 Foot Pool is about a km east of central Dun Laoghaire.

The Harbour

The 1290-metre East and 1548-metre West piers, each ending in a lighthouse from the 1850s, have always been popular sites for walking (more popular along the East Pier), bird-watching and fishing (particularly from the end of the West Pier). You can also ride a bicycle out along the piers (bottom level only). In the last century the practice of 'scorching' – riding out along the pier at breakneck speed – became so prevalent that bicycles were banned for some time.

The East Pier has an 1890s bandstand and a memorial to Captain Boyd and the crew of the Dun Laoghaire lifeboat who were drowned in a rescue attempt. Near the end of the pier is the 1852 anemometer, one of the first of these wind-speed measuring devices to be installed anywhere in the world. The East Pier ends at the East

Pier Battery with a lighthouse and a gun saluting station, which is useful when visiting VIPs arrive by sea.

The harbour has long been a popular yachting centre and the Royal Irish Yacht Club's building, dating from around 1850, was the first purpose-built yacht club in Ireland. The Royal St George Yacht Club's building dates from 1863 and that of the National Yacht Club from 1876. The world's first one-design sailing boat class started life at Dun Laoghaire with a dinghy design known as the Water Wag. A variety of specifically Dublin Bay one-design classes still race here as do Mirrors and other popular small sailing boats.

Carlisle Pier, also known as the Mailboat Pier, opened in 1859 and was modified to handle drive on/drive off car ferries in 1970. St Michael's Pier, also known as the Car Ferry Pier, was added in 1969. Over on the West Pier side of the harbour are two anchored lightships which have now been replaced by automatic buoys.

National Maritime Museum

The National Maritime Museum is housed in the Mariner's Church, built in 1837 'for the benefit of sailors in men-of-war, merchant ships, fishing boats and yachts'. The window in the chancel is a replica of the 'Five Sisters' window at York Minster in England. The museum is open May to September from 2 to 5.30 pm Tuesday to Sunday; entry is IR£1.20 (children 60p).

Exhibits include a French ship's longboat captured at Bantry in 1796 from Wolfe Tone's abortive invasion. The huge clockwork-driven Great Baily Light Optic came from the Baily Lighthouse on Howth Peninsula. It operated from 1902 until 1972, when it was replaced with an electrically powered lens.

There's a model of the *Great Eastern* (1858), the early steam-powered vessel built by English engineer Isambard Kingdom Brunel. Although it proved a commercial failure as a passenger ship, it successfully laid the first transatlantic telegraph cable to run between Ireland and North America. There are also various items from the German submarine U19 which landed Sir Roger Casement in Kerry in 1916 (see the Sandycove section). These were donated 50 years after the event by the U-boat's captain, Raimund Weisbach.

Around the Town

Nothing remains of the *dún* or fort that gave Dun Laoghaire its name as it was totally destroyed during the construction of the railway line. The railway line from

Dun Laoghaire towards Dalkey was built along the route of an earlier line known as 'The Metals'. This line was used to bring stone for the harbour construction from the quarries at Dalkey Hill. By means of a pulley system, the laden trucks trundling down to the harbour pulled the empty ones back up to the quarry.

On the waterfront is a curious monument to King George IV to commemorate his visit in 1821. It consists of an obelisk balanced on four stone balls, one of which is missing as a result of an IRA bomb attack. On the other side of the coast road is the *Christ the King* sculpture, which was created in Paris in 1926, bought in 1949 and then put in storage until 1978 because the religious authorities decided they didn't like it.

Sandycove

Only a km south of Dun Laoghaire is Sandycove, with a pretty little beach and the Martello Tower that houses the James Joyce Museum. Sir Roger Casement, who attempted to organise a German-backed Irish opposition force during WW I, was born here in 1864. He was captured after being landed in County Kerry from a German U-boat and executed by the British as a traitor in 1916.

James Joyce Museum South of Dun Laoghaire in Sandycove is the Martello Tower where the action begins in James Joyce's epic novel *Ulysses*. It now houses a James Joyce Museum with photographs, letters, documents, various editions of Joyce's work and two death masks of Joyce on display. The museum was opened in 1962 by Sylvia Beach, the Paris-based publisher who first dared to put *Ulysses* into print.

A string of Martello towers were built around the coast of Ireland between 1804 and 1815 to counter a feared invasion by Napoleon's forces. The granite tower stands 12 metres high with walls 2.5 metres thick and was copied from a tower at Cape Mortella in Corsica. Originally, the entrance to the tower led straight into what is now the 'upstairs'. Other tower sites included Dalkey Island, Killiney and Bray, all to the south of Dun Laoghaire, and to the north, Howth and Ireland's Eye, the island off Howth.

In 1904 Oliver St John Gogarty, 'stately, plump' Buck Mulligan in *Ulysses*, rented the tower from the army for the princely sum of £8 a year and Joyce stayed there briefly. The stay was actually less than a week as another guest, Samuel Chenevix Trench (who appears in *Ulysses* as the Englishman Haines), had a nightmare one night and dealt with it by drawing his revolver and taking a shot at the fireplace. Gogarty took the gun from him, yelled 'Leave him to me' and fired at the saucepans on the shelf above Joyce's bed. Relations between Gogarty and Joyce had been uneasy after Joyce had accused him of snobbery in a poem, so Joyce took this incident as a hint that his presence was not welcome and left the next morning. He was soon to leave Ireland as well, eloping to the Continent with Nora Barnacle in 1904. Trench's aim did not improve, as just five years later he shot himself, fatally, in the head.

There are fine views from the tower. To the south-east you can see Dalkey Island with its signal tower and Killiney Hill with its obelisk. Howth Head is visible on the northern side of Dublin Bay. Right next to the tower is the house of architect Michael Scott, who owned the tower from 1950 until it was turned into a museum. There's another Martello Tower not far to the south near Bullock Harbour.

The tower is open May to September from 10 am to 1 pm and 2 to 5 pm Monday to Friday, 10 am to 5 pm Saturdays and 2 to 6 pm Sundays. In April and October it's still open weekdays but not on weekends. Entry is IR£1.75 (students IR£1.40, children 90p). At other times of the year the tower is only open on weekdays and then only to groups for a flat fee of IR£40. Contact Patsy O'Connell at Dublin Tourism (☎ 280 8571) for more details.

You can get to the tower by a 30-minute walk along the seafront from Dun Laoghaire Harbour, a 15-minute walk from Sandycove DART Station or a five-minute walk from Sandycove Ave West, which is served by bus No 8.

The 40 Foot Pool Just below the Martello Tower is the 40 Foot Pool, an open-air sea water bathing pool that probably took its name from the army regiment, the Fortieth Foot, which was stationed at the tower until it was disbanded in 1904. At the close of the first chapter of *Ulysses*, Buck Mulligan heads off to the 40 Foot Pool for a morning swim. A morning wake-up here is still a Dun Laoghaire tradition, winter or summer. In fact a winter dip is not that much braver than a summer one since the water temperature only varies by about 5°C, winter or summer. Basically, it's bloody cold whatever the time of year.

When it was recently suggested that in these enlightened times a public stretch of water like this should be open to both sexes, the '40 foot gentlemen' put up strong opposition. They eventually compromised with the ruling that a 'togs must be worn' sign would now apply after 9 am. Prior to that time nudity prevails and swimmers are still predominantly '40 foot gentlemen', and the odd brave woman.

Activities

A series of walks in the Dun Laoghaire area make up the signposted Dun Laoghaire Way. The *Heritage Map of Dun Laoghaire* includes a map and notes on the seven separate walks.

Scuba divers head for the waters around Dalkey Island. Oceantec (☎ 280 1083, fax 284 3885) is a dive shop at 10/11 Marine Terrace in Dun Laoghaire. They rent diving equipment at IR£17.50 for half a day; a local dive costs IR£27.50.

Places to Stay

B&Bs Rosmeen Gardens is packed with B&Bs. To get there, walk south along George's St, the main shopping street, and Rosmeen Gardens is the first street after Glenageary Rd Lower, directly opposite People's Park. *Mrs Callanan* (☎ 280 6083) is at No 1, *Rathoe* (☎ 280 8070) is at No 12, *Rosmeen House* (☎ 280 7613) is at No 13, *Mrs McGloughlin* (☎ 280 4333) is at No 27, *Annesgrove* (☎ 280 9801) is at No 28 and *Mrs Dunne* (☎ 280 3360) is at No 30. Prices here are IR£16 to IR£18 for singles, IR£28 to IR£35 for doubles.

There are also some B&Bs on Northumberland Ave, like *Innisfree* (☎ 280 5598) at No 31. Close to the harbour is *Bayside* (☎ 280 4660) at Seafront, 5 Haddington Terrace, which is slightly more expensive with singles for IR£20, doubles from IR£30. Others can be found on Mellifont and Corrig avenues.

Hotels Dun Laoghaire has a number of attractively situated seaside hotels. The port's premier hotel is the A-rated *Royal Marine Hotel* (☎ 280 1911, fax 280 1089) on Royal Marine Rd, only two minutes' walk from the Dun Laoghaire car ferry terminal. There are 104 rooms, all of which have attached bathrooms, costing IR£100/120 for singles/doubles.

Also pleasantly located on Royal Marine Rd is the small *Port View Hotel* (☎ 280 1663, fax 280 0447). About half of the 20 rooms have en suite bathrooms and these better rooms cost IR£29.50/49 for singles/doubles. The larger *Hotel Pierre* (☎ 280 0291, fax 284 3332), is also close to the waterfront at 3 Victoria Terrace. There are 36 rooms, almost all of them with en suite facilities at

IR£29/50. Close by on Haddington Terrace is the *Kingston Hotel* (☎ 280 1810, fax 280 1237) with 24 rooms, all with attached bathroom, costing IR£32/55.

Places to Eat

Fast Food Branches of *McDonald's*, *La Pizza* and *Abrakebabra* can all be found on George's St. Just off George's St on Patrick St is the *Ritz Café* for traditional fish and chips.

Restaurants *Outlaw's* (☎ 284 2817) at 62 George's St Upper offers steak, burgers and other 'Wild West' fare. *Café Society* (☎ 280 1100) at 19 George's St Upper has a standard menu offering dishes like steaks or chicken Kiev. *Darby O'Gill* on George's St Upper, on the corner of Northumberland Ave, offers a very similar menu but with a little Irish flavour.

Dilshad Tandoori Restaurant (☎ 284 4604) on Convent Rd has a very standard Indian menu but the tandoori dishes have a good reputation. Alternatively, there's the *Krishna Indian Restaurant* (☎ 280 1855) on the 1st floor at 47 George's St.

Near the harbour *Restaurant Na Mara* (☎ 280 6787) is in what used to be railway station and offers more expensive food with the emphasis on seafood. *Trudi's* (☎ 280 5318) at 107 George's St Lower is another fancier restaurant which offers excellent and slightly adventurous food. Count on paying around IR£20 to IR£25 per person, including drinks. It's open in the evening from Tuesday to Saturday.

On Marine Parade, between Dun Laoghaire and Sandycove, is *La Vie en Rose* (☎ 280 9873), which serves old-fashioned but high-quality French cuisine. Prices are also rather high and it's open Tuesday to Friday for lunch, Monday to Saturday for dinner.

Finally, many Dubliners suggest that a trip beyond Dun Laoghaire to Bray is worthwhile purely to eat at *The Tree of Idleness* (see the Bray section).

Entertainment

Popular pubs include *Cooney's* at 88 George's St Lower and *Dunphy's*, right across the road at No 41. Farther out along George's St is *Smyth's*, with its very original interior. The Hotel Pierre is noted for its jazz performances, and the Purty Loft on the Old Dunleary Rd often has traditional Irish music or rock.

Getting There & Away

See the introductory Getting There & Away chapter for details of the ferries between Dun Laoghaire and Holyhead in the UK.

Bus No 7, 7A or 8 or the DART rail service will take you from Dublin to Dun Laoghaire. It only takes 15 to 20 minutes to cover the 12 km by DART with a one-way fare of IR£1.

DALKEY

South of Sandycove is Dalkey, which has the remains of a number of old castles. Bulloch Castle overlooking Bullock Harbour was built by St Mary's Abbey in Dublin in the 12th century. On Castle St in Dalkey are two castles – the Goat Castle and Archibold's Castle. On the same street is the ancient St Begnet's Church, dating from the 9th century. Dalkey Quarry is now a popular site for rock climbers, but it originally provided most of the stone used to construct the gigantic piers at Dun Laoghaire Harbour.

Dalkey has several holy wells, including St Begnet's Holy Well on Dalkey Island which is reputed to cure rheumatism. The island has an area of nine hectares and lies just a few hundred metres offshore. The waters around the island are popular with local scuba divers. A number of rocky swimming pools are also to be found along the coast at Dalkey.

Dalkey Harbour (TW)

BRAY

The arrival of the railway in the 1850s turned Bray – only 19 km south of Dublin – into another seaside excursion for Dubliners. Its central position between the city and the Wicklow Hills is an attraction, but basically it's not a very attractive seaside town, its long seafront parade providing a home for fast-food places and amusement arcades.

The young James Joyce lived here between 1888 and 1891, and, as in Sandycove near Dun Laoghaire, there's a Martello Tower. From Bray Head there are fine views to the south of the Great Sugar Loaf, a prominent peak in the Wicklow Mountains. There's a cliff walk leading eight km south to the pleasant coastal resort of Greystones. The National Aquarium is at the Seafront in Bray and is open from 10 am to 9 pm daily. Entry is IR£2, (children IR£1.50, family tickets IR£6).

One attraction for which it is worth making the foray out from Dublin to Bray is *The Tree of Idleness* (☎ 286 3498, 286 8183), a seafront restaurant with delicious Greek-Cypriot food.

HOWTH

The bulbous Howth Peninsula delineates the northern end of Dublin Bay. Howth town is only 15 km from central Dublin and is easily reached by DART train or by simply following the Clontarf Rd out around the north bay shoreline. En route you pass Clontarf, site of the pivotal clash between Celtic and Viking forces at the Battle of Clontarf in 1014. Farther along is North Bull Island, a wildlife sanctuary where many migratory birds pause in winter. Howth is a popular excursion from Dublin and has developed as a residential suburb (see Map 16 at the back of this book).

History

Howth's name (which rhymes with 'both') has Viking origins, and comes from the Danish word *hoved* or head. Howth Harbour dates from 1807-09 and was the main Dublin harbour for the packet boats from England. The Howth Rd was built to ensure rapid transfer of incoming mail and dispatches from the harbour to the city. The replacement of sailing packets with steam packets in 1818 reduced the transit time from Holyhead to seven hours. Howth's period of importance was short, however, because by 1813 the harbour was already showing signs of silting up and was finally superseded by Dun Laoghaire in 1833. Howth's most famous arrival was King George IV, who visited Ireland in 1821 and is chiefly remembered because he staggered off the boat in a highly inebriated state. He did manage to leave his footprint at the point where he stepped ashore on the West Pier.

In 1914 Robert Erskine Childers' yacht *Asgard* brought a cargo of 900 rifles in to the port to arm nationalist supporters. During the Civil War, Childers was on the IRA side and was court-martialled and executed by firing squad for the illegal possession of a revolver. The *Asgard* is now on display at Kilmainham Jail. Howth's popularity as a seaside escape from Dublin made the Howth electric trams famous, but they were withdrawn in the late 1950s.

Howth Town

Howth is a pretty little town built on steep streets running down to the waterfront. Although the harbour's role as a shipping port has long gone, Howth is now a major fishing centre and yachting harbour.

St Mary's Abbey stands in ruins near the centre and was originally founded in 1042, supposedly by the Viking King Sitric, who also founded the original church on the site of Christ Church Cathedral in Dublin. It was amalgamated with the monastery on Ireland's Eye in 1235. Some parts of the ruins date from that time but most of it was built in the 15th and 16th centuries. The tomb of Christopher St Lawrence (Lord Howth), in the south-east corner, dates from around 1470. There are instructions on the gate about where to obtain the key to the abbey.

Howth Castle & Desmesne

Howth Castle's demesne, an Irish term meaning 'grounds', was acquired by the Norman noble Sir Almeric Tristram in 1177 and has remained in the family ever since, though the unbroken chain of male succession finally came to an end in 1909. The family name was changed to St Lawrence when Sir Almeric won a battle at, so he believed, St Lawrence's behest.

Originally built in 1564, the St Lawrence family's Howth Castle has been much restored and rebuilt over the years, most recently in 1910 by the British architect Sir Edwin Lutyens. A legend relates that in 1575 Grace O'Malley, the 'Queen' of western Ireland, dropped by the castle on her way back from a visit to England's Queen Elizabeth I. When the family claimed they were

Howth Harbour (JM)

busy having dinner and refused her entry, she kid-
napped the son and only returned him when Lord
Howth promised that in future his doors would always
be open at meal times. As a result, so it is claimed, for
many years the castle extended an open invitation to
hungry passers-by. Despite Grace O'Malley's actions,
the castle is no longer open, but the gardens can be
visited in spring and summer and there's a popular golf
course beyond the castle.

The castle gardens are noted for their rhododendrons,
which bloom in May and June, for their azaleas and for
a long stretch of 10-metre-high beech hedges which were
planted back in 1710. The castle grounds also have the
ruins of 16th century Corr Castle and an ancient dolmen
known as Aideen's Grave. It is said that Aideen died of
a broken heart after her husband was killed at the Battle
of Gavra near Tara in 184 AD, but that's probably mere
legend as the dolmen is thought to be much older.
Dolmens, Neolithic grave memorials, are constructed of
three vertical stones topped by a table stone. The table
stone here is estimated to weigh over 70 tonnes. Dolmens are found all over Ireland, and also in Europe,
Britain and northern Africa.

The castle is only a short walk from the centre of
Howth.

Transport Museum

The National Transport Museum has a range of exhibits,
including double-decker buses, fire engines and trams.
A Hill of Howth tram which operated from 1901 to 1959
is in the process of being restored. In June, July and

Martello Tower, Ireland's Eye (TW)

August the museum is open Monday to Friday from 10 am to 6 pm. Throughout the year it is open Saturday and Sunday from 2 to 6 pm in summer, 2 to 5 pm in winter. Entry is IR£1 (children 50p). You can reach the museum by entering the castle gates and turning right just before the castle.

Around the Peninsula

The 171-metre Summit offers views across Dublin Bay to the Wicklow Hills. From the Summit you can walk to the top of the Ben of Howth, which has a cairn said to mark a 2000-year- old Celtic royal grave. The 1814 Baily Lighthouse at the south- east corner is on the site of an old stone fort or 'bailey' and can be reached by a dramatic clifftop walk. There was an earlier hilltop beacon here in 1670.

Ireland's Eye

Only a short distance offshore from Howth is Ireland's Eye, a rocky sea-bird sanctuary with the ruins of a 6th century monastery. There's a Martello Tower at the north-west end of the island, where boats from Howth land, while the east end plummets into the sea in a spectacularly sheer rock face. As well as the sea birds wheeling overhead, you can see young birds on the ground during the nesting season. Seals can also be spotted around the island.

Boats (☎ 31 4200 for information) shuttle out to the island from the East Pier of Howth Harbour during the summer, most frequently on weekend afternoons. The cost is IR£3 (children IR£1.50) return. Don't wear shorts if you're planning to visit the monastery ruins, as they are surrounded by a thicket of stinging nettles. And do bring your garbage back with you – far too many island visitors don't.

Farther north from Ireland's Eye is Lambay Island, a more remote and even more important sea-bird sanctuary.

Places to Stay

A night in Howth would make a pleasant seaside escape from central Dublin and, like Dun Laoghaire to the south, it's within easy commuting distance of the centre.

There are several B&Bs along Thormanby and Nashville Rds with typical overnight costs of IR£14 to IR£16 per person. Mrs Rickard's *Gleann-na-Smol* (☎ 32 2936) is on Nashville Rd, Mrs Dunne's *Morven* (☎ 32 2164) is farther along on Nashville Park, while Mrs Hobb's *Hazelwood* (☎ 39 1391) and Mrs McMahon's *Highfield* (☎ 32 3936) are both on Thormanby Rd.

The *St Lawrence Hotel* (☎ 32 2643) on Harbour Rd, directly overlooking the harbour, has 12 rooms, all with attached bathroom. Singles/doubles cost IR£26/52 including breakfast.

On the Dublin side of Howth village there are good views of Ireland's Eye from the *Howth Lodge Hotel* (☎ 39 0288) where the 17 rooms, all with attached bathroom, cost IR£44.50/59 for singles/doubles. By the golf course in the grounds of Howth Castle is the *Deer Park Hotel* (☎ 32 2624), a larger 48-room establishment charging IR£37/58.

Places to Eat

If you want to buy food and prepare it yourself, Howth has fine seafood and you can buy it, fresh from the trawler, at the string of seafood shops along the West Pier.

The *Pizza Place* (☎ 32 2255) at 12 West Pier has reasonably priced pizzas and pasta dishes along with a great selection of Italian ice creams. Other economical alternatives include Howth's plentiful supply of pubs, like the *Pier House* (☎ 32 4510) on the East Pier. The *Abbey Tavern* (☎ 39 0307) by St Mary's Abbey has traditional Irish entertainment in the evenings. The *St Lawrence Hotel* (☎ 32 2643) by the harbour has a carvery restaurant that is open daily.

King Sitric (☎ 32 5235) at the East Pier is well known for its fine seafood and is open for lunch and dinner

Monday to Saturday. Main dinner courses cost IR£16 to
IR£18 or you can have a set dinner menu for IR£22.

Entertainment

Howth's pubs are noted for their jazz performances. You
can try *The Cock Tavern*, the *Royal Howth Hotel*, the *Waterside Inn*, the *Pier House*, the *Abbey Tavern* and others –
they're all likely to have something on and are all in the
centre.

Getting There & Away

The easiest and quickest way to get to Howth from
Dublin is by the DART, which will whisk you out there
in just over 20 minutes for a fare of IR£1.

Excursions

Ireland is so small that almost anywhere on the island could be within day-trip distance – it's no problem to zip up to Belfast for the day, for example. Bus Éireann have day tours from Dublin as far afield as Kilkenny, Waterford and even Lough Erne in Northern Ireland. The places described in this chapter, however, are all easy and popular day trips from the capital and feature on many day-tour itineraries. See the Tours section in the Getting Around chapter for details on where to book Bus Éireann tours.

Just south of the city in County Wicklow, the gardens of Powerscourt House are strong contenders for the title of Ireland's most beautiful gardens. Wicklow also boasts the medieval monastery site of Glendalough, quite possibly the most interesting medieval monastery in the country. To complete the threesome, Wicklow has the Wicklow Way, a superb 10 to 12-day walk (shorter sections can also be tackled), which may well be the best in Ireland.

Inland from Dublin, only 20 km from the city centre, Castletown near Maynooth has a fine stately home from the days of the Anglo-Irish ascendancy plus two unusual associated follies (see the Castletown section). Malahide Castle, one of the most interesting old homes in Ireland, is a similar distance north of the city.

The varied sites of the Boyne Valley make an excellent day excursion from Dublin. Apart from the sites associated with the 1690 Battle of the Boyne, the valley also has a number of prehistoric grave sites, including the magnificent Newgrange, probably Europe's largest and most impressive Neolithic passage grave (a burial place with a passageway leading to one or more chambers). Near Newgrange you can also see another fine monastic site at Mellifont and some of Ireland's most magnificent high crosses at Monasterboice. The town of Drogheda makes a good base for the Boyne Valley and also has a number of interesting sites in its own right.

Inland from the Boyne Valley sites are the ancient site of Tara, and the castle and medieval ruins of Trim and Kells, the original monastic home of the Book of Kells.

POWERSCOURT

Near the picture postcard village of Enniskerry and about 22 km south of Dublin, the house at Powerscourt was designed by Richard Castle but accidentally burnt down in 1974, just after a major renovation had been completed. The owners now live in one wing but it's the magnificent garden which attracts the crowds. Even with modern power equipment, it takes a small army of gardeners to keep the vegetation in line. Stepping down the hill in front of the shell of the house, the gardens are backed by the peak of the Great Sugar Loaf, rising to a 506-metre-high point on the horizon. The Japanese call it 'borrowed scenery' and Powerscourt also has a small Japanese garden, as well as curiosities like a pets' cemetery. The original owners of Powerscourt also had a town house in Dublin which is now the Powerscourt Town-house Shopping Centre.

Opening hours in summer are 9.30 am to 5.30 pm daily, and entry is IR£2.50 (students IR£2, children IR£1). The estate's noted waterfall, the highest in Ireland at almost 120 metres (398 feet), is farther south and entry is IR£1.50 (IR£1, 80p). There's a six-km walking path from the estate to the falls.

Getting There & Away

Bus No 44 runs regularly from Dublin to Enniskerry and takes about 1½ hours. There's a Bus Éireann tour to Powerscourt on Sundays from May to mid-September. It departs from Dublin at 2.15 pm, returns at 6 pm and costs IR£10 (children IR£5).

Powerscourt (TW)

GLENDALOUGH

St Kevin may rank as one of Ireland's least friendly hermit monks, as he is reputed to have pushed a monastic groupie (who disturbed his isolation) over a cliff edge into a lake. The monastery he reluctantly founded in Glendalough has, however, certainly lasted. From its establishment early in the 6th century, it grew to be one of the most important monasteries in Ireland, surviving Viking raids in the 9th and 10th centuries and an English incursion in 1398 before final suppression in the 16th century.

The site is entered through Ireland's only surviving monastic gateway. The ruins include a round tower, the cathedral, a fine high cross and the curious St Kevin's Church. The latter is sometimes referred to as the kitchen because of its chimney-like tower. Beyond the monastic site is Upper Lake, with a cave known as St Kevin's Bed, where the saint is said to have retreated. On the south shore of the lake and accessible only by boat is Teampall na Scellig, an oratory or small church-like building used for private prayer. There are other reminders of St Kevin around the lake.

Glendalough (pronounced 'glenda-lock') translates as the 'glen of two lakes'. It's close enough to Dublin to attract big tourist crowds in summer. Entry to the visitors' centre (not to the site, which is free) is IR£1 (children 40p). The centre has some interesting displays, including a model of the monastery in its prime, and a fine audiovisual display is regularly shown. From mid-June to mid-September it's open from 10 am to 7 pm daily, but closes earlier during the rest of the year and all day on Monday from November to mid-March.

Places to Stay & Eat

The *Glendalough International Youth Hostel* (☎ 0404-45342) is near the site and costs IR£5.50 a night. At the village of Laragh, three km east of the monastic site, the *Old Mill Hostel* (☎ 0404-45156) has private rooms, dorm beds at IR£5.30 and camping at IR£3. Laragh has restaurants, pubs and plenty of B&Bs.

Getting There & Away

St Kevin's Bus Service (☎ 281 8119) runs daily between St Stephen's Green in Dublin and the site. From Dublin the bus departs at 11.30 am from outside the Royal College of Surgeons on St Stephen's Green West. From

Glendalough departures are at 4.15 pm and cost IR£5 one-way or IR£8 return.

Bus Éireann has a tour to Glendalough and Wicklow daily except Friday from April to September. The tour departs at 10.30 am, returns at 5.45 pm and costs IR£12 (children IR£6). You can pick the tour up from Dun Laoghaire at 11 am. There's a tour to Glendalough, Avondale Forest Park and Charles Stewart Parnell's home, and to the Wicklow Hills on Fridays from June to mid-September. It departs at 9.30 am, returns at 4.30 pm and also costs IR£12 (children IR£6).

THE WICKLOW WAY

Running for 132 km from County Dublin through County Wicklow to County Carlow, this is the longest established and one of the most popular of Ireland's long-distance walks. It's well documented in leaflets and guidebooks. Much of the trail traverses country above 500 metres in altitude, so you should be prepared for rapid changes in the weather. If you don't feel up to tackling the whole 10 to 12-day walk, the three-day section from Enniskerry (near Powerscourt) to Glendalough is probably the most attractive and has easy transport at each end. At the Dublin end the walk starts at Marlay Park in Rathfarnham.

There are An Óige hostels along the route at *Glencree* (☎ 01-86 4037), *Knockree* (☎ 01-86 4036), *Glendalough*, *Glenmalure* (no phone) and *Aghavannagh* (☎ 0402-36366), as well as numerous B&Bs.

RUSSBOROUGH HOUSE

Russborough House at Blessington in County Wicklow was designed by the architect Richard Castle and built between 1740 and 1750. The house is renowned for its superb plasterwork by the Francini brothers and for the Beit painting collection, which features works by Goya, Gainsborough, Rubens and Vermeer. Russborough House is open on Sundays and public holidays from Easter to October, daily in summer. Buses depart regularly from Dublin and take about 1½ hours to complete the 29-km trip.

KILDARE

St Brigid's Church in Kildare has the remains of an ancient fire temple in its grounds, and the second-highest round tower in Ireland. In summer you can

Japanese Garden, Kildare (TW)

climb it between 10 am and 1 pm Monday to Saturday, or between 2 and 5 pm on any day.

Just south of the town is the National Stud, where for IR£2 (students IR£1.50, children IR£1) you can learn all about breeding very expensive racehorses. Next to the stud, and with the same entry charges again, is the curious Japanese Garden, the result of Ireland's short-lived mania for building Japanese gardens early this century. The stud and the gardens are open from 10.30 am to 5 pm Monday to Friday, to 6 pm on Saturday, and from 2 to 6 pm on Sunday.

If you need a meal in Kildare, the very popular *Silken Thomas* pub has middling to average pub food at average to above-average prices, and there are numerous other pubs. Buses from Dublin take about an hour for the 55-km trip.

CASTLETOWN

Castletown House near Maynooth was designed in 1722 for William Conolly, Speaker of the Irish House of Commons, and is another fine example of an imposing Anglo-Irish home. The neighbouring village of Celbridge, which has a tree-lined avenue that leads directly to the house, was built as an adjunct to the house. Descendants of Conolly continued to live at Castletown House until 1965.

Lady Louisa Conolly commissioned the stucco work in the house and the unusual print room, but she also had a passion for building follies. There's a curious tower known as the Obelisk which was designed by

Richard Castle and is framed in the view to the north from the Long Gallery. Off to the east, on private property just outside Leixlip, is the even more curious conical Wonderful Barn.

The opening hours vary and the house is closed on Saturday in winter. Entry is IR£2.50 (students IR£2, children IR£1). Castletown is 21 km inland from Dublin. Buses leave about every hour and take a little over an hour to get there.

SWORDS

The village of Swords is 16 km north of Dublin and five km west of Malahide. The Archbishop of Dublin built a fortified palace here in the 12th century, but the castellated walls date from the 15th century and numerous other modifications were made over the centuries. The windows to the right of the main entrance date from around 1250.

Swords also had an ancient monastery but today only its 23-metre-high round tower remains and that was rebuilt several times between 1400 and 1700. It stands in the grounds of the Church of Ireland. The body of Brian Ború was kept overnight in the monastery after his death in 1014 at the Battle of Clontarf, when his forces defeated the Vikings.

Buses from Dublin depart every half-hour or so and take less than an hour.

MALAHIDE

Malahide is virtually a suburb of Dublin, swallowed by the city's northward expansion. The well-kept 101 hectares of the Malahide Demesne, which contains Malahide Castle, is the town's principal attraction. The Talbot Botanic Gardens are next to the castle and the extensive Fry Model Railway is in the castle grounds.

Malahide Castle

Despite the vicissitudes of Irish history, the Talbot family managed to keep Malahide Castle (π 45 2655, 45 2337) under their control from 1185 to 1976 apart from a short interlude while Cromwell was around (1649-60). The castle is the usual hotchpotch of additions and renovations, and the oldest part of it is a three-storey 12th century tower house. The façade is flanked by circular towers which were tacked on in 1765.

The castle is packed with furniture and paintings, and Puck, the family ghost, is still in residence. The 16th century oak room with its decorative carvings is one of the castle's high points, along with the medieval Great Hall with family portraits and a minstrel gallery.

The castle's opening hours vary through the year. All year it's open Monday to Friday from 10 am to 12.45 pm and 2 to 5 pm. From November to March it's also open on weekends and holidays from 2 to 5 pm. From April to October weekend hours are extended: Saturdays 11 am to 6 pm and Sundays and holiday 2 to 6 pm. Entry is IR£2.50 (students IR£1.90, children IR£1.25). A family ticket for two adults and up to four children costs IR£7. Combined tickets are available for the castle and railway (see the next section).

The parkland around the castle is open daily from 10 am to 5 pm in the middle of winter and to 9 pm at the height of summer.

Fry Model Railway

Ireland's biggest model railway layout covers 240 square metres and in O-gauge (track width of 32 mm) authentically displays much of Dublin and Ireland's rail and public transport system, including the DART line and Irish Sea ferry services. There's also a separate room exhibiting railway models and other memorabilia. Unfortunately, the operators suffer from the over-seriousness that sometimes afflicts grown men with complicated toys, and rather than let you simply look and admire you're herded into the working railway room in groups and subjected to a demonstration.

The railway has rather complex and variable opening hours. From April to September it's open Monday to Thursday from 10 am to 1 pm and 2 to 5 pm, Saturday 11 am to 1 pm and 2 to 6 pm, Sunday and holidays 2 to 6 pm. In June, July and August it's also open on Friday from 10 am to 1 pm and 2 to 5 pm. From October to March it's open on weekends and holidays from 2 to 5 pm. Entry is IR£2.10 (students IR$1.50, children IR£1.15). You can get combined castle and railway tickets for IR£4 (IR£3, IR£2). Family tickets for two adults and up to four children cost IR£6.25 for the railway or IR£10 for the railway and castle.

Getting There & Away

Bus No 42 from Talbot St takes about 45 minutes to get to Malahide. Alternatively, take a Drogheda train to the Malahide town station, only 10 minutes' walk from the park. Malahide is 13 km north of Dublin.

NEWBRIDGE HOUSE

North of Malahide at Donabate is Newbridge House (☎ 43 6534, 43 6535), a historic Georgian mansion with fine plasterwork by Robert West and a traditional farm. It's open April to October from 10 am to 1 pm and 2 to 5 pm Tuesday to Friday, 11 am to 6 pm Saturdays, 2 to 6 pm Sundays and public holidays. During November and March it's open only on Saturday, Sunday and holidays from 2 to 5 pm. Entry is IR£2.20 (students IR£1.80, children IR£1.20). A family ticket for two adults and up to four children costs IR£6.50.

The 144 hectares of Newbridge Demesne, of which the house is the centrepiece, is open from 10 am to 5 pm in midwinter and to 9 pm in midsummer.

Getting There & Away

Donabate is 19 km north of Dublin. Bus No 33B runs from Eden Quay in central Dublin to Donabate village. You can also get there on the suburban rail service from Connolly or Pearse St Stations.

SKERRIES

The seaside resort of Skerries is 30 km north of Dublin. St Patrick is said to have made his arrival in Ireland here at Red Island, now joined to the mainland. There's a good cliff walk south from Skerries to the bay of Loughshinny. At low tide you can walk to Shenick's, a small island off Skerries. Colt and St Patrick's are two other small islands, the latter with an old church ruin. Farther offshore is Rockabill with a lighthouse. The 7th century oratory and holy well of St Moibhi and the ruins of Baldongan Castle are all near the town.

Getting There & Away

Buses depart from Dublin about every hour and take just over an hour to reach Skerries. Trains from Connolly Station are less frequent but slightly faster.

DROGHEDA

Straddling the River Boyne about five km inland from the sea, the interesting little town of Drogheda was captured by the Danes in 911 and later fortified by the Normans. By the 14th century it was one of Ireland's four major towns; bits and pieces of the medieval walls and early monastic buildings lie scattered around the town.

Drogheda (TW)

In 1649 Drogheda was the scene of Cromwell's best remembered Irish slaughter. He met with stiff resistance and when his forces eventually overran the town the defenders were shown no mercy. It's estimated that nearly 3000 people were massacred, including innocent civilians and children. When 100 of the town's inhabitants hid in the steeple of St Peter's Church, Cromwell's men simply burnt the church down. 'A righteous judgement of God upon these barbarous wretches,' was Cromwell's summation of the butchery. Drogheda also took the losing side at the Battle of the Boyne in 1690 but quickly surrendered the day after James II was defeated.

It took many years for the town to recover from these events, but in the last century a number of Catholic churches were built. The massive railway viaduct and string of quayside buildings hint at the town's brief Victorian-era industrial boom, when it was a centre for brewing and for the manufacture of cotton and linen.

Orientation & Information

Drogheda makes an excellent base for visiting Boyne Valley sites. The town itself straddles the River Boyne, with the main shopping area along West and Laurence Sts. The area of town south of the river is dominated by the mysterious Millmount mound, which supposedly covers a passage grave. There's a tourist information office (☎ 041-37070) near the junction of West and George's Sts.

Things to See

Dominating the centre of town is **St Peter's Roman Catholic Church** (1791) on West St. In a glass case on the left side of the church you can see the head of St Oliver Plunkett (1629-81). He was executed by the perfidious English after being wrongly accused of being a conspirator in the Popish Plot of 1678 (a supposed Catholic conspiracy to murder Charles II and massacre Protestants).

Straddling Laurence St, the eastward extension of West St, is **St Laurence Gate**, the finest surviving portion of the city walls. The only other remaining city gate is the 13th century **Butter Gate**.

You have to cross the river to **Millmount** for the finest views over the town. Topping the hill is the 14th century **Magdalene Tower**, which was originally part of a Dominican friary founded in 1224 and which played a dramatic role in the 1922 Civil War. The **Millmount Museum** has interesting displays about the town and its history. The museum is open from 2 to 6 pm Tuesday to Sunday in summer, and entry is 50p (children 20p). You can drive up to the hilltop or ascend via the steps from St Mary's Bridge.

Places to Stay & Eat

There are no hostels in Drogheda but there are quite a few B&Bs in and around the town. Apart from pubs and cafés, try the *Snackmaster Restaurant*, just off West St, which is run by a friendly Egyptian.

Getting There & Away

Drogheda is only 40 km north of Dublin, on the main N1 route to Belfast. From Dublin buses depart about every two hours from the Busáras and take over an hour. In Drogheda the Bus Éireann station is on New St, just south of the river. The railway station is also just south of the river and east of the centre, off the Dublin Rd. Buses depart from Connolly Station in Dublin about every two hours and take less than an hour. If you take the train between Dublin and Belfast, the railway crosses the river just downstream from Drogheda on a huge railway viaduct.

Drogheda is the central jumping-off point for a visit to the Boyne Valley sites. There's a Bus Éireann tour which visits Newgrange, Mellifont, Monasterboice, Tara and Slane. It operates on Sunday, Tuesday and Thursday from mid-May to September. The tour departs from

Dublin at 10 am, returns at 5.45 pm and costs IR£12 (children IR£6).

Getting Around

Drogheda's attractions are all in or near the centre of town and within easy walking distance. If you want to visit the places around Drogheda and don't have your own transport, you can hire a taxi on Laurence St.

BOYNE VALLEY

There are many historic markers along the Boyne Valley which are sites of the Battle of the Boyne, the epic struggle between the forces of the Catholic King James II and the Protestant King William of Orange. The defeat of the Catholic forces was to have long-running and tragic consequences for Ireland. Despite their importance, the sites are of limited interest unless you're a student of Irish history, but the fertile valley has other very worthwhile attractions.

Boyne Valley Passage Tombs

The prehistoric passage tombs of the Boyne Valley are collectively known as Brugh na Bóinne or Boyne Palace. At first it was surmised that they were the grave sites of the kings of Tara (who ruled in the first few centuries AD), but it is now known that they predate that period of Irish history by many centuries. At that time this fertile valley sheltered some of Ireland's earliest farming communities. Apart from the huge site at Newgrange, there are two lesser, but still extremely impressive, sites at Dowth and Knowth.

These ancient passage tombs were the largest things built in Ireland until the Normans came and built their castles, and the country between the three major tombs is littered with countless other ancient mounds and standing stones. Over the centuries the tombs have been plundered by everybody from Vikings to Victorian treasure hunters and the mounds have decayed and been covered by grass and trees.

Newgrange The finest Celtic passage tomb in Ireland is a huge flattened mound near the River Boyne about 10 km west of Drogheda. It's believed to date from around 4000 to 3000 BC, making it older than the pyramids of Egypt. The site was extensively restored in the 1970s and you can walk down the narrow passage to the tomb chamber, about a third of the way into the colossal mound. At dawn on the mornings of the winter solstice, the rising sun's rays shine directly down the long passage and illuminate the tomb chamber for about 15 minutes. There's no need to apply years ahead for the limited number of viewing positions during the winter solstice, and then hope that the sky is not overcast, because modern science provides a simulated winter sunrise for every party of visitors.

The grass-covered mound is about 80 metres in diameter and 13 metres high and is faced by a pebbled wall which in turn is encircled by huge horizontal stones, many of them finely decorated with curious designs, such as whorls, spirals, zigzags and circles. Farther out from the mound is a circle of standing stones, many of which have been broken off or removed. From the entrance, with its extravagantly incised entrance stone, the passage leads 19 metres into the mound to the cross-shaped central chamber. This has huge standing stones and dished stones in which burnt bones of the bodies buried here were originally found. Above the chamber massive stones form a ceiling.

Newgrange is about 13 km west of Drogheda, just north of the River Boyne. The site (☎ 041-24488) is open between 10 am and 7 pm from June to mid-September. Opening hours are 10 am to 1 pm and 2 to 5 pm from mid-March to May and mid-September to October. From November to March, in the depths of winter, the hours are 10 am to 1 pm and 2 to 4.30 pm (closed Tuesdays). The admission fee is IR£1.50 (children 60p) and includes a very good guided tour. In summer, particularly on Sundays, Newgrange can get fairly crowded so you should try to come early or late. The last tours leave about half an hour before closing time.

Dowth Between Newgrange and Drogheda is Dowth, where the circular mound is several hundred years younger than Newgrange and is not currently open to the public. It's smaller at about 63 metres in diameter but slightly higher at 14 metres. An eight-metre-long passage leads into the central chamber, which, like that of Newgrange, is cross-shaped. Dowth was excavated by archaeologists from the Royal Irish Academy in 1847 and for a time it even had a teahouse on top.

Knowth The third major burial mound is between Newgrange and Slane. Modern excavations commenced at Knowth in 1962 and a 35-metre-long passage to the central chamber was soon cleared. This passage was much longer than that at Newgrange, but in 1968 an

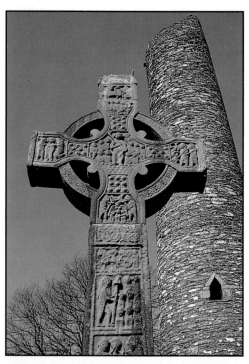

Top: West Cross, Monasterboice (TW)
Bottom: Mellifont Abbey (TW)

extraordinary discovery was made when a second passage was unearthed. There are 18 smaller passage graves around the main mound. The site is famous for the art discovered there, which includes ornate kerbstones. Knowth is open from 9.30 am to 6.30 pm daily from June to September. Entry is IR£1 (children 40p).

DONORE & DULEEK

In 1429 King Henry VI offered a £10 grant to anybody who would build a castle within the area known as the Pale, which essentially meant the counties of Dublin, Kildare, Meath and Louth. To ensure that there would be no cheating, minimum dimensions were stipulated. The result can be seen here at Donore, which has a miniature castle that was just barely big enough to claim the £10.

Duleek claims to have had Ireland's first stone church, founded by the energetic and peripatetic St Patrick; the town's name comes from *An Damh Liag*, meaning 'the stone church'. Duleek's 12th century abbey ruins contain a number of excellent effigies and tombstones. Outside is a 10th century high cross.

There are bus services to these towns from Drogheda.

MELLIFONT ABBEY

Mellifont Abbey, about 10 km north-west of Drogheda, was Ireland's original Cistercian monastery and in its prime was the most magnificent and important centre of this monastic sect. The abbey was founded in 1142 by the Archbishop of Armagh, who, dismayed by local corruption in the order, brought in a new troupe of monks from France. They were deliberately established at this remote location, far from any distracting influences. The French and Irish monks failed to get on and the visitors soon returned to the Continent, but within 10 years nine more Cistercian monasteries followed and Mellifont eventually became the mother house for more than 20 lesser monasteries.

Only fragments of the settlement remain but the plan of the extensive monastery can be easily traced. The buildings are clustered around an open cloister garth or courtyard. Other buildings include a cross-shaped church, a chapter house, an east range which would once have had the monks' dormitories above it, and a south range which would have had the refectory or dining area, the kitchen and the warming room. The most recognisable building is the lavabo, an octagonal washing house for the monks.

Entry is 80p (children 30p) and the grounds are open from 10 am to 6 pm during the summer months.

MONASTERBOICE

Just off the N1 road, about 10 km north of Drogheda, is Monasterboice with an intriguing little enclosure containing a cemetery, two ancient, though unimportant, church ruins, a fine, though topless, round tower and two of the best high crosses in Ireland. Monasterboice can be reached directly from Mellifont though the route is rather difficult.

The high crosses, depicting biblical scenes, are superb examples of Celtic art with an important didactic use for an often illiterate populace. Like Greek statuary, they may once have been brightly painted, but all trace of colour has long disappeared. Muiredach's Cross is the older, dating from the early 10th century, and is also in better condition. The newer West Cross stands 6.5 metres high, making it one of the highest high crosses, but it's much more worn, with only a dozen or so of its 50 panels still legible.

The original monastic settlement is said to have been founded by St Buithe in the 5th century. This saint was a follower of St Patrick and his name somehow got converted to Boyne, so the river is named after him. Although he's a little-known saint, it is said that he made a direct ascent to heaven via a ladder lowered from above.

SLANE

At the junction of the N2 and N51, 15 km west of Drogheda, Slane is perched on a hillside overlooking the River Boyne. It's a picturesque town with a curious quartet of identical houses facing each other at the junction. A local tale relates that they were built for four sisters who had developed an intense mutual dislike and kept watch on each other from their doorways.

On the Slane Castle estate are the 16th century Hermitage and the Old Mill Transport Museum. St Patrick is said to have announced the arrival of Christianity from the top of Slane Hill. The ruins of a 16th century church occupy the site of St Patrick's original church.

There are buses to Slane several times a day from Dublin (a one-hour trip) or Drogheda (less than half an hour).

KELLS

Almost every visitor to Ireland pays homage to the Book of Kells in Dublin's Trinity College, but far fewer pause to see the town of Kells, where the book came from. Little remains of the ancient monastic site, but there are some fine high crosses, a 1000-year-old round tower, the perhaps equally ancient St Columba's Oratory with its enormously thick walls, and an interesting exhibit in the gallery of the church.

St Columba established the monastic settlement here in the 6th century, and in 807 it was joined by monks from a sister monastery on the remote Scottish island of Iona who were retreating from a Viking onslaught. They brought with them the famous Book of Kells, now housed in Dublin's Trinity College. Kells proved little safer, for Viking raids soon spread to Ireland, and Kells was plundered on several occasions.

Things to See

The comparatively modern **St Columba's Church** stands on the grounds of the old monastic settlement. There's an exhibit about the settlement and its famous illuminated book in the church's gallery. In the churchyard the 30-metre-high round tower lacks its original roof but is known to date back to at least 1076, because a murder took place in the tower in that year. Best preserved of the several high crosses in the churchyard is the 9th century **South Cross** or **Cross of SS Patrick and Columba**. A medieval **church tower** stands beside the modern church and has a number of interesting tombstones set into its walls.

Round the corner from the church is **St Columba's Oratory**, a squat and solid survivor from the old monastic settlement. The original entrance door to this 1000-year-old building was over two metres above ground level. Inside, a ladder leads to a low attic room under the roofline. If it's locked up, the brown house near the stop sign has the keys.

The **Market Cross** was placed in Cross St by Jonathan Swift, and in 1798 the English garrison executed rebels by hanging them from the crosspiece.

Getting There & Away

Kells is 63 km north-west of Dublin and buses leave several times daily from the Busáras.

Top: Abbey Ruins, Slane (TW)
Bottom: Marcy Regan's Pub, Trim (TW)

HILL OF TARA

Near the Dublin-Navan N3 road, Tara was already a place of legend 1000 years ago, when it was held to be the palace and fort of the original High Kings of Ireland. The High Kings were priest-kings who ruled over the many over-kings and kings but had no law-making powers. Only mounds and depressions in the grass mark where the Iron Age hill fort and surrounding ringforts once stood. The rather romantic names that have been attached to the various features do not have any basis in fact.

Behind St Patrick's Church, the Rath of the Synods has four concentric ditches and banks. South of this is the large Royal Enclosure, which was once a hill fort and contains a passage tomb, similar to the tombs of Newgrange. It has been dubbed the Mound of the Hostages. The Royal Seat, an ancient ringfort, and Cormac's House are also within the Royal Enclosure. The Stone of Destiny in Cormac's House is claimed to be the inauguration stone of the kings of Tara. Another hill fort stands south of the Royal Enclosure.

To the north of the site is the Banquet Hall, which was probably the entranceway to the Hill of Tara. To the north-west of this feature are three smaller circular enclosures. The Office of Public Works is planning to open an interpretive centre at the site.

TRIM

A pleasant little town on the River Boyne, Trim has several interesting sites, all of them in ruins. Few visitors pause here to inspect the ruins of Ireland's largest Anglo-Norman castle, a sprawling construction with a huge keep. The original Trim Castle was completed in the late 12th century but was destroyed only a year later and in the succeeding centuries had a dramatic history. The town surrendered to Cromwell's forces in 1649, but not before the town walls, parts of the castle walls and the Yellow Steeple had been severely damaged.

Information

In summer there's a tourist office, right next to the castle entrance, which sells a handy little *Trim Tourist Trail* walking tour booklet. Trim's name, *truim*, which means 'ford of the elder trees' is appropriate as there was an ancient ford over the river at this point.

Things to See

The ruins of **Trim Castle** can be reached either by a riverside path or through the Town Gate. King John visited Trim in 1210, giving the castle its alternative name of King John's Castle. Geoffrey de Greneville, who was responsible for the second stage of the keep's construction between 1220 and 1225, was a keen crusader and later became a monk at the Dominican Abbey, just outside the town's northern wall.

The open grassy area at the heart of the castle is dominated by de Greneville's massive stone keep. Just outside the central keep are the remains of an earlier wall and moat. The main outer wall, still standing today, dates from around 1250. The finest stretch of the outer wall is from the Dublin Gate to the River Boyne. The outer wall has five towers and a number of sally gates from which sorties could 'sally' out to meet the enemy.

Across the river from the castle are the ruins of the Augustinian **St Mary's Abbey**, originally built in the 12th century but rebuilt after a fire in 1368. Part of the abbey cloister was converted into a manor house known as Talbot Castle in 1415 and the Talbot coat of arms can be seen on the north wall. The building was later used as a school whose pupils included Arthur Wellesley, later the Duke of Wellington, Jonathan Swift, and his friend Stella Johnson. Just north of the abbey building is the **Yellow Steeple**, dating from the 1368 restoration but damaged in the Cromwell takeover of 1649.

East of the town there's an interesting group of ruins around **Newtown Cathedral** in Newtown Cemetery. The 13th century **Chapel of the Victorines** encloses the 16th century tomb effigies of Sir Lucas Dillon and his wife, Lady Jane Bathe, known locally as 'the jealous man and woman'. The other buildings here are the **Cathedral of SS Peter and Paul** and **Newtown Abbey**, also known as the Abbey of the Canons Regular of St Victor.

Just over the river from these ruins is the **Crutched Friary**. Built as a hospital after the crusades by the Knights of St John of Jerusalem, there are ruins of the keep and traces of a watchtower and other buildings. The bridge beside the friary is thought to be the second oldest in Ireland and *Marcy Regan's Pub* beside the bridge is claimed to be the second-oldest pub.

Getting There & Away

Trim is about 45 km north-west of Dublin. Buses depart from the Busáras in Dublin several times daily and take about an hour.

Index

MAP LEGEND

BOUNDARIES

_ . _ International Boundaries

_ . . _ Internal Boundaries

SYMBOLS

⊠ Post Office

✈ Airport

i Tourist Information

⊖ Bus Station, Terminal

♱ Church

Cathedral

Mosque, Temple

▌ Pub

∴ Archaeological Site

✚ Hospital

※ Lookout

Ⱥ Camping Area

ൔ Lighthouse

▲ Mountain or Hill

N2 Highway Route Number

Railway Station

ROUTES

——— Major Roads

——— Minor Roads

City Streets

+—+—+ Railways

– – – Ferry Routes

· · · · · Walking Tours

HYDROGRAPHIC FEATURES

Rivers, Creeks, Canals

Lakes, Reservoirs

Coastline

OTHER FEATURES

Parks, Gardens and National Parks

Shopping Centres and Market Places

▾ Places to Eat

■ Places to Stay

Pedestrian Street, Mall

Cemetery

Urban Area

Note: Not all the symbols displayed above will necessarily appear in this book

MAP 12

Heritage Tour Bus Route

0   150   300 m

→ Bus Route
·····

1 Municipal Art Gallery &
  Dublin Writers' Museum
2 General Post Office
  (GPO)
3 Bank of Ireland
4 Trinity College
5 Civic Museum
6 Leinster House
  (Irish Parliament)
7 National Museum
8 National Gallery
9 Newman House
10 Dublin Castle
11 Christ Church Cathedral
12 St Patrick's Cathedral
13 Marsh's Library
14 St Audoen's Church
15 Four Courts

◖ BUS STOPS

A Dublin Bus Office
B Parnell Square — Garden
  of Remembrance
C Dublin Tourism Office
D Trinity College
E National Gallery
  (Merrion St Upper)
F St Stephen's Green North
G Dawson St
H Dublin Castle
I St Patrick's Cathedral
J Christ Church Cathedral

Dorset St Upper
Bolton St
Parnell St
O'Connell St
Gardiner St Lower
Talbot St
Capel St
Henry St
Mary St
Abbey St Mid
Abbey St Lr
Eden Quay
Custom House Qu
To St Michan's Church
Ormond Qy Lr
Burgh Quay
City Qua
15
Ormond Qy Up
Wellington Quay
Aston Quay
Olier St
Townsend
Wood Essex Qy
Temple Bar
Pearse St
Dame St
D
4
Westland Rw
J
11
H
Wicklow St
14
10
G
E
B
Sth Gt George's St
William St South
Grafton St
Dawson St
Kildare St
6
F
7
Aungler St
Patrick St
12
St Stephen's Green
13
Baggot St
I
Kevin St Upper
9

Top: Four Courts (JM)
Bottom: Lamp Posts (JM)

Temple Bar

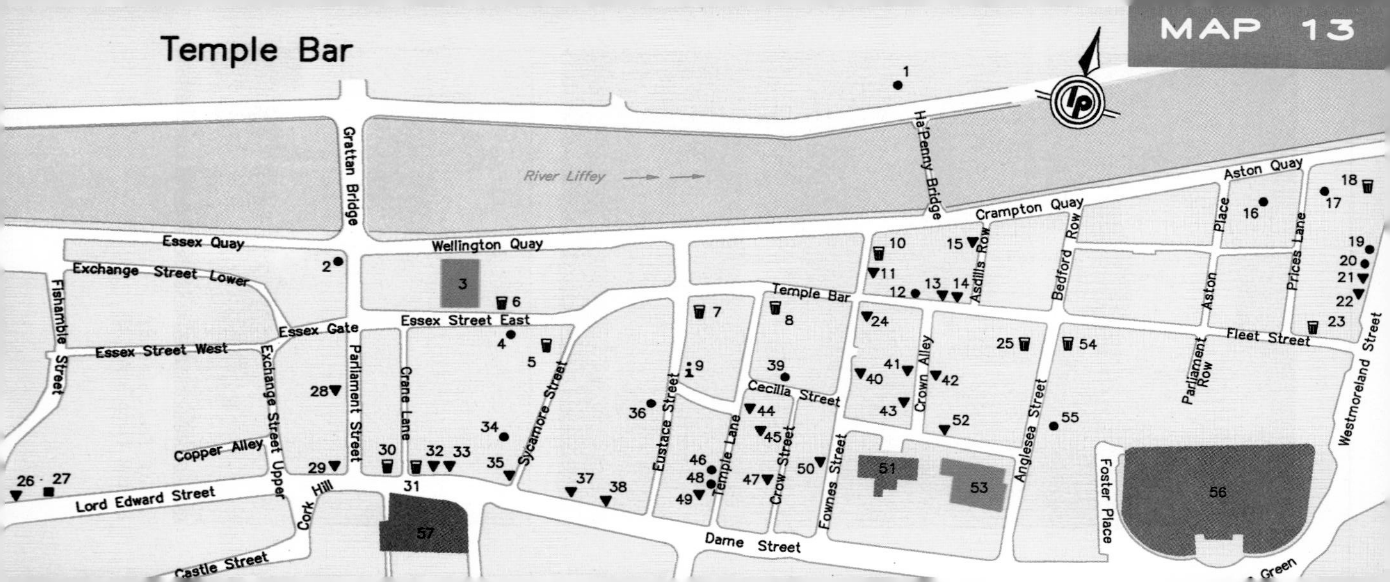
River Liffey
Grattan Bridge
Ha'Penny Bridge
Essex Quay
Wellington Quay
Crampton Quay
Aston Quay
Exchange Street Lower
Exchange Street Upper
Fishamble Street
Essex Street West
Essex Gate
Essex Street East
Parliament Street
Crane Lane
Copper Alley
Lord Edward Street
Cork Hill
Castle Street
Sycamore Street
Eustace Street
Temple Lane
Temple Bar
Cecilia Street
Crow Street
Fownes Street
Crown Alley
Asdills Row
Bedford Row
Anglesea Street
Aston Place
Prices Lane
Fleet Street
Parliament Row
Westmoreland Street
Foster Place
Dame Street
Green
1
2
3
4
5
6
7
8
9
10
11
12
13
14
15
16
17
18
19
20
21
22
23
24
25
26
27
28
29
30
31
32
33
34
35
36
37
38
39
40
41
42
43
44
45
46
47
48
49
50
51
52
53
54
55
56
57

MAP 13 TEMPLE BAR

■ PLACES TO STAY

3 The Clarence Hotel
27 Kinlay House
53 Bloom's Hotel
29 Pizza on the Corner
32 San Marino

▼ PLACES TO EAT

11 Cellary
13 The Elephant & Castle
14 Gallagher's Boxty House
15 Omar Khayyam Restaurant
21 Beshoff's (Fish & Chips)
22 Bewley's Café
24 Temple & Fownes
   Sandwich Bar
26 The Refectory
   (Kinlay House)
28 Poco Loco
33 Les Frères Jacques
35 Da Lorenzo Restaurant
37 Fans Cantonese
   Restaurant
38 Café Carolina
40 Pasta Nostra
41 Bad Ass Café
42 Rock Garden Café
43 Paddy Garibaldi's
44 Fat Freddy's Pizza
45 Well Fed Café/Dublin
   Resource Centre
47 Tante Zoë's
   Cajun Food
49 La Mezza Luna
50 Little Lisbon
52 Coffer's Restaurant

♥ PUBS

5 Bad Bob's
   Backstage Bar
6 The Garage Bar
7 The Norseman
8 The Temple Bar
10 Ha'penny Bridge Inn
18 Daniel O'Connell
23 The Palace Bar
25 The Auld Dubliner
30 The Oak
31 The Crane
54 The Oliver St John Gogarty

OTHER

1 The Hags with the Bags
2 Sunlight Chambers
4 Project Arts Centre
9 Temple Bar Information
   Office
12 Rory's Fishing Tackle
16 Virgin Megastore
17 USIT Travel Office
19 B&I Lines Office
20 Sealink Stena Office
34 Olympia Theatre
36 Friend's Meeting House
39 Claddagh Records
46 Hare Krishna Centre
48 City Cycle Tours
51 Central Bank
55 Stock Exchange
56 Bank of Ireland
57 City Hall

MAP 14

Around Grafton St

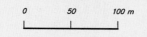

0   50   100 m

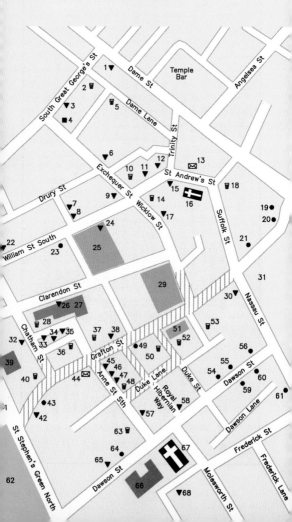

MAP 14 AROUND GRAFTON ST

■ **PLACES TO STAY**

4 Central Hotel
27 Westbury Hotel

▼ **PLACES TO EAT**

1 The Broker's
   Restaurant
3 Bewley's Café
6 Restaurant Pasta
   Pasta
7 The Bistro
8 Cooke's
9 Munchies
11 Cedar Tree
12 QV2
15 Trocadero
17 Cornucopia
22 Eastern Tandoori
24 Restaurant Mahler
26 Rajdoot Tandoori
   Restaurant
30 Judge Roy Bean
32 Pasta Fresca
33 Topo Gigio
34 Pizza Stop
35 Little Caesar's Pizza
38 Bewley's Oriental
   Café
42 Captain America
45 The Coffee Inn
46 Eddie Rocket's Diner
47 Independent Pizza
   Company
57 Subs n Salad
58 Fitzer's
65 La Stampa
68 Polo One

☕ **PUBS**

2 Dame Tavern
5 The Stag's Head
10 The Old Stand
14 International Bar

18 O'Neills
28 Neary's
36 McDaid's
37 Bruxelles
40 The Chatham
48 John Kehoe's
50 Davy Byrne's
52 The Bailey
53 Lillie's Bordello
   Nightclub
63 McGonagle's
   Nightclub

OTHER

13 Post Office
16 St Andrew's Church
19 Thomas Cook
20 American Express
21 Molly Malone Statue
23 Dublin Civic Museum
25 Powerscourt Shopping
   Centre
29 Switzer's Department
   Store
31 Trinity College
39 Gaiety Theatre
41 St Stephen's Green
   Shopping Centre
43 Aer Lingus Office
44 Post Office
49 Dublin Bookshop
51 Brown Thomas
   Department Store
54 TAP, Iberia & Swissair
   Office
55 Hodges Figgis
   Bookshop
56 Alitalia Office
59 Waterstones Bookshop
60 Ryanair Office
61 Fred Hanna Bookshop
62 St Stephen's Green
64 Forbidden Planet
66 Mansion House
67 St Ann's Church

MAP 15

Dun Laoghaire

0   250   500 m

1
2
3
4
5
6
Crofton Rd
10
i 9
11
12
28
13
14
Queen's Rd
7
8
30
29
to Dublin
15
16
17
George's St Lower
18 19
Royal Marine
31
Convent Rd
20
21 22
Patrick St
Mulgrave St
25
26
23
24
George's St Upper
High Ter
32
33
34
35
Adelaide St
Mellifont Ave
36
To Sandycove
& James Joyc
Museum
Windsor Ter
People's
Park
27
Northumberland Ave
37
38
North
Clarinda Park West
Corrig Ave
Clarinda Park East
Glenageary Rd Lower
Rosmeen Gdns
39
Summerhill Rd
Rosmeen Park
Patrick St
Mulgrave
Terrace
Tivoli Rd
Corrig Rd

MAP 15   DUN LAOGHAIRE

■ PLACES TO STAY

14	Port View Hotel
24	Royal Marine Hotel
27	Innisfree B&B
32	Bayside Guest House
34	Kingston Hotel
35	Hotel Pierre
39	Rosmeen Gardens B&Bs

▼ PLACES TO EAT

11	Restaurant Na Mara
15	Trudi's Restaurant
20	Dilshad Tandoori Restaurant
21	Ritz Café (Fish & Chips)
26	Café Society & Darby O'Gill
38	Outlaws Restaurant

▉ PUBS

16	Cooney's
17	Dunphy's

OTHER

1	Lighthouse
2	Anemometer
3	Lifeboat Memorial
4	East Pier
5	Car Ferry Pier
6	Royal Irish Yacht Club
7	Carlisle or Mailboat Pier
8	Bandstand
9	Tourist Office
10	DART Station
12	Royal St George Yacht Club
13	GPO
18	Pembrey's Bookshop
19	St Michael's Church
22	Eason Bookshop
23	Dun Laoghaire Shopping Centre
25	Aer Lingus
28	King George IV Monument
29	National Yacht Club
30	Compass Pointer
31	Christ the King Sculpture
33	National Maritime Museum
36	Oceantec Dive Shop
37	Star Laundry

Dun Laoghaire (TW)

MAP 16

Ireland's
Eye

1 Boat Landing Point
2 Martello Tower
3 Monastic Ruins
4 Lighthouse
5 King George IV
  Footprint
6 West Pier
7 East Pier
8 Pizza Place
9 Fishing Boats
10 Yacht Marina
11 Howth DART Station
12 St Lawrence Hotel
13 Waterside Inn
14 St Mary's Abbey
15 Pier House
16 King Sitric
   Restaurant
17 The Cock Tavern
18 Abbey Tavern
19 National Transport
   Museum
20 Howth Castle
21 Royal Howth Hotel
22 The Deer Park Hotel

Howth

0   250   500 m

Harbour

To Howth Lodge
Hotel & Dublin

Howth Rd

Harbour Rd

To the Nose
of Howth

Balscadden Rd

O'Malley Rd

Main St

Nashville Rd

Balkill Rd

Thormanb

To the
Summi

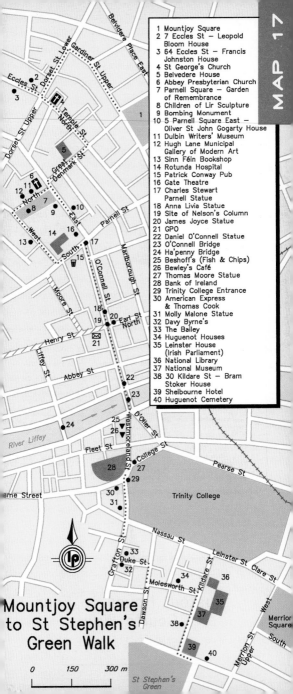

1 Mountjoy Square
2 7 Eccles St — Leopold
   Bloom House
3 64 Eccles St — Francis
   Johnston House
4 St George's Church
5 Belvedere House
6 Abbey Presbyterian Church
7 Parnell Square — Garden
   of Remembrance
8 Children of Lir Sculpture
9 Bombing Monument
10 5 Parnell Square East —
   Oliver St John Gogarty House
11 Dublin Writers' Museum
12 Hugh Lane Municipal
   Gallery of Modern Art
13 Sinn Féin Bookshop
14 Rotunda Hospital
15 Patrick Conway Pub
16 Gate Theatre
17 Charles Stewart
   Parnell Statue
18 Anna Livia Statue
19 Site of Nelson's Column
20 James Joyce Statue
21 GPO
22 Daniel O'Connell Statue
23 O'Connell Bridge
24 Ha'penny Bridge
25 Beshoff's (Fish & Chips)
26 Bewley's Café
27 Thomas Moore Statue
28 Bank of Ireland
29 Trinity College Entrance
30 American Express
   & Thomas Cook
31 Molly Malone Statue
32 Davy Byrne's
33 The Bailey
34 Huguenot Houses
35 Leinster House
   (Irish Parliament)
36 National Library
37 National Museum
38 30 Kildare St — Bram
   Stoker House
39 Shelbourne Hotel
40 Huguenot Cemetery

Mountjoy Square
to St Stephen's
Green Walk

0   150   300 m

MAP 18

O'Connell St
Capel St
Bachelor's Walk
Ormond Quay Lower
Aston Quay
River Liffey
Ormond Quay Upper
Wellington Quay
40
39
Wood Qy   Essex Qy
28
38
37
32
31
College St
27
Dame St
30
26
36
Ld Edward St
29
Suffolk St   Nas
35
33
Wicklow St
34
Duke St
South Gt George's St
William St South
Clarendon St
Grafton St
Winetavern St
Christ Ch Pl

1 Custom House
2 Liberty Hall
3 Abbey Theatre
4 Busáras & Eblana Theatre
5 International Financial Services Centre
6 Talbot Memorial Bridge
7 Loop Line Railway Bridge
8 St Mark's Church
9 Pearse Station
10 St Andrew's Church
11 Oscar Wilde's Birthplace
12 Sweny's Chemist Shop
13 Wildes' Residence

14 Irish Architectural Association
15 Former UK Embassy
16 St Stephen's Church
17 No 29 Fitzwilliam St Lower (Georgian House)
18 Electricity Supply Board Office
19 Government Buildings
20 Duke of Wellington's Birthplace
21 Natural History Museum
22 Leinster House
23 National Gallery
24 Kildare St Club
25 Arts & Social Science Building

26 Statue of Molly Malone
27 American Express & Thomas Cook
28 Bank of Ireland
29 St Andrew's Church
30 Thingmote Site
31 Central Bank
32 Olympia Theatre
33 City Hall
34 Dublin Castle
35 Christ Church Cathedral
36 Dublin Music Hall Doorway
37 Dublin Corporation Civic Offices
38 St Francis' Church
39 O'Donovan Rossa Bridge
40 Four Courts

Custom House to Four Courts Walk

0   250   500 m

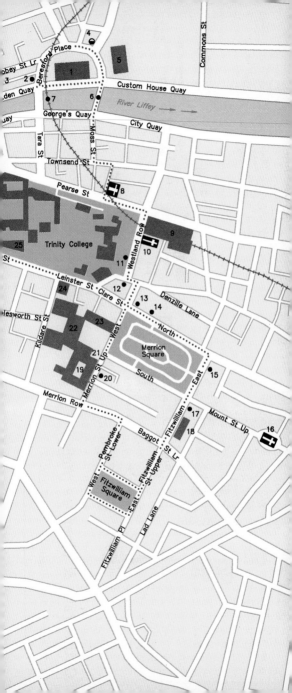

MAP 19

Cathedrals & Liberties Walk

Dublin Castle

Werburgh St

Essex Qy

Fishamble St

Ld Edward St

Bride St

6
7

3   4

Wood Qy

9

Christ Church Place

8

1

2

Kevin St Upper

Winetavern St

Patrick St

Nicholas St

Dean St

Merchant's Quay

High St

10

5

Inns Quay

12

Back Lane

11

16

Arran Quay

13

14

18

River Liffey

15

Francis St

The Coombe

Newmarket

Usher's Quay

20

Cornmarket

19

17

21

Meath St

Usher's Island

Cork St

22

Crane St

24

23

Thomas St West

Watling St

26

Rainsford St

Bellevue St

St James's Gate Brewery

27

James's St

25

Echlin St

Steeven's Lane

29

28

30

St John's Rd West

500 m

250

0

MAP 19 CATHEDRALS & LIBERTIES WALK

1 St Patrick's Cathedral
2 The Deanery
3 Marsh's Library
4 Kevin St Garda Station
5 Cabbage Garden
6 St Werburgh's Church
7 Hoey's Court Location
8 Christ Church Cathedral
9 Dublin Corporation
   Civic Offices
10 Tailor's Hall
11 Christchurch Festival Market
12 St Audoen's
   (Catholic)

13 St Audoen's
   (Protestant)
14 Iveagh Market
15 Tivoli Theatre
16 St Nicholas Without
   (Catholic)
17 Coombe Maternity
   Hospital Gate
18 St Nicholas Without
   (Protestant)
19 St Catherine's Church
   (Catholic)
20 SS John & Augustine Church

21 National College of
   Art & Design (NCAD)
22 St Catherine's Church
   (Protestant)
23 Windmill Tower
24 Guinness Hop Store
25 Site of St James's
   St Harbour
26 St James's Gate
   Brewery Entrance
27 St James's Church
28 St Patrick's Hospital
29 Steevens' Hospital
30 Heuston Station

See Temple Bar, Map 13

Bachelor's Walk

Aston Quay

Dame St

4

See Around Grafton St, Map 14

Colle

Dublin Castle

6

South Gt George's St

Grafton St

5

Aungier St

King St

Dawson St

12

14

Peter Row

13

York St

15

West

North

38

St Stephen's Green

Cuffe St

Wexford St

St

South

39

Camden St Lower

Harcourt

40

41

42

44

45

Earlsfort Terrace

43

Hatch St

Camden St Upper

48

Harrington St   Harcourt Rd   Adelaide Rd

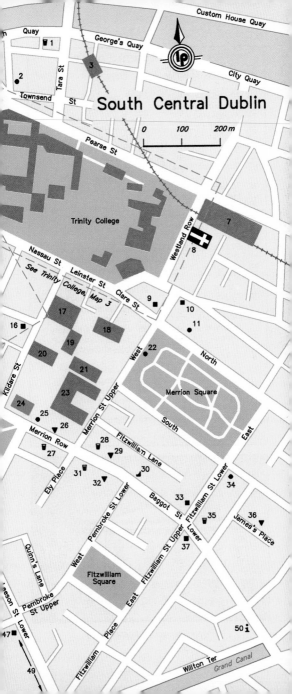

South Central Dublin

Custom House Quay

George's Quay

City Quay

Quay

Townsend St

Tara St

1

2

3

0   100   200 m

Pearse St

Trinity College

Westland Row

7

8

Nassau St

Leinster St

See Trinity College Map 3

Clare St

9

10

11

16

17

18

Kildare St

19

20

21

22

West

North

Merrion Square

23

24

25

26

South

East

Merrion Row

27

28

Fitzwilliam Lane

29

31

30

32

Ely Place

33

34

Baggot St Lower

35

James's Place

36

37

Pembroke St Lower

West

Fitzwilliam St Upper

Fitzwilliam St Lower

Quinn's Lane

Fitzwilliam Square

East

Pembroke St Upper

Leeson St Lower

47

50

Fitzwilliam Place

49

Wilton Ter

Grand Canal

MAP 20 SOUTH CENTRAL DUBLIN

■ PLACES TO STAY

9	Mont Clare Hotel
10	Davenport Hotel
13	Avalon House
16	Buswell's Hotel
24	Shelbourne Hotel
30	Georgian House
33	Longfield's Hotel
37	Fitzwilliam Guest House
42	Russell Court Hotel
43	Harcourt Hotel
45	Hotel Conrad
46	Stephen's Hall
47	Leeson Court Hotel

▼ PLACES TO EAT

26	Galligan's Café
29	Miller's Pizza Kitchen
32	Ayumi-ya Restaurant
36	Restaurant Patrick Guilbaud
48	Oisin's

🍺 PUBS

1	John Mulligan's
5	Break for the Border
27	O'Donoghue's
28	Doheny & Nesbitt's
31	Baggot Inn
35	Henry Grattan

OTHER

2	Cinema Screen (College St)
3	Tara St Station
4	City Hall
6	Royal Chapel
7	Pearse Station
8	St Andrew's Church
11	Architectural Association
12	Whitefriars Carmelite Church
14	St Stephen's Green Shopping Centre
15	Royal College of Surgeons
17	National Library
18	National Gallery
19	Leinster House (Irish Parliament)
20	National Museum
21	Natural History Museum
22	Rutland Fountain
23	Government Buildings
25	Huguenot Cemetery
34	No 29 Fitzwilliam St Lower (Georgian House)
38	Unitarian Church
39	Newman House
40	Newman Chapel
41	Iveagh House
44	National Concert Hall
49	Nightclubs
50	Irish Tourist Board Office

Royal College of Surgeons (TW)

Top: Art Show, Temple Bar (TW)
Bottom: Amateur Artists, St Stephen's Green (TW)

MAP 21

Excursions

0   15   30 km

† Monasterboice

Kells

Mellifont Abbey

Slane   Knowth   Drogheda
Dowth
Newgrange   Donore

Navan   River Boyne   Duleek

Hill
of Tara

Trim   N3   N2

N1
Skerries

Lam
Isla

Donabate
Royal Canal   Swords
Maynooth   Dublin   Malahide
N4   Airport   Ireland's
Castletown   Leixlip   Glasnevin   Eye
House   Drumcondra   Howth
Clontarf

Robertstown   Grand Canal   DUBLIN

Dun Laoghai
Sallins   N7   Dalkey
River Liffey   Marlay Park   Killiney
Naas   N81

Kildare   Bray

Blessington   Lough   Enniskerry
Bray   Powerscourt Deme
Rossborough   Glencree Youth Hostel   ▲ Great Sugar Lo
House   Poulaphouca   (506
Reservoir   Lough Tay   Greystone
Knockree
Youth Hostel   Vartry
Lough Dan   Reservoir
Lough Nahanagan
Glendalough †
N9   Upper   Laragh
Lake
Glenmalure Youth Hostel   ■
Aghavannagh   ■
Youth Hostel   Wicklow

Wicklow Way   N11

St George's
Channel

To Clonegal →

IRISH
SEA

Top: Newgrange (TW)
Bottom: Statue, Powerscourt (TW)

MAP 22

DART & Suburban Rail Plan

Ⓐ Western Suburban
Ⓑ Northern Suburban
Ⓒ Dart
Ⓓ South—Eastern Suburban

Ⓑ Dundalk
Drogheda
Laytown
Mosney
Gormanston
Balbriggan
Skerries
Rush—Lusk
Donabate
Malahide
Portmarnock
Howth Junction
Bayside
Sutton
Howth Ⓒ
Kilbarrack
Raheny
Harmonstown
Killester
Connolly Station
Tara Street
Pearse Station
Lansdowne Road
Sandymount
Sydney Parade
Booterstown
Blackrock
Seapoint
Salthill & Monkstown
Dun Laoghaire
Sandycove & Glasthule
Glenageary
Dalkey
Killiney
Shankill
Bray
Greystones
Kilcoole
Wicklow
Rathdrum
Arklow Ⓓ

Ⓐ Mullingar
Enfield
Maynooth
Leixlip Louisa Bridge
Leixlip Confey
Clonsilla
Coolmine
Blanchardstown/
Castleknock
Ashtown
Broombridge

Top: Howth Harbour (JM)
Bottom: Sea birds, Ireland's Eye (TW)

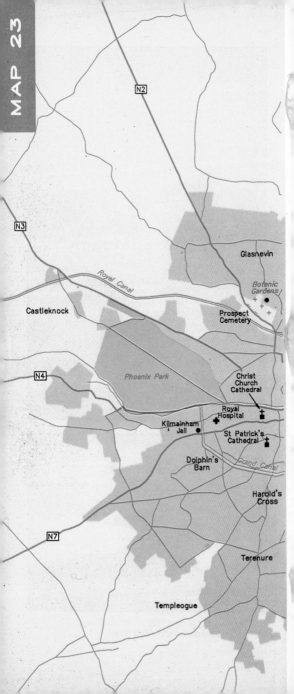

MAP 23

N2

N3

Glasnevin

Royal Canal

Botanic
Gardens

Castleknock

Prospect
Cemetery

N4

Phoenix Park

Christ
Church
Cathedral

Royal
Hospital

Kilmainham
Jail

St Patrick's
Cathedral

Dolphin's
Barn

Grand Canal

Harold's
Cross

N7

Terenure

Templeogue